C-603 CAREER EXAMINATION SERIES

This is your
PASSBOOK for...

Postal Supervisor Exam 642 (USPS)

Test Preparation Study Guide
Questions & Answers

COPYRIGHT NOTICE

This book is SOLELY intended for, is sold ONLY to, and its use is RESTRICTED to individual, bona fide applicants or candidates who qualify by virtue of having seriously filed applications for appropriate license, certificate, professional and/or promotional advancement, higher school matriculation, scholarship, or other legitimate requirements of education and/or governmental authorities.

This book is NOT intended for use, class instruction, tutoring, training, duplication, copying, reprinting, excerption, or adaptation, etc., by:

1) Other publishers
2) Proprietors and/or Instructors of "Coaching" and/or Preparatory Courses
3) Personnel and/or Training Divisions of commercial, industrial, and governmental organizations
4) Schools, colleges, or universities and/or their departments and staffs, including teachers and other personnel
5) Testing Agencies or Bureaus
6) Study groups which seek by the purchase of a single volume to copy and/or duplicate and/or adapt this material for use by the group as a whole without having purchased individual volumes for each of the members of the group
7) Et al.

Such persons would be in violation of appropriate Federal and State statutes.

PROVISION OF LICENSING AGREEMENTS – Recognized educational, commercial, industrial, and governmental institutions and organizations, and others legitimately engaged in educational pursuits, including training, testing, and measurement activities, may address request for a licensing agreement to the copyright owners, who will determine whether, and under what conditions, including fees and charges, the materials in this book may be used them. In other words, a licensing facility exists for the legitimate use of the material in this book on other than an individual basis. However, it is asseverated and affirmed here that the material in this book CANNOT be used without the receipt of the express permission of such a licensing agreement from the Publishers. Inquiries re licensing should be addressed to the company, attention rights and permissions department.

All rights reserved, including the right of reproduction in whole or in part, in any form or by any means, electronic or mechanical, including photocopying, recording, or by any information storage and retrieval system, without permission in writing from the Publisher.

Copyright © 2024 by
National Learning Corporation

212 Michael Drive, Syosset, NY 11791
(516) 921-8888 • www.passbooks.com
E-mail: info@passbooks.com

PUBLISHED IN THE UNITED STATES OF AMERICA

PASSBOOK® SERIES

THE *PASSBOOK® SERIES* has been created to prepare applicants and candidates for the ultimate academic battlefield – the examination room.

At some time in our lives, each and every one of us may be required to take an examination – for validation, matriculation, admission, qualification, registration, certification, or licensure.

Based on the assumption that every applicant or candidate has met the basic formal educational standards, has taken the required number of courses, and read the necessary texts, the *PASSBOOK® SERIES* furnishes the one special preparation which may assure passing with confidence, instead of failing with insecurity. Examination questions – together with answers – are furnished as the basic vehicle for study so that the mysteries of the examination and its compounding difficulties may be eliminated or diminished by a sure method.

This book is meant to help you pass your examination provided that you qualify and are serious in your objective.

The entire field is reviewed through the huge store of content information which is succinctly presented through a provocative and challenging approach – the question-and-answer method.

A climate of success is established by furnishing the correct answers at the end of each test.

You soon learn to recognize types of questions, forms of questions, and patterns of questioning. You may even begin to anticipate expected outcomes.

You perceive that many questions are repeated or adapted so that you can gain acute insights, which may enable you to score many sure points.

You learn how to confront new questions, or types of questions, and to attack them confidently and work out the correct answers.

You note objectives and emphases, and recognize pitfalls and dangers, so that you may make positive educational adjustments.

Moreover, you are kept fully informed in relation to new concepts, methods, practices, and directions in the field.

You discover that you are actually taking the examination all the time: you are preparing for the examination by "taking" an examination, not by reading extraneous and/or supererogatory textbooks.

In short, this PASSBOOK®, used directedly, should be an important factor in helping you to pass your test.

GENERAL SUMMARY INFORMATION ON EXAM 642
U. S. Postal Service

The new supervisor selection assessment, Exam 642, is based on a recent job analysis that included job observations, focus groups, interviews, and supervisor surveys. The job analysis also included interviews with USPS personnel who are aware of upcoming changes to the job. Therefore, Exam 642 is based on the most current information we have about the supervisor job.

This online exam is divided into two parts, one that is unproctored and one that is administered in a proctored environment. Eligible employees who submit an application through *eCareer* will receive an email invitation with instructions for the unproctored portion of the exam. Applicants are responsible for monitoring their emails to ensure they read and take action as soon as the email is received. **Applicants must complete the entire assessment process 14 days from the date that the email message is sent.** Applicants can take the unproctored assessment in their own homes. Applicants who pass this portion are then asked to schedule a date and time to take the proctored portion at a testing center.

The unproctored portion of the exam consists of the following two parts:

Part A: Situational Judgment assesses judgment in circumstances similar to those at work. Scenarios describe work-related situations and provide a list of potential responses.

Part B: Personal Characteristics consists of items that assess several personal characteristics or tendencies that relate to effective performance as a supervisor.

Table 1. Summary of unproctored portion of Exam 642E

1. Test Part	2. Number of Items	3. Time Allowed	4. Subject Matter
Part A: Situational Judgment	48	60	Assesses your judgment in situations similar to those at work.
Part B: Personal Characteristics	63	30	Assesses several personal characteristics or tendencies related to performing effectively.

The proctored portion of the exam consists of the following three parts:

Part A: Sentence Sequencing tests the ability to arrange information in a logical and understandable manner. Applicants select the correct sentence order to create a paragraph that is well organized, clear, and coherent.

Part B: Business Math tests math ability. The problems are drawn from the types of documents Postal supervisors are required to use on the job.

Part C: Logic Passages tests reading comprehension and reasoning ability.

Table 2. Summary of proctored portion of Exam 642

1. Test Part	2. Number of Items	3. Time Allowed	4. Subject Matter
Part A: Sentence Sequencing	20	25	Tests your ability to arrange information in a logical and understandable manner.
Part B: Business Math	13	35	Tests your math ability
Part C: Logic Passages	20	15	Tests your reading comprehension and your reasoning ability.

The table below lists the contents of Exam 642E.

Test Part	Number of Items	Time Allowed	Subject Matter Covered
Part A: Situational Judgment	48	60	Assesses your judgment in situations similar to those at work.
Part B: Personal Characteristics	63	30	Assess several personal characteristics or tendencies related to performing effectively as an employee in this organization.

Below are sample questions like the ones that will be on the assessment. Study these carefully. This will give you practice with the different kinds of items on the assessment. You will also have an opportunity to view sample questions and complete practice tests during the actual assessment administration.

SAMPLE QUESTIONS

Part A: Situational Judgment

Part A, Situational Judgment, assesses your judgment in situations similar to those at work. Each situation consists of a scenario describing a work-related situation, and two questions asking "what you would do," based on a list of alternate responses supplied below. Carefully read each scenario and the list of responses. Then select the one response that best represents what you would *"most likely do"* and the one response that represents what you would *"least likely do."* Responding to these situations does not require or assume specific postal procedural or job knowledge.

> Office productivity is down. You have the same number of employees and the workload has not increased.

S1. Which of the following *would you most likely* do?———

S2. Which of the following *would you least likely* do?———

  a) Talk with your employees to try and determine if there are attitudinal problems or operational problems that are leading to this decrease.
  b) Assess if there have been changes occurring in how goods are being produced that are causing productivity to decrease.
  c) Ask your manager to hire more people so that productivity can be maintained.
  d) Mention the situation to your employees, and inform them that if it continues to be a problem that more formal action will be taken against those employees not performing up to their potential.
  e) Inform employees that unless productivity levels return to normal, part-time workers will be hired which will cut into the number of total hours that a given employee can work.

> Your manager informs you that someone you supervise has made comments about you being unfair to your employees.

S3. Which of the following *would you most likely* do?———

S4. Which of the following *would you least likely* do?———

  a) Confront that employee and ask why he or she went over your head to complain.
  b) Hold a meeting with all of the people you supervise and ask if they have any problems they want to discuss
  c) Work hard to make sure that you treat all employees fairly.
  d) Meet with the employee and ask for more information about the problem
  e) Tell your manager that the individual who complained cannot be trusted.

> Your team is working under a very tight deadline and one of your workers injures himself and must go home, leaving you severely understaffed

S5. Which of the following *would you most likely* do?———

S6. Which of the following *would you least likely* do?———

    a) Ask everyone to work extra hours until the work is completed.
    b) Ask the injured employee if he can work from home.
    c) Let your employees leave at their normal time and stay to finish the work yourself.
    d) Contact your client and ask if you can extend the deadline.
    e) Request that a member of another work team assist until the deadline is met.

Part B: Personal Characteristics

The items in this test part assess several personal characteristics or tendencies related to performing effectively as an employee in this organization.

Read each item carefully, and decide which of the response choices is most true about *you*. For some items, more than one statement may describe you. However, be sure to mark one and only one response for each item. It is important to consider and respond to each item, even if you are not completely sure which response is best. Also, it is generally best to work at a fairly rapid pace.

Whenever possible, respond to the items in terms of what you have done, felt or believed in a work setting. If you cannot relate the item to your work experiences, base your response on other experiences that are similar to work, such as school or volunteer activities. For example, if an item involves how often you have gotten into arguments with others, respond in terms of how often you have gotten into arguments with co-workers. If you have not held a job before, or if the item cannot be related to your work experiences, draw on whatever experiences are necessary to choose the response choice that best describes you.

This test part includes items in two different formats. Some items include four response choices ranging from "Strongly Agree" to "Strongly Disagree." Other items include four response choices ranging from "Very Often" to "Rarely or Never." Each item shows the rating scale response options on the page. Read each page carefully before you respond.

For items S7 and S10, respond to each statement by choosing the letter that describes you best.

S7. You like work that challenges you.

A = Strongly Agree
B = Agree
C = Disagree
D = Strongly Disagree

S8. You prefer a rigid work schedule.

A = Strongly Agree
B = Agree
C = Disagree
D = Strongly Disagree

S9. You finish your work on time or before it is due.

A = Very Often
B = Often
C = Sometimes
D = Rarely or Never

S10. You share your ideas with your coworkers

A = Very Often
B = Often
C = Sometimes
D = Rarely or Never

SAMPLE TEST QUESTIONS

Test Instructions

During the test session, read all instructions very carefully. One of the purposes of the test is to see how quickly and accurately you can work. Therefore, each section of the test will be timed. Where appropriate, a countdown clock will be displayed on your computer screen. When time runs out for a particular part, the test will automatically advance to the next part. If you finish a section before the timer runs out, you will have an opportunity to review your answers for that part. Once a timed section has ended, you will not be allowed to return to that section.

There are 3 parts to this examination:
- Part A: Sentence Sequencing
- Part B: Business Math
- Part C: Logic Passages

Each section contains several multiple-choice questions. During the actual test session, you will select your response to each question by clicking the button (small circle) next to your answer.

The total time for the assessment is **approximately 1 1/2 hours**. Again, please be sure to take care of any personal needs before you check in to the test. The table below lists the contents of Exam 642.

Test Part	Number of Items	Time Allowed	Subject Matter Covered
Part A: Sentence Sequencing	20	25	Tests your ability to arrange information in a logical and understandable manner.
Part B: Business Math	13	35	Tests your math ability.
Part C: Logic Passages	20	15	Tests your reading comprehension and your reasoning ability.

On the following pages are sample questions like the ones that will be on the test. Study these carefully. This will give you practice with the different kinds of items on the test. You will have an opportunity to view sample questions and complete practice tests during the actual test session.

There is no penalty for guessing. Therefore, it is generally to your advantage to respond to each item, even if you have to guess.

Sample Exercise: Parts A, B, and C

Part A: Sentence Sequencing

Part A, Sentence Sequencing, tests your ability to arrange information in a logical and understandable manner. For each item, select the correct sentence order to create a paragraph that is well-organized, clear, and coherent. Read all of the sentences carefully before making your response.

For question S1, select the correct sentence order to create a paragraph that is well-organized, clear, and coherent.

S1.
1) As you begin your exercise program you should start slowly and build up gradually.
2) If you are consistent in exercising regularly, you could see results in 12 weeks.
3) Before using exercise machines at home or in the health club you should first talk with your doctor.
4) After two to three weeks of repeating your routine you can increase the resistance and length of time.

   a) 3, 2, 4, 1
   b) 4, 1, 2, 3
   c) 3, 1, 4, 2
   d) 2, 3, 1, 4

The correct answer for sample question S1 is C.

Part B: Business Math

Part B, Business Math, tests your math ability. The business math problems are drawn from the types of documents Postal supervisors are required to use on the job. However, the contents of these questions are for **testing purposes only**. The regulations and/or procedures described in the problems may be fictional and require no knowledge of Postal service policies or procedures. DO NOT answer these questions based on your local practices; answer the questions based **SOLELY** on the information supplied.

For questions S3 and S4, read the following report. Based on the information provided, choose the best answer from the options listed.

SYSTEM RUN REPORT

Machines A & B Totals		Machine B Total	
Number of Records	4,871	Number of Records	2,436
Productive Records	4,620	Productive Records	2,339
Read Reject Records	197	Read Reject Records	97
Type 1 Rejects	0	Type 1 Rejects	0
Type 2 Rejects	5	Type 2 Rejects	4
Type 3 Rejects	192	Type 3 Rejects	93
Miscellaneous Rejects	54		

S3. What is the number of Read Reject Records for Machines A & B?
   a. 197
   b. 294
   c. 394
   d. 448

S4. How would you calculate the number of Productive Records for Machine A?
   a. (Number of Records for Machines A & B) - (Number of Records for Machine B)
   b. (Productive Records for Machine A & B) - (Productive Records for Machine B)
   c. [(Number of Records for Machines A & B)] - [(Read Reject Records for Machines A & B) +(Miscellaneous Rejects for Machines A & B)]
   d. (Number of Records for Machine B) - (Number of Productive Records for Machine B)

The correct answer for sample questions S3 is A and S4 is B.

Part C: Logic Passages

Part C, Logic Passages, tests your reading comprehension and your reasoning ability. This section contains reading passages. Each passage is followed by several questions about the passage. For each question, *use only the information provided in the passage to identify the best answer.* You do not need previous experience or knowledge of the job to answer the questions correctly. Each passage contains all the information you need to answer the questions.

The passage contains several facts, each followed by some conclusions. Read the facts, then read each conclusion, and decide if

- A. The conclusion is definitely **TRUE** – that is, the conclusion follows logically from the facts presented,
- B. The conclusion is definitely **FALSE** – that is, you can tell from the facts that the conclusion must be false, or
- C. You **CAN'T TELL** – that is, you would need more information to tell if the conclusion is true or false.

Read the following passage and answer questions S4 through S6 based on the information provided.

Assume the following statements are true:

- At the Midtown Post Office, all day-shift employees take turns delivering mail and working behind the counter.
- During the swing-shift at the Midtown Post Office, all employees work behind the counter only.
- Cal is an employee at the Midtown Post Office.
- Sam is a day-shift employee.

Based on the facts above, decide whether each statement is true, false, or you cannot tell.

> A = True
> B = False
> C = Can't Tell

S5. If Cal works during the day shift, then he only works behind the counter.

S6. If Sam works at the Midtown Post Office, then she delivers mail and works behind the counter.

S7. If Sam works at the Greenwood Post Office, then she delivers mail and works behind the counter.

The correct answer for sample questions S5 is B, S6 is A, and S7 is C.

HOW TO TAKE A TEST

I. YOU MUST PASS AN EXAMINATION

A. WHAT EVERY CANDIDATE SHOULD KNOW

Examination applicants often ask us for help in preparing for the written test. What can I study in advance? What kinds of questions will be asked? How will the test be given? How will the papers be graded?

As an applicant for a civil service examination, you may be wondering about some of these things. Our purpose here is to suggest effective methods of advance study and to describe civil service examinations.

Your chances for success on this examination can be increased if you know how to prepare. Those "pre-examination jitters" can be reduced if you know what to expect. You can even experience an adventure in good citizenship if you know why civil service exams are given.

B. WHY ARE CIVIL SERVICE EXAMINATIONS GIVEN?

Civil service examinations are important to you in two ways. As a citizen, you want public jobs filled by employees who know how to do their work. As a job seeker, you want a fair chance to compete for that job on an equal footing with other candidates. The best-known means of accomplishing this two-fold goal is the competitive examination.

Exams are widely publicized throughout the nation. They may be administered for jobs in federal, state, city, municipal, town or village governments or agencies.

Any citizen may apply, with some limitations, such as the age or residence of applicants. Your experience and education may be reviewed to see whether you meet the requirements for the particular examination. When these requirements exist, they are reasonable and applied consistently to all applicants. Thus, a competitive examination may cause you some uneasiness now, but it is your privilege and safeguard.

C. HOW ARE CIVIL SERVICE EXAMS DEVELOPED?

Examinations are carefully written by trained technicians who are specialists in the field known as "psychological measurement," in consultation with recognized authorities in the field of work that the test will cover. These experts recommend the subject matter areas or skills to be tested; only those knowledges or skills important to your success on the job are included. The most reliable books and source materials available are used as references. Together, the experts and technicians judge the difficulty level of the questions.

Test technicians know how to phrase questions so that the problem is clearly stated. Their ethics do not permit "trick" or "catch" questions. Questions may have been tried out on sample groups, or subjected to statistical analysis, to determine their usefulness.

Written tests are often used in combination with performance tests, ratings of training and experience, and oral interviews. All of these measures combine to form the best-known means of finding the right person for the right job.

II. HOW TO PASS THE WRITTEN TEST

A. NATURE OF THE EXAMINATION

To prepare intelligently for civil service examinations, you should know how they differ from school examinations you have taken. In school you were assigned certain definite pages to read or subjects to cover. The examination questions were quite detailed and usually emphasized memory. Civil service exams, on the other hand, try to discover your present ability to perform the duties of a position, plus your potentiality to learn these duties. In other words, a civil service exam attempts to predict how successful you will be. Questions cover such a broad area that they cannot be as minute and detailed as school exam questions.

In the public service similar kinds of work, or positions, are grouped together in one "class." This process is known as *position-classification*. All the positions in a class are paid according to the salary range for that class. One class title covers all of these positions, and they are all tested by the same examination.

B. FOUR BASIC STEPS

1) Study the announcement

How, then, can you know what subjects to study? Our best answer is: "Learn as much as possible about the class of positions for which you've applied." The exam will test the knowledge, skills and abilities needed to do the work.

Your most valuable source of information about the position you want is the official exam announcement. This announcement lists the training and experience qualifications. Check these standards and apply only if you come reasonably close to meeting them.

The brief description of the position in the examination announcement offers some clues to the subjects which will be tested. Think about the job itself. Review the duties in your mind. Can you perform them, or are there some in which you are rusty? Fill in the blank spots in your preparation.

Many jurisdictions preview the written test in the exam announcement by including a section called "Knowledge and Abilities Required," "Scope of the Examination," or some similar heading. Here you will find out specifically what fields will be tested.

2) Review your own background

Once you learn in general what the position is all about, and what you need to know to do the work, ask yourself which subjects you already know fairly well and which need improvement. You may wonder whether to concentrate on improving your strong areas or on building some background in your fields of weakness. When the announcement has specified "some knowledge" or "considerable knowledge," or has used adjectives like "beginning principles of..." or "advanced ... methods," you can get a clue as to the number and difficulty of questions to be asked in any given field. More questions, and hence broader coverage, would be included for those subjects which are more important in the work. Now weigh your strengths and weaknesses against the job requirements and prepare accordingly.

3) Determine the level of the position

Another way to tell how intensively you should prepare is to understand the level of the job for which you are applying. Is it the entering level? In other words, is this the position in which beginners in a field of work are hired? Or is it an intermediate or advanced level? Sometimes this is indicated by such words as "Junior" or "Senior" in the class title. Other jurisdictions use Roman numerals to designate the level – Clerk I, Clerk II, for example. The word "Supervisor" sometimes appears in the title. If the level is not indicated by the title, check the description of duties. Will you be working under very close supervision, or will you have responsibility for independent decisions in this work?

4) Choose appropriate study materials

Now that you know the subjects to be examined and the relative amount of each subject to be covered, you can choose suitable study materials. For beginning level jobs, or even advanced ones, if you have a pronounced weakness in some aspect of your training, read a modern, standard textbook in that field. Be sure it is up to date and has general coverage. Such books are normally available at your library, and the librarian will be glad to help you locate one. For entry-level positions, questions of appropriate difficulty are chosen -- neither highly advanced questions, nor those too simple. Such questions require careful thought but not advanced training.

If the position for which you are applying is technical or advanced, you will read more advanced, specialized material. If you are already familiar with the basic principles of your field, elementary textbooks would waste your time. Concentrate on advanced textbooks and technical periodicals. Think through the concepts and review difficult problems in your field.

These are all general sources. You can get more ideas on your own initiative, following these leads. For example, training manuals and publications of the government agency which employs workers in your field can be useful, particularly for technical and professional positions. A letter or visit to the government department involved may result in more specific study suggestions, and certainly will provide you with a more definite idea of the exact nature of the position you are seeking.

III. KINDS OF TESTS

Tests are used for purposes other than measuring knowledge and ability to perform specified duties. For some positions, it is equally important to test ability to make adjustments to new situations or to profit from training. In others, basic mental abilities not dependent on information are essential. Questions which test these things may not appear as pertinent to the duties of the position as those which test for knowledge and information. Yet they are often highly important parts of a fair examination. For very general questions, it is almost impossible to help you direct your study efforts. What we can do is to point out some of the more common of these general abilities needed in public service positions and describe some typical questions.

1) General information

Broad, general information has been found useful for predicting job success in some kinds of work. This is tested in a variety of ways, from vocabulary lists to questions about current events. Basic background in some field of work, such as sociology or economics, may be sampled in a group of questions. Often these are principles which have become familiar to most persons through exposure rather than through formal training. It is difficult to advise you how to study for these questions; being alert to the world around you is our best suggestion.

2) Verbal ability

An example of an ability needed in many positions is verbal or language ability. Verbal ability is, in brief, the ability to use and understand words. Vocabulary and grammar tests are typical measures of this ability. Reading comprehension or paragraph interpretation questions are common in many kinds of civil service tests. You are given a paragraph of written material and asked to find its central meaning.

3) Numerical ability

Number skills can be tested by the familiar arithmetic problem, by checking paired lists of numbers to see which are alike and which are different, or by interpreting charts and graphs. In the latter test, a graph may be printed in the test booklet which you are asked to use as the basis for answering questions.

4) Observation

A popular test for law-enforcement positions is the observation test. A picture is shown to you for several minutes, then taken away. Questions about the picture test your ability to observe both details and larger elements.

5) Following directions

In many positions in the public service, the employee must be able to carry out written instructions dependably and accurately. You may be given a chart with several columns, each column listing a variety of information. The questions require you to carry out directions involving the information given in the chart.

6) Skills and aptitudes

Performance tests effectively measure some manual skills and aptitudes. When the skill is one in which you are trained, such as typing or shorthand, you can practice. These tests are often very much like those given in business school or high school courses. For many of the other skills and aptitudes, however, no short-time preparation can be made. Skills and abilities natural to you or that you have developed throughout your lifetime are being tested.

Many of the general questions just described provide all the data needed to answer the questions and ask you to use your reasoning ability to find the answers. Your best preparation for these tests, as well as for tests of facts and ideas, is to be at your physical and mental best. You, no doubt, have your own methods of getting into an exam-taking mood and keeping "in shape." The next section lists some ideas on this subject.

IV. KINDS OF QUESTIONS

Only rarely is the "essay" question, which you answer in narrative form, used in civil service tests. Civil service tests are usually of the short-answer type. Full instructions for answering these questions will be given to you at the examination. But in case this is your first experience with short-answer questions and separate answer sheets, here is what you need to know:

1) Multiple-choice Questions

Most popular of the short-answer questions is the "multiple choice" or "best answer" question. It can be used, for example, to test for factual knowledge, ability to solve problems or judgment in meeting situations found at work.

A multiple-choice question is normally one of three types—
- It can begin with an incomplete statement followed by several possible endings. You are to find the one ending which *best* completes the statement, although some of the others may not be entirely wrong.
- It can also be a complete statement in the form of a question which is answered by choosing one of the statements listed.

- It can be in the form of a problem – again you select the best answer.

Here is an example of a multiple-choice question with a discussion which should give you some clues as to the method for choosing the right answer:

When an employee has a complaint about his assignment, the action which will *best* help him overcome his difficulty is to
   A. discuss his difficulty with his coworkers
   B. take the problem to the head of the organization
   C. take the problem to the person who gave him the assignment
   D. say nothing to anyone about his complaint

In answering this question, you should study each of the choices to find which is best. Consider choice "A" – Certainly an employee may discuss his complaint with fellow employees, but no change or improvement can result, and the complaint remains unresolved. Choice "B" is a poor choice since the head of the organization probably does not know what assignment you have been given, and taking your problem to him is known as "going over the head" of the supervisor. The supervisor, or person who made the assignment, is the person who can clarify it or correct any injustice. Choice "C" is, therefore, correct. To say nothing, as in choice "D," is unwise. Supervisors have and interest in knowing the problems employees are facing, and the employee is seeking a solution to his problem.

2) True/False Questions

The "true/false" or "right/wrong" form of question is sometimes used. Here a complete statement is given. Your job is to decide whether the statement is right or wrong.

SAMPLE: A roaming cell-phone call to a nearby city costs less than a non-roaming call to a distant city.

This statement is wrong, or false, since roaming calls are more expensive.
This is not a complete list of all possible question forms, although most of the others are variations of these common types. You will always get complete directions for answering questions. Be sure you understand *how* to mark your answers – ask questions until you do.

V. RECORDING YOUR ANSWERS

Computer terminals are used more and more today for many different kinds of exams.
For an examination with very few applicants, you may be told to record your answers in the test booklet itself. Separate answer sheets are much more common. If this separate answer sheet is to be scored by machine – and this is often the case – it is highly important that you mark your answers correctly in order to get credit.
An electronic scoring machine is often used in civil service offices because of the speed with which papers can be scored. Machine-scored answer sheets must be marked with a pencil, which will be given to you. This pencil has a high graphite content which responds to the electronic scoring machine. As a matter of fact, stray dots may register as answers, so do not let your pencil rest on the answer sheet while you are pondering the correct answer. Also, if your pencil lead breaks or is otherwise defective, ask for another.

Since the answer sheet will be dropped in a slot in the scoring machine, be careful not to bend the corners or get the paper crumpled.

The answer sheet normally has five vertical columns of numbers, with 30 numbers to a column. These numbers correspond to the question numbers in your test booklet. After each number, going across the page are four or five pairs of dotted lines. These short dotted lines have small letters or numbers above them. The first two pairs may also have a "T" or "F" above the letters. This indicates that the first two pairs only are to be used if the questions are of the true-false type. If the questions are multiple choice, disregard the "T" and "F" and pay attention only to the small letters or numbers.

Answer your questions in the manner of the sample that follows:

32. The largest city in the United States is
    A. Washington, D.C.
    B. New York City
    C. Chicago
    D. Detroit
    E. San Francisco

1) Choose the answer you think is best. (New York City is the largest, so "B" is correct.)
2) Find the row of dotted lines numbered the same as the question you are answering. (Find row number 32)
3) Find the pair of dotted lines corresponding to the answer. (Find the pair of lines under the mark "B.")
4) Make a solid black mark between the dotted lines.

VI. BEFORE THE TEST

Common sense will help you find procedures to follow to get ready for an examination. Too many of us, however, overlook these sensible measures. Indeed, nervousness and fatigue have been found to be the most serious reasons why applicants fail to do their best on civil service tests. Here is a list of reminders:

- Begin your preparation early – Don't wait until the last minute to go scurrying around for books and materials or to find out what the position is all about.
- Prepare continuously – An hour a night for a week is better than an all-night cram session. This has been definitely established. What is more, a night a week for a month will return better dividends than crowding your study into a shorter period of time.
- Locate the place of the exam – You have been sent a notice telling you when and where to report for the examination. If the location is in a different town or otherwise unfamiliar to you, it would be well to inquire the best route and learn something about the building.
- Relax the night before the test – Allow your mind to rest. Do not study at all that night. Plan some mild recreation or diversion; then go to bed early and get a good night's sleep.
- Get up early enough to make a leisurely trip to the place for the test – This way unforeseen events, traffic snarls, unfamiliar buildings, etc. will not upset you.
- Dress comfortably – A written test is not a fashion show. You will be known by number and not by name, so wear something comfortable.

- Leave excess paraphernalia at home – Shopping bags and odd bundles will get in your way. You need bring only the items mentioned in the official notice you received; usually everything you need is provided. Do not bring reference books to the exam. They will only confuse those last minutes and be taken away from you when in the test room.
- Arrive somewhat ahead of time – If because of transportation schedules you must get there very early, bring a newspaper or magazine to take your mind off yourself while waiting.
- Locate the examination room – When you have found the proper room, you will be directed to the seat or part of the room where you will sit. Sometimes you are given a sheet of instructions to read while you are waiting. Do not fill out any forms until you are told to do so; just read them and be prepared.
- Relax and prepare to listen to the instructions
- If you have any physical problem that may keep you from doing your best, be sure to tell the test administrator. If you are sick or in poor health, you really cannot do your best on the exam. You can come back and take the test some other time.

VII. AT THE TEST

The day of the test is here and you have the test booklet in your hand. The temptation to get going is very strong. Caution! There is more to success than knowing the right answers. You must know how to identify your papers and understand variations in the type of short-answer question used in this particular examination. Follow these suggestions for maximum results from your efforts:

1) Cooperate with the monitor
The test administrator has a duty to create a situation in which you can be as much at ease as possible. He will give instructions, tell you when to begin, check to see that you are marking your answer sheet correctly, and so on. He is not there to guard you, although he will see that your competitors do not take unfair advantage. He wants to help you do your best.

2) Listen to all instructions
Don't jump the gun! Wait until you understand all directions. In most civil service tests you get more time than you need to answer the questions. So don't be in a hurry. Read each word of instructions until you clearly understand the meaning. Study the examples, listen to all announcements and follow directions. Ask questions if you do not understand what to do.

3) Identify your papers
Civil service exams are usually identified by number only. You will be assigned a number; you must not put your name on your test papers. Be sure to copy your number correctly. Since more than one exam may be given, copy your exact examination title.

4) Plan your time
Unless you are told that a test is a "speed" or "rate of work" test, speed itself is usually not important. Time enough to answer all the questions will be provided, but this does not mean that you have all day. An overall time limit has been set. Divide the total time (in minutes) by the number of questions to determine the approximate time you have for each question.

5) Do not linger over difficult questions

If you come across a difficult question, mark it with a paper clip (useful to have along) and come back to it when you have been through the booklet. One caution if you do this – be sure to skip a number on your answer sheet as well. Check often to be sure that you have not lost your place and that you are marking in the row numbered the same as the question you are answering.

6) Read the questions

Be sure you know what the question asks! Many capable people are unsuccessful because they failed to *read* the questions correctly.

7) Answer all questions

Unless you have been instructed that a penalty will be deducted for incorrect answers, it is better to guess than to omit a question.

8) Speed tests

It is often better NOT to guess on speed tests. It has been found that on timed tests people are tempted to spend the last few seconds before time is called in marking answers at random – without even reading them – in the hope of picking up a few extra points. To discourage this practice, the instructions may warn you that your score will be "corrected" for guessing. That is, a penalty will be applied. The incorrect answers will be deducted from the correct ones, or some other penalty formula will be used.

9) Review your answers

If you finish before time is called, go back to the questions you guessed or omitted to give them further thought. Review other answers if you have time.

10) Return your test materials

If you are ready to leave before others have finished or time is called, take ALL your materials to the monitor and leave quietly. Never take any test material with you. The monitor can discover whose papers are not complete, and taking a test booklet may be grounds for disqualification.

VIII. EXAMINATION TECHNIQUES

1) Read the general instructions carefully. These are usually printed on the first page of the exam booklet. As a rule, these instructions refer to the timing of the examination; the fact that you should not start work until the signal and must stop work at a signal, etc. If there are any *special* instructions, such as a choice of questions to be answered, make sure that you note this instruction carefully.

2) When you are ready to start work on the examination, that is as soon as the signal has been given, read the instructions to each question booklet, underline any key words or phrases, such as *least, best, outline, describe* and the like. In this way you will tend to answer as requested rather than discover on reviewing your paper that you *listed without describing*, that you selected the *worst* choice rather than the *best* choice, etc.

3) If the examination is of the objective or multiple-choice type – that is, each question will also give a series of possible answers: A, B, C or D, and you are called upon to select the best answer and write the letter next to that answer on your answer paper – it is advisable to start answering each question in turn. There may be anywhere from 50 to 100 such questions in the three or four hours allotted and you can see how much time would be taken if you read through all the questions before beginning to answer any. Furthermore, if you come across a question or group of questions which you know would be difficult to answer, it would undoubtedly affect your handling of all the other questions.

4) If the examination is of the essay type and contains but a few questions, it is a moot point as to whether you should read all the questions before starting to answer any one. Of course, if you are given a choice – say five out of seven and the like – then it is essential to read all the questions so you can eliminate the two that are most difficult. If, however, you are asked to answer all the questions, there may be danger in trying to answer the easiest one first because you may find that you will spend too much time on it. The best technique is to answer the first question, then proceed to the second, etc.

5) Time your answers. Before the exam begins, write down the time it started, then add the time allowed for the examination and write down the time it must be completed, then divide the time available somewhat as follows:
   - If 3-1/2 hours are allowed, that would be 210 minutes. If you have 80 objective-type questions, that would be an average of 2-1/2 minutes per question. Allow yourself no more than 2 minutes per question, or a total of 160 minutes, which will permit about 50 minutes to review.
   - If for the time allotment of 210 minutes there are 7 essay questions to answer, that would average about 30 minutes a question. Give yourself only 25 minutes per question so that you have about 35 minutes to review.

6) The most important instruction is to *read each question* and make sure you know what is wanted. The second most important instruction is to *time yourself properly* so that you answer every question. The third most important instruction is to *answer every question*. Guess if you have to but include something for each question. Remember that you will receive no credit for a blank and will probably receive some credit if you write something in answer to an essay question. If you guess a letter – say "B" for a multiple-choice question – you may have guessed right. If you leave a blank as an answer to a multiple-choice question, the examiners may respect your feelings but it will not add a point to your score. Some exams may penalize you for wrong answers, so in such cases *only*, you may not want to guess unless you have some basis for your answer.

7) Suggestions
   a. Objective-type questions
      1. Examine the question booklet for proper sequence of pages and questions
      2. Read all instructions carefully
      3. Skip any question which seems too difficult; return to it after all other questions have been answered
      4. Apportion your time properly; do not spend too much time on any single question or group of questions

5. Note and underline key words – *all, most, fewest, least, best, worst, same, opposite,* etc.
6. Pay particular attention to negatives
7. Note unusual option, e.g., unduly long, short, complex, different or similar in content to the body of the question
8. Observe the use of "hedging" words – *probably, may, most likely,* etc.
9. Make sure that your answer is put next to the same number as the question
10. Do not second-guess unless you have good reason to believe the second answer is definitely more correct
11. Cross out original answer if you decide another answer is more accurate; do not erase until you are ready to hand your paper in
12. Answer all questions; guess unless instructed otherwise
13. Leave time for review

  b. Essay questions
    1. Read each question carefully
    2. Determine exactly what is wanted. Underline key words or phrases.
    3. Decide on outline or paragraph answer
    4. Include many different points and elements unless asked to develop any one or two points or elements
    5. Show impartiality by giving pros and cons unless directed to select one side only
    6. Make and write down any assumptions you find necessary to answer the questions
    7. Watch your English, grammar, punctuation and choice of words
    8. Time your answers; don't crowd material

8) Answering the essay question

Most essay questions can be answered by framing the specific response around several key words or ideas. Here are a few such key words or ideas:

M's: manpower, materials, methods, money, management
P's: purpose, program, policy, plan, procedure, practice, problems, pitfalls, personnel, public relations

  a. Six basic steps in handling problems:
    1. Preliminary plan and background development
    2. Collect information, data and facts
    3. Analyze and interpret information, data and facts
    4. Analyze and develop solutions as well as make recommendations
    5. Prepare report and sell recommendations
    6. Install recommendations and follow up effectiveness

  b. Pitfalls to avoid
    1. *Taking things for granted* – A statement of the situation does not necessarily imply that each of the elements is necessarily true; for example, a complaint may be invalid and biased so that all that can be taken for granted is that a complaint has been registered

2. *Considering only one side of a situation* – Wherever possible, indicate several alternatives and then point out the reasons you selected the best one
3. *Failing to indicate follow up* – Whenever your answer indicates action on your part, make certain that you will take proper follow-up action to see how successful your recommendations, procedures or actions turn out to be
4. *Taking too long in answering any single question* – Remember to time your answers properly

IX. AFTER THE TEST

Scoring procedures differ in detail among civil service jurisdictions although the general principles are the same. Whether the papers are hand-scored or graded by machine we have described, they are nearly always graded by number. That is, the person who marks the paper knows only the number – never the name – of the applicant. Not until all the papers have been graded will they be matched with names. If other tests, such as training and experience or oral interview ratings have been given, scores will be combined. Different parts of the examination usually have different weights. For example, the written test might count 60 percent of the final grade, and a rating of training and experience 40 percent. In many jurisdictions, veterans will have a certain number of points added to their grades.

After the final grade has been determined, the names are placed in grade order and an eligible list is established. There are various methods for resolving ties between those who get the same final grade – probably the most common is to place first the name of the person whose application was received first. Job offers are made from the eligible list in the order the names appear on it. You will be notified of your grade and your rank as soon as all these computations have been made. This will be done as rapidly as possible.

People who are found to meet the requirements in the announcement are called "eligibles." Their names are put on a list of eligible candidates. An eligible's chances of getting a job depend on how high he stands on this list and how fast agencies are filling jobs from the list.

When a job is to be filled from a list of eligibles, the agency asks for the names of people on the list of eligibles for that job. When the civil service commission receives this request, it sends to the agency the names of the three people highest on this list. Or, if the job to be filled has specialized requirements, the office sends the agency the names of the top three persons who meet these requirements from the general list.

The appointing officer makes a choice from among the three people whose names were sent to him. If the selected person accepts the appointment, the names of the others are put back on the list to be considered for future openings.

That is the rule in hiring from all kinds of eligible lists, whether they are for typist, carpenter, chemist, or something else. For every vacancy, the appointing officer has his choice of any one of the top three eligibles on the list. This explains why the person whose name is on top of the list sometimes does not get an appointment when some of the persons lower on the list do. If the appointing officer chooses the second or third eligible, the No. 1 eligible does not get a job at once, but stays on the list until he is appointed or the list is terminated.

X. HOW TO PASS THE INTERVIEW TEST

The examination for which you applied requires an oral interview test. You have already taken the written test and you are now being called for the interview test – the final part of the formal examination.

You may think that it is not possible to prepare for an interview test and that there are no procedures to follow during an interview. Our purpose is to point out some things you can do in advance that will help you and some good rules to follow and pitfalls to avoid while you are being interviewed.

What is an interview supposed to test?

The written examination is designed to test the technical knowledge and competence of the candidate; the oral is designed to evaluate intangible qualities, not readily measured otherwise, and to establish a list showing the relative fitness of each candidate – as measured against his competitors – for the position sought. Scoring is not on the basis of "right" and "wrong," but on a sliding scale of values ranging from "not passable" to "outstanding." As a matter of fact, it is possible to achieve a relatively low score without a single "incorrect" answer because of evident weakness in the qualities being measured.

Occasionally, an examination may consist entirely of an oral test – either an individual or a group oral. In such cases, information is sought concerning the technical knowledges and abilities of the candidate, since there has been no written examination for this purpose. More commonly, however, an oral test is used to supplement a written examination.

Who conducts interviews?

The composition of oral boards varies among different jurisdictions. In nearly all, a representative of the personnel department serves as chairman. One of the members of the board may be a representative of the department in which the candidate would work. In some cases, "outside experts" are used, and, frequently, a businessman or some other representative of the general public is asked to serve. Labor and management or other special groups may be represented. The aim is to secure the services of experts in the appropriate field.

However the board is composed, it is a good idea (and not at all improper or unethical) to ascertain in advance of the interview who the members are and what groups they represent. When you are introduced to them, you will have some idea of their backgrounds and interests, and at least you will not stutter and stammer over their names.

What should be done before the interview?

While knowledge about the board members is useful and takes some of the surprise element out of the interview, there is other preparation which is more substantive. It *is* possible to prepare for an oral interview – in several ways:

1) Keep a copy of your application and review it carefully before the interview

This may be the only document before the oral board, and the starting point of the interview. Know what education and experience you have listed there, and the sequence and dates of all of it. Sometimes the board will ask you to review the highlights of your experience for them; you should not have to hem and haw doing it.

2) Study the class specification and the examination announcement

Usually, the oral board has one or both of these to guide them. The qualities, characteristics or knowledges required by the position sought are stated in these documents. They offer valuable clues as to the nature of the oral interview. For example, if the job involves supervisory responsibilities, the announcement will usually indicate that knowledge of modern supervisory methods and the qualifications of the candidate as a supervisor will be tested. If so, you can expect such questions, frequently in the form of a hypothetical situation which you are expected to solve. NEVER go into an oral without knowledge of the duties and responsibilities of the job you seek.

3) Think through each qualification required

Try to visualize the kind of questions you would ask if you were a board member. How well could you answer them? Try especially to appraise your own knowledge and background in each area, *measured against the job sought*, and identify any areas in which you are weak. Be critical and realistic – do not flatter yourself.

4) Do some general reading in areas in which you feel you may be weak

For example, if the job involves supervision and your past experience has NOT, some general reading in supervisory methods and practices, particularly in the field of human relations, might be useful. Do NOT study agency procedures or detailed manuals. The oral board will be testing your understanding and capacity, not your memory.

5) Get a good night's sleep and watch your general health and mental attitude

You will want a clear head at the interview. Take care of a cold or any other minor ailment, and of course, no hangovers.

What should be done on the day of the interview?

Now comes the day of the interview itself. Give yourself plenty of time to get there. Plan to arrive somewhat ahead of the scheduled time, particularly if your appointment is in the fore part of the day. If a previous candidate fails to appear, the board might be ready for you a bit early. By early afternoon an oral board is almost invariably behind schedule if there are many candidates, and you may have to wait. Take along a book or magazine to read, or your application to review, but leave any extraneous material in the waiting room when you go in for your interview. In any event, relax and compose yourself.

The matter of dress is important. The board is forming impressions about you – from your experience, your manners, your attitude, and your appearance. Give your personal appearance careful attention. Dress your best, but not your flashiest. Choose conservative, appropriate clothing, and be sure it is immaculate. This is a business interview, and your appearance should indicate that you regard it as such. Besides, being well groomed and properly dressed will help boost your confidence.

Sooner or later, someone will call your name and escort you into the interview room. *This is it.* From here on you are on your own. It is too late for any more preparation. But remember, you asked for this opportunity to prove your fitness, and you are here because your request was granted.

What happens when you go in?

The usual sequence of events will be as follows: The clerk (who is often the board stenographer) will introduce you to the chairman of the oral board, who will introduce you to the other members of the board. Acknowledge the introductions before you sit down. Do not be surprised if you find a microphone facing you or a stenotypist sitting by. Oral interviews are usually recorded in the event of an appeal or other review.

Usually the chairman of the board will open the interview by reviewing the highlights of your education and work experience from your application – primarily for the benefit of the other members of the board, as well as to get the material into the record. Do not interrupt or comment unless there is an error or significant misinterpretation; if that is the case, do not hesitate. But do not quibble about insignificant matters. Also, he will usually ask you some question about your education, experience or your present job – partly to get you to start talking and to establish the interviewing "rapport." He may start the actual questioning, or turn it over to one of the other members. Frequently, each member undertakes the questioning on a particular area, one in which he is perhaps most competent, so you can expect each member to participate in the examination. Because time is limited, you may also expect some rather abrupt switches in the direction the questioning takes, so do not be upset by it. Normally, a board member will not pursue a single line of questioning unless he discovers a particular strength or weakness.

After each member has participated, the chairman will usually ask whether any member has any further questions, then will ask you if you have anything you wish to add. Unless you are expecting this question, it may floor you. Worse, it may start you off on an extended, extemporaneous speech. The board is not usually seeking more information. The question is principally to offer you a last opportunity to present further qualifications or to indicate that you have nothing to add. So, if you feel that a significant qualification or characteristic has been overlooked, it is proper to point it out in a sentence or so. Do not compliment the board on the thoroughness of their examination – they have been sketchy, and you know it. If you wish, merely say, "No thank you, I have nothing further to add." This is a point where you can "talk yourself out" of a good impression or fail to present an important bit of information. Remember, *you close the interview yourself.*

The chairman will then say, "That is all, Mr. _____, thank you." Do not be startled; the interview is over, and quicker than you think. Thank him, gather your belongings and take your leave. Save your sigh of relief for the other side of the door.

How to put your best foot forward

Throughout this entire process, you may feel that the board individually and collectively is trying to pierce your defenses, seek out your hidden weaknesses and embarrass and confuse you. Actually, this is not true. They are obliged to make an appraisal of your qualifications for the job you are seeking, and they want to see you in your best light. Remember, they must interview all candidates and a non-cooperative candidate may become a failure in spite of their best efforts to bring out his qualifications. Here are 15 suggestions that will help you:

1) Be natural – Keep your attitude confident, not cocky

If you are not confident that you can do the job, do not expect the board to be. Do not apologize for your weaknesses, try to bring out your strong points. The board is interested in a positive, not negative, presentation. Cockiness will antagonize any board member and make him wonder if you are covering up a weakness by a false show of strength.

2) Get comfortable, but don't lounge or sprawl

Sit erectly but not stiffly. A careless posture may lead the board to conclude that you are careless in other things, or at least that you are not impressed by the importance of the occasion. Either conclusion is natural, even if incorrect. Do not fuss with your clothing, a pencil or an ashtray. Your hands may occasionally be useful to emphasize a point; do not let them become a point of distraction.

3) Do not wisecrack or make small talk

This is a serious situation, and your attitude should show that you consider it as such. Further, the time of the board is limited – they do not want to waste it, and neither should you.

4) Do not exaggerate your experience or abilities

In the first place, from information in the application or other interviews and sources, the board may know more about you than you think. Secondly, you probably will not get away with it. An experienced board is rather adept at spotting such a situation, so do not take the chance.

5) If you know a board member, do not make a point of it, yet do not hide it

Certainly you are not fooling him, and probably not the other members of the board. Do not try to take advantage of your acquaintanceship – it will probably do you little good.

6) Do not dominate the interview

Let the board do that. They will give you the clues – do not assume that you have to do all the talking. Realize that the board has a number of questions to ask you, and do not try to take up all the interview time by showing off your extensive knowledge of the answer to the first one.

7) Be attentive

You only have 20 minutes or so, and you should keep your attention at its sharpest throughout. When a member is addressing a problem or question to you, give him your undivided attention. Address your reply principally to him, but do not exclude the other board members.

8) Do not interrupt

A board member may be stating a problem for you to analyze. He will ask you a question when the time comes. Let him state the problem, and wait for the question.

9) Make sure you understand the question

Do not try to answer until you are sure what the question is. If it is not clear, restate it in your own words or ask the board member to clarify it for you. However, do not haggle about minor elements.

10) Reply promptly but not hastily

A common entry on oral board rating sheets is "candidate responded readily," or "candidate hesitated in replies." Respond as promptly and quickly as you can, but do not jump to a hasty, ill-considered answer.

11) Do not be peremptory in your answers

A brief answer is proper – but do not fire your answer back. That is a losing game from your point of view. The board member can probably ask questions much faster than you can answer them.

12) Do not try to create the answer you think the board member wants

He is interested in what kind of mind you have and how it works – not in playing games. Furthermore, he can usually spot this practice and will actually grade you down on it.

13) Do not switch sides in your reply merely to agree with a board member

Frequently, a member will take a contrary position merely to draw you out and to see if you are willing and able to defend your point of view. Do not start a debate, yet do not surrender a good position. If a position is worth taking, it is worth defending.

14) Do not be afraid to admit an error in judgment if you are shown to be wrong

The board knows that you are forced to reply without any opportunity for careful consideration. Your answer may be demonstrably wrong. If so, admit it and get on with the interview.

15) Do not dwell at length on your present job

The opening question may relate to your present assignment. Answer the question but do not go into an extended discussion. You are being examined for a *new* job, not your present one. As a matter of fact, try to phrase ALL your answers in terms of the job for which you are being examined.

Basis of Rating

Probably you will forget most of these "do's" and "don'ts" when you walk into the oral interview room. Even remembering them all will not ensure you a passing grade. Perhaps you did not have the qualifications in the first place. But remembering them will help you to put your best foot forward, without treading on the toes of the board members.

Rumor and popular opinion to the contrary notwithstanding, an oral board wants you to make the best appearance possible. They know you are under pressure – but they also want to see how you respond to it as a guide to what your reaction would be under the pressures of the job you seek. They will be influenced by the degree of poise you display, the personal traits you show and the manner in which you respond.

ABOUT THIS BOOK

This book contains tests divided into Examination Sections. Go through each test, answering every question in the margin. We have also attached a sample answer sheet at the back of the book that can be removed and used. At the end of each test look at the answer key and check your answers. On the ones you got wrong, look at the right answer choice and learn. Do not fill in the answers first. Do not memorize the questions and answers, but understand the answer and principles involved. On your test, the questions will likely be different from the samples. Questions are changed and new ones added. If you understand these past questions you should have success with any changes that arise. Tests may consist of several types of questions. We have additional books on each subject should more study be advisable or necessary for you. Finally, the more you study, the better prepared you will be. This book is intended to be the last thing you study before you walk into the examination room. Prior study of relevant texts is also recommended. NLC publishes some of these in our Fundamental Series. Knowledge and good sense are important factors in passing your exam. Good luck also helps. So now study this Passbook, absorb the material contained within and take that knowledge into the examination. Then do your best to pass that exam.

EXAMINATION SECTION

EXAMINATION SECTION

TEST 1

DIRECTIONS: Each question or incomplete statement is followed by several suggested answers or completions. Select the one that BEST answers the question or completes the statement. *PRINT THE LETTER OF THE CORRECT ANSWER IN THE SPACE AT THE RIGHT.*

1. Assume that a supervisor finds that his employees have become fatigued from doing a very long and repetitious job.
   The one of the following which would be the BEST way to relieve this fatigue is to
   A. assign other work so that the employees can switch to different assignments in the middle of the day
   B. let the employees listen to a radio while they work
   C. break the job down into very small parts so that each employee can concentrate on one simple task
   D. allow the employees to take frequent rest periods

   1.____

2. Assume that one of your subordinates is injured and will be out for at least six weeks.
   Of the following, the BEST way to handle the work normally assigned to this person is to
   A. allow the work to remain uncompleted until the injured person returns, since he is the one who can BEST do this work
   B. divide this work equally among the persons under your supervision who can do this work
   C. do all the work yourself
   D. give the injured person's work to the most efficient member of your staff

   2.____

3. Suppose that another supervisor tells you about a new way to organize some of your unit's work. The idea sounds good to you. However, before you were in this unit, a similar plan was tried and it failed.
   The MOST important thing for you to do FIRST is to
   A. find out why the previous attempt failed
   B. suggest that the other supervisor tell his idea to top management
   C. try the plan to see whether it works
   D. find proof that the plan has worked elsewhere

   3.____

4. One of your subordinates comes to you with a grievance. You discuss it with him so that you may fully understand the problem as he sees it. However, since you are uncertain as to the proper answer, you should
   A. tell him that you cannot help him with this problem
   B. tell him that you will have to check further and make an appointment to see him again
   C. send him to see your immediate superior for a solution to the problem
   D. ask him to find out from his co-workers whether this problem has come up before

   4.____

5. A supervisor reprimanded one of his subordinates severely for making a serious error in judgment while performing an assignment for which he had volunteered.
The supervisor's action was
   A. *incorrect*, chiefly because in the future the worker will probably try to avoid taking on responsibility
   B. *correct*, chiefly because this will insure that the worker will not make the same mistake in the future
   C. *correct*, chiefly because the worker should be discouraged from using his own judgment on the job
   D. *incorrect*, chiefly because the reprimand came too late to correct the error that had already been made

5.____

6. Of the following, the BEST way for a supervisor to inform all his subordinates of a change in lunch rules is, in MOST cases, to
   A. call a staff meeting
   B. tell each one individually
   C. issue a memorandum
   D. tell one or two employees to pass the word around

6.____

7. For a supervisor to assign work giving only general instructions to his subordinate would be advisable when
   A. the supervisor is confident that the worker knows how to do the job
   B. the assignment is a simple one
   C. the subordinate is himself a supervisory employee
   D. errors in the work will not cause serious delay

7.____

8. One of the DISADVANTAGES of setting minimum standards of performance for custodial employees is that
   A. such standards eliminate the basis for evaluating employees
   B. the custodial employees may keep their performance at the minimum level
   C. standards are always subject to change
   D. the supervisor may feel that his initiative is being restricted

8.____

9. One of your subordinates has been functioning below his usual level. You feel that something of a personal nature may be affecting his work. When you ask him casually whether anything is wrong, he says everything is fine.
As a next step, it would be BEST to
   A. make frequent casual and humorous comments about the poor quality of his work but refrain, at this time, from any serious discussion
   B. warn him that failure to maintain his customary level of performance might result in disciplinary action
   C. express your concern privately and reveal your interest in the reason for his change in work performance
   D. discuss with him the work of another employee, suggesting that the other employee would be a good example to follow

9.____

10. Assume you are teaching a new job to one of your subordinates. After you have demonstrated the job, you can BEST maintain the worker's interest by
    A. showing him training films about the job
    B. giving him printed material that explains why the job is important
    C. having him observe other workers do the job
    D. letting him attempt to do the job by himself under supervision

10.____

11. *Insubordination is sometimes a protest against inferior or arbitrary leadership.*
    For the supervisor, the MOST basic implication of the above statement is:
    A. Accusations of insubordination are easy to make, but usually difficult to prove.
    B. Insubordination cannot be permitted if an organization wishes to remain effective.
    C. When an employee discusses an order instead of carrying it out, he has not understood it.
    D. When an employee questions an order, review it to make sure it is reasonable.

11.____

12. In appraising a subordinate's mistakes, a supervisor should ALWAYS consider the
    A. absolute number of mistakes, without regard to severity
    B. number of mistakes in proportion to the number of decisions made
    C. total number of mistakes made by other, regardless of assignment
    D. number of mistakes which were discovered upon higher review

12.____

13. If you are the supervisor of an office in which the work frequently involves lifting heavy boxes, you should instruct your staff in the proper method of lifting to avoid injury.
    In giving these instructions, you should stress that a person lifting heavy objects MUST
    A. keep his feet close together
    B. bend at the waist
    C. keep his back as straight as possible
    D. use his back muscles to straighten up

13.____

14. Of the following, the BEST qualified supervisor is one who
    A. knows the basic principles and procedures of all the jobs which he supervises
    B. has detailed working knowledge of all aspects of the job he supervises but knows little about principles of supervision
    C. is able to do exceptionally well at least one of the jobs which he supervises and as some knowledge of the others
    D. knows little or nothing about most of the jobs which he supervises but knows the principles of supervision

14.____

15. The rate at which an employee will learn will vary according to a number of considerations.
    Of the following, which is LEAST likely to be controllable by the supervisor or the trainer? The
    A. manner in which the material is presented
    B. state of readiness of the learner
    C. scheduling of practice sessions
    D. nature of the material

16. When considering whether to use written material rather than oral instructions as a means of giving instructions to employees, the one of the following which should be given GREATEST consideration is the employees'
    A. personal preferences
    B. attitude toward supervision
    C. general educational level
    D. salary level

17. Assume that one of your subordinates has been assigned to attend job training classes.
    The one of the following which would probably be the BEST evidence of the success of the course is that the employee
    A. feels that he has learned something
    B. continues to study after the course is over
    C. has had a good class record
    D. improves in his work performance

18. Of the following, the situation LEAST likely to result if a supervisor shows favoritism toward particular employees is
    A. laxity in the work of the favored employees
    B. resentment from the other, less-favored employees
    C. increased ability among the favored employees
    D. lowering of morale among employees

19. The one of the following reasons for evaluating employees' performance, whether done formally or informally, which is NOT considered to be POSITIVE in nature is to
    A. give individual counsel to employees
    B. motivate employees toward improvement
    C. provide recognition of superior service
    D. set penalties for substandard performance

20. Assume that, because there has been an unexpected and temporary increase in the short-term work of your unit, you have had temporarily assigned to you several staff members from another agency.
    Of the following, in dealing with these employees, it would be LEAST advisable to
    A. assign them to long-term projects
    B. organize tasks so that they can begin work immediately
    C. set standards, making allowances to give them time to learn your ways
    D. direct them in the same way, in general, as you do your regular staff

21. It has been suggested that one way to increase employee productivity would be to require employees dealing with the public to have proficiency in a relevant foreign language.
    Of the following, the MAJOR reason for implementing such a proposal, from the viewpoint of effective public administration, would be to
    A. encourage the foreign-born to learn English
    B. exchange information more rapidly and accurately
    C. increase the public prestige of the agency
    D. stimulate ethnic pride among all groups

21.____

22. Assume that the clerk who normally keeps your unit's records will be on vacation for four weeks.
    If other clerks are equally qualified to keep these records, your BEST choice to replace the clerk would be the person who
    A. has skills which are needed least for other duties during this period
    B. volunteers for this work
    C. is next in turn for a special assignment
    D. has handled this task before

22.____

23. Assume that you have under your supervision several young clerical employees who have the bad habit of fooling around when they should be working.
    Of the following, the BEST disciplinary action to take would be to
    A. ignore it; these young people will outgrow it
    B. join in the fun briefly in order to bring it to a quicker end each time it occurs
    C. bring to their attention the fact that this behavior is not acceptable and if it continues shift the make-up of the group to keep these young persons apart
    D. warn them that this type of behavior is reason for dismissal and be quick to make an example of the first one who starts it again

23.____

24. Seeking the advice of community leaders has human relations value for a public agency in planning or executing its programs CHIEFLY because it
    A. allows for the keeping of careful records concerning individual suggestions
    B. lets community leaders know that the agency has regard for their opinions
    C. permits the agency to state in writing which programs seem most appropriate
    D. unifies community leaders against the programs of competing private agencies

24.____

25. Good community relations is often action-oriented.
    Which of the following activities of a public agency is LEAST likely to be considered as action-oriented by the people of a local community?
    A. Conducting a survey to gather information about the local community
    B. Extending the use of a facility to those previously excluded
    C. Providing a service that was formerly non-existent
    D. Removing something considered objectionable by the local community

25.____

KEY (CORRECT ANSWERS)

1.	A	11.	D
2.	B	12.	B
3.	A	13.	C
4.	B	14.	A
5.	A	15.	B
6.	C	16.	C
7.	A	17.	D
8.	B	18.	D
9.	C	19.	D
10.	D	20.	A

21. B
22. A
23. C
24. B
25. A

TEST 2

DIRECTIONS: Each question or incomplete statement is followed by several suggested answers or completions. Select the one that BEST answers the question or completes the statement. *PRINT THE LETTER OF THE CORRECT ANSWER IN THE SPACE AT THE RIGHT.*

1. Methods of communication with employees are of three types: oral, written, and visual.
   A MAJOR advantage of the written word is that it
   A. insures that content will remain unchanged no matter how many persons may be involved in its transmission
   B. facilitates two-way communication in delicate or confidential situations
   C. strengthens chain-of-command procedures in transmission of information and instruction by requiring the use of prescribed channels
   D. encourages the active participation of employees in the solution of complicated problems

2. The use of the conference technique in training often requires more preparatory work on the part of the trainer than does a good lecture PRIMARILY because
   A. a conference would cover material of a more technical nature
   B. the trainer will be required to supply more printed material to the participants
   C. a conference usually involves a greater number of trainees
   D. the trainer must be prepared for a wide variety of possible occurrences

3. The one of the following which is NOT an advantage of the lecture over most other methods of training is that it can be given
   A. over the radio or on record
   B. to large numbers of trainees
   C. without interruptions
   D. with little preparation

4. Of the following, the one which is LEAST appropriate as a purpose for using an employee attitude survey is to
   A. develop a supervisory training program
   B. learn the identity of dissatisfied employees
   C. re-evaluate employee relations policies
   D. re-orient publications designed for employees

5. The competent trainer seeks to become knowledgeable both in the work of the agency and in the duties of the positions for which he is to conduct training. Of the following, the GREATEST practical value that result when the trainer gains such knowledge is that
   A. he will be more likely to instruct employees to perform their work in a manner consistent with actual practice
   B. all levels of staff will be favorably impressed by a display of interest in the agency and its work
   C. employees will become familiar with the trainer and will not consider him an outsider
   D. the trainer will gain an accurate picture of the capacity of each employee for training

6. Assume that you, the supervisor of a small office, are involved in planning the reorganization of your bureau's work. Management has decided not to inform your staff of the reorganization until the plans are completed.
If one of your subordinates tells you that he has heard a rumor about reorganization of the department, you should reply that
   A. the reorganization involves the bureau, not the department
   B. you haven't heard anything about departmental reorganization and that he should stop spreading rumors
   C. you will inform your staff at the appropriate time if any definite plans are made involving a reorganization
   D. you do not know what is being planned but will ask your superior for details

7. Of the following training methods, the one in which the trainee's role is usually LEAST active is the _____ method.
   A. case-study
   B. conference
   C. group discussion
   D. lecture

8. Differences in morale between two work groups can sometimes be attributed to differences in the supervision they receive.
Of the following, the behavior MOST characteristic of a supervisor of a group with high morale is that he
   A. assigns the least difficult tasks to employees with the most seniority
   B. is concerned primarily with his ultimate responsibility, production
   C. delegates authority and responsibility to his staff
   D. is lenient with his workers when they violate rules

9. Informal performance evaluations of individual employees, prepared systematically and regularly over a period of several years, are considered to be useful to a supervisor PRIMARILY because
   A. he will be able to assign tasks based only on these records
   B. unlike formal records, since they are fitted to the characteristics of individual employees, they provide for quick comparisons
   C. he need not discuss them with employees, since they are informal
   D. whatever personnel action he recommends can be substantiated by cumulative records

10. When instructing first-line supervisors in the proper method of evaluating the performance of probationary employees, it is LEAST important for a higher-level supervisor to
    A. explain in detail the standards to be used
    B. inform them of the possibility of higher management review
    C. caution them concerning common errors of evaluation
    D. mention the purposes of probationary employee evaluation

11. Assume that your agency is considering abolishing its official performance rating system but that you, a supervisor of a fairly large office, would like to devise a system for your own use.
    The FIRST step in setting up a system would be to
    A. decide what factors and personal characteristics are important and should be rated
    B. compare several rating methods to see which would be easiest to use
    C. have a private conference with each employee to discuss his performance
    D. set specific standards of employee performance, allowing your workers to make suggestions

11.____

12. The basic organizational structure of a municipal agency may have come about for several reasons.
    Of the following, the MOST important influence on the nature of its structure is the agency's
    A. professional attitude
    B. public reputation
    C. overall goal
    D. staff morale

12.____

13. The term *formal organization* refers to that organization structure agreed upon by top management whereas the term *informal organization* refers to the more spontaneous and flexible organizational ties developed by subordinates.
    The one of the following which BEST describes the usual *informal organization* is that it represents a(n)
    A. destructive system of relationships which should be eliminated
    B. concealed system of relationships whose goals are the same as management's
    C. actual system of relationships which should be recognized
    D. dysfunctional system of relationships which should be ignored

13.____

14. The reluctance of supervisors to delegate work to subordinates when they should is GENERALLY due to the supervisor's
    A. feelings of insecurity in work situations
    B. need to acquire additional experience
    C. inability to exercise control over his subordinates
    D. lack of technical knowledge

14.____

15. Assume that you have just been made the supervisor of a group of people you did not know before.
    For you to talk casually with each of your new subordinates with the purpose of getting to know them personally would be
    A. *advisable*, chiefly because subordinates have more confidence in a supervisor who shows personal interest in them
    B. *inadvisable*, chiefly because subordinates resent having their supervisor ask about their outside interests
    C. *advisable*, chiefly because one of the supervisor's main concerns should be to help his subordinates with their personal problems
    D. *inadvisable*, chiefly because a supervisor should not allow his relations with his subordinates to be influenced by their personalities

15.____

16. It has been found that high-producing subdivisions of organizations usually have supervisors whose behavior is employee-centered, whereas low-producing units usually have supervisors whose behavior is work-centered.
Therefore, it could be concluded from these findings that
    A. a high-producing unit may cause a supervisor to be authoritarian
    B. a low-producing unit may cause a supervisor to be work-centered
    C. close supervision usually increases production
    D. employee-centered leadership may reduce production

17. A recent study in managerial science showed that, as the amount of praise increased and amount of criticism decreased, the supervisor was more likely to be perceived by his subordinates as being
    A. concerned with their career advancement
    B. production oriented, through subtle intimidation
    C. seeking personal satisfaction, irrespective of production
    D. uncertain of the subordinates' reliability

18. The power to issue directives or instructions to employees is derived from employees as much as from management.
It follows MOST logically from this statement that
    A. attitudes toward management can be changed
    B. emphasis on discipline is needed
    C. authority is dependent upon acceptance
    D. employees should be properly supervised for work to be done

19. "In the decision-making process, it is a rare problem that has only one possible solution. Such a solution should be suspected of being nothing but a plausible argument for a preconceived idea."
The author of the foregoing quotation apparently does NOT believe that
    A. there is usually only one possible solution to a problem
    B. the risks involved in any solution should be weighed against expected gains
    C. each alternative should be evaluated to determine the effort needed
    D. actions should be based on the urgency of problems

20. The supervisor who relies on punitive discipline to enforce his authority is putting limits on the potential of his leadership. Fear of punishment may secure obedience, but it destroys initiative. Such a supervisor's autocratic methods have cut off upward communications.
Of the following, the major DISADVANTAGE of such autocratic behavior is that
    A. difficulties in the supervision of his subordinates will arise if limits are placed on the supervisor's responsibility
    B. policies that affect the public will be changed too frequently
    C. the supervisor will apply punishment subjectively rather than objectively
    D. instructions will be obeyed to the letter, regardless of changing circumstances

21. The need for a supervisor to carefully coordinate and direct the work of his unit increases as the work becomes
    A. more routine
    B. more specialized
    C. less complex
    D. less technical

    21.____

22. The MAIN goal of discipline as used by a supervisor should be to
    A. keep the employees' respect
    B. influence behavior, so that work will be completed properly
    C. encourage the employees to work faster
    D. set an example for others

    22.____

23. One of your subordinates has exhibited discourtesy and non-cooperation on several occasions.
    Of the following, the MOST appropriate attitude for you to adopt in dealing with this problem is that
    A. disciplinary measures for such an individual generally creates additional problems
    B. failure to correct such behavior may lead to worse offenses
    C. it is a mistake to make an issue out of minor infractions
    D. the harsher the medicine, the faster the cure

    23.____

24. Assume that an employee has complained to you, his supervisor, that he cannot concentrate on his work because two of his co-workers make too much noise. You pay particular attention to these employees for several days and do not find them making excessive noise.
    The NEXT step you should take in handling this grievance is to
    A. have a talk with all three employees, urging them to cooperate and be considerate of one another
    B. arrange for the complainant to change his work location to a place away from the two co-workers
    C. talk to the complainant to find out if the complaint he made to you is the real cause of his dissatisfaction
    D. tell the complainant that you have found his grievance to be unfounded

    24.____

25. In planning the application of an existing agency program to a local community, it is generally necessary to discover relevant problems and possibilities for service.
    Of the following, the BEST way to learn about such problems and possibilities for service would usually be to
    A. begin the program on a full-scale basis and await reactions
    B. seek opinions and advice from community residents and leaders
    C. hold staff meetings with agency employees who have worked in similar communities
    D. study official federal reports about already completed programs of the same kind

    25.____

KEY (CORRECT ANSWERS)

1.	A	11.	A
2.	D	12.	C
3.	D	13.	C
4.	B	14.	A
5.	A	15.	A
6.	C	16.	B
7.	D	17.	A
8.	C	18.	C
9.	D	19.	A
10.	B	20.	D

21.	B
22.	B
23.	B
24.	C
25.	B

TEST 3

DIRECTIONS: Each question or incomplete statement is followed by several suggested answers or completions. Select the one that BEST answers the question or completes the statement. *PRINT THE LETTER OF THE CORRECT ANSWER IN THE SPACE AT THE RIGHT.*

1. Which of the following characteristics would be LEAST detrimental to a supervisor in his efforts to set up and maintain good relations with other supervisors with whom he must deal in the course of his duties?
   A. Not getting involved in consultation on any supervisory problems they might have
   B. Indicating that they should improve their supervising methods and offering suggestions on how to do so
   C. Emphasizing his own role as a member of management
   D. Sharing information which has proved useful in his unit

1.____

2. Both trainers and supervisors might agree that there is usually a best way to do a particular job. Yet a supervisor or instructor sometimes does not teach a new employee the best way, the most efficient way, to do a complex job. Sometimes, in such cases, the supervisor temporarily changes the sequence of operations, increases the number of steps needed to do a job, or makes other changes in the method, which then deviates from the one considered most efficient.
   When is such a difference in approach MOST justified when teaching a new employee a complex job?
   A. When the changes in approach correspond to the learning ability of the new employee
   B. When the new employee's performance on the job is closely supervised to compensate for a change in approach
   C. Where the steps in performing the task have not been defined in a manual of procedures
   D. When the instructor has ideas of improving upon the methods for doing the job

2.____

3. Considerable thought in the field of management is directed toward the advantages and disadvantages of authoritarian methods of influencing behavior, and, in the so-called authoritarian model, a nucleus of rather consistent ideas prevail.
   Which of the following is LEAST characteristic of an administrative system based on the authoritarian model?
   A. A conviction of a need for order and efficiency in a world consisting mainly of people who lack direction and incentive
   B. Rules and contracts are the basis for action, and decisions are made on an impersonal basis
   C. The right to give orders and instructions is inherent in the hierarchical arrangement of an organizational structure
   D. Realization that subordinates' needs for affiliation and recognition can contribute to management's objectives

3.____

4. Of the following, the FIRST step in planning an operation is to
   A. obtain relevant information
   B. identify the goal to be achieved
   C. consider possible alternatives
   D. make necessary assignments

5. A supervisor who is extremely busy performing routine tasks is MOST likely making incorrect use of what basis principle of supervision?
   A. Homogeneous Assignment
   B. Span of Control
   C. Work Distribution
   D. Delegation of Authority

6. Controls help supervisors to obtain information from which they can determine whether their staffs are achieving planned goals.
   Which one of the following would be LEAST useful as a control device?
   A. Employee diaries
   B. Organization charts
   C. Periodic inspections
   D. Progress charts

7. A certain employee has difficulty in effectively performing a particular portion of his routine assignments, but his overall productivity is average.
   As a direct supervisor of this individual, your BEST course of action would be to
   A. attempt to develop the investigator's capacity to execute the problematical facets of his assignments
   B. diversify the investigator's work assignments in order to build up his confidence
   C. reassign the investigator to less difficult tasks
   D. request in a private conversation that the investigator improve his work output

8. A supervisor who uses persuasion as a means of supervising a unit would GENERALLY also use which of the following practices to supervise his unit?
   A. Supervises and control the staff with an authoritative attitude to indicate that he is a *take-charge* individual
   B. Make significant changes in the organizational operations so as to improve job efficiency
   C. Remove major communication barriers between himself, subordinates, and management
   D. Supervise everyday operations while being mindful of the problems of his subordinates

9. Whenever a supervisor in charge of a unit delegates a routine task to a capable subordinate, he tells him exactly how to do it.
   This practice is GENERALLY
   A. *desirable*, chiefly because good supervisors should be aware of the traits of their subordinates and delegate responsibilities to them accordingly
   B. *undesirable*, chiefly because only non-routine tasks should be delegated
   C. *desirable*, chiefly because a supervisor should frequently test the willingness of his subordinates to perform ordinary tasks
   D. *undesirable*, chiefly because a capable subordinate should usually be allowed to exercise his own discretion in doing a routine job

10. The one of the following activities through which a supervisor BEST demonstrates leadership ability is by
    A. arranging periodic staff meetings in order to keep his subordinates informed about professional developments in the field of investigation
    B. frequently issuing definite orders and directives which will lessen the need for subordinates to make decisions in handling any investigations assigned to them
    C. devoting the major part of his time to supervising subordinates so as to stimulate continuous improvement
    D. setting aside time for self-development and research so as to improve the investigative techniques and procedures of his unit

10.____

11. The following three statements relate to supervision of employees:
    I. The assignment of difficult tasks that offer a challenge is more conducive to good morale than the assignment of easy tasks.
    II. The same general principles of supervision that apply to men are equally applicable to women.
    III. The best restraining program should cover all phases of an employee's work in a general manner.
    Which of the following choices lists ALL of the above statements that are generally CORRECT?
    A. II, III B. I C. I, II D. I, II, III

11.____

12. Which of the following examples BEST illustrates the application of the *exception principle* as a supervisory technique? A(n)
    A. complex job is divided among several employees who work simultaneously to complete the whole job in a shorter time
    B. employee is required to complete any task delegated to him to such an extent that nothing is left for the superior who delegated the task except to approve it
    C. superior delegates responsibility to a subordinate but retains authority to make the final decisions
    D. superior delegates all work possible to his subordinates and retains that which requires his personal attention or performance

12.____

13. Assume that you are a supervisor. Your immediate superior frequently gives orders to your subordinates without your knowledge.
    Of the following, the MOST direct and effective way for you to handle this problem is to
    A. tell your subordinates to take orders only from you
    B. submit a report to higher authority in which you cite specific instances
    C. discuss it with your immediate superior
    D. find out to what extent you authority and prestige as a supervisor have been affected

13.____

14. In an agency which has as its primary purpose the protection of the public against fraudulent business practices, which of the following would GENERALLY be considered an auxiliary or staff rather than a line function?

14.____

A. Interviewing victims of frauds and advising them about their legal remedies
B. Daily activities directed toward prevention of fraudulent business practices
C. Keeping records and statistics about business violations reported and corrected
D. Follow-up inspections by investigators after corrective action has been taken

15. A supervisor can MOST effectively reduce the spread of false rumors through the *grapevine* by
    A. identifying and disciplining any subordinate responsible for initiating such rumors
    B. keeping his subordinates informed as much as possible about matters affecting them
    C. denying false rumors which might tend to lower staff morale and productivity
    D. making sure confidential matters are kept secure from access by unauthorized employees

16. A supervisor has tried to learn about the background, education, and family relationships of his subordinates through observation, personal contact, and inspection of their personnel records.
    These supervisory actions are GENERALLY
    A. *inadvisable*, chiefly because they may lead to charges of favoritism
    B. *advisable*, chiefly because they may make him more popular with his subordinates
    C. *inadvisable*, chiefly because his efforts may be regarded as an invasion of privacy
    D. *advisable*, chiefly because the information may enable him to develop better understanding of each of his subordinates

17. In an emergency situation, when action must be taken immediately, it is BEST for the supervisor to give orders in the form of
    A. direct commands, which are brief and precise
    B. requests, so that his subordinate will not become alarmed
    C. suggestions, which offer alternative courses of action
    D. implied directive, so that his subordinates may use their judgment in carrying them out

18. When demonstrating a new and complex procedure to a group of subordinates, it is ESSENTIAL that a supervisor
    A. go slowly and repeat the steps involved at least once
    B. show the employees common errors and the consequences of such errors
    C. go through the process at the usual speed so that the employees can see the rate at which they should work
    D. distribute summaries of the procedure during the demonstration and instruct his subordinates to refer to them afterwards

19. The PRIMARY value of office reports and procedures is to
    A. assist top management in controlling key agency functions
    B. measure job performance
    C. save time and labor
    D. control the activities and use of time of all staff members

20. Of the following, which is considered to be the GREATEST advantage of the oral report? It
    A. allows for accurate transmission of information from one individual to another
    B. presents an opportunity to discuss or clarify any immediate questions raised by the receiver of the report
    C. requires less office work to maintain records on actions taken when an oral report is involved
    D. takes only a short amount of time to plan and prepare material for an oral report

21. A supervisor who is to make a report about a job he has done can make an oral report of a written report.
    Of the following, which is the BEST time to make an oral report? When
    A. the work covers an emergency situation
    B. a record is needed for the files
    C. the report is channeled to other departments
    D. the report covers additional work he will do

22. Suppose that a new employee has been assigned to you. It is your responsibility to see to it that he understands how to fill out properly the forms he is required to use.
    What would be the BEST way to do this?
    A. Explain the use of each form to the new technician and show him how to fill them out
    B. Give the new employee a copy of each form he must use so that he can learn by studying them
    C. Ask an experienced worker to explain clearly to him how the forms should be filled out
    D. Tell the new employee that filling out forms is simple and he should follow the instructions on each form

23. As a supervisor, you want to have your staff take part in improving work methods.
    Of the following, the BEST way to do this is to
    A. make critical appraisals of their work frequently
    B. encourage them to make suggestions
    C. make no change without their approval
    D. hold regular staff meetings

24. A good relationship with other supervisors is important to a senior supervisor. Close cooperation among supervisory personnel is MOST likely to result in
    A. increasing the probability for support of supervisory actions and decisions
    B. stimulating supervisors to achieve higher status in the organization
    C. helping to control the flow of work within a unit
    D. a clearer definition of the responsibilities of individual supervisors

25. Which of the following is MOST likely to gain a supervisor the respect and cooperation of his staff?
    A. Assigning the most difficult jobs to the experienced staff members
    B. Giving each staff member the same number of assignments
    C. Assigning jobs according to each staff member's ability
    D. Giving each staff member the same types of assignments

KEY (CORRECT ANSWERS)

1.	D	11.	C
2.	A	12.	D
3.	D	13.	C
4.	B	14.	C
5.	D	15.	B
6.	B	16.	D
7.	A	17.	A
8.	D	18.	A
9.	D	19.	A
10.	C	20.	B

21. A
22. A
23. B
24. A
25. C

EXAMINATION SECTION
TEST 1

DIRECTIONS: Each question or incomplete statement is followed by several suggested answers or completions. Select the one that BEST answers the question or completes the statement. *PRINT THE LETTER OF THE CORRECT ANSWER IN THE SPACE AT THE RIGHT.*

1. A supervisor was given a booklet that showed a new work method that could save time. He didn't tell his men because he thought that they would get the booklet anyway.
   For the supervisor to have acted like this is a
   A. *good* idea, because he saves time and both of talking to the men
   B. *bad* idea, because he should make sure his men know about better work methods
   C. *good* idea, because the men would rather read about it themselves
   D. *bad* idea, because a supervisor should always show his men every memo he gets from higher authority

   1.____

2. A supervisor found it necessary to discipline two subordinates. One man had been operating his equipment in a wrong way, while the other man came to work late for three days in a row. The supervisor decided to talk to both men together.
   For the supervisor to deal with the problems in this way is a
   A. *good* idea because each man will learn about the difficulties of the other person and how to solve such difficulties
   B. *bad* idea because the supervisor should wait until he can bring a larger group together and save time in discussing such questions
   C. *good* idea because he will be able to get the men to see that their problems are related
   D. *bad* idea because he should meet with each man separately and give him his full attention

   2.____

3. A supervisor should try to make his men feel their jobs are important in order to
   A. get the men to say good things about their supervisor to his own superior
   B. get the men to think in terms of advancing to better jobs
   C. let higher management in the agency know that the supervisor is efficient
   D. help the men to be able to work more efficiently and enthusiastically

   3.____

4. A supervisor should know approximately how long it takes to do a particular kind of job CHIEFLY because he
   A. will know how much time to take if he has to do it himself
   B. will be able to tell his men to do it even faster
   C. can judge the performance of the person doing the job
   D. can retrain experienced employees in better work habits

   4.____

5. Supervisors often get their employees' opinions about better work methods because
   A. the men will know that they are respected
   B. the men would otherwise lose all their confidence in the supervisor
   C. the supervisor might find in this way a good suggestion he could use
   D. this is the best method for improvement of work methods

6. Right after you have trained your subordinates in doing a new job, you find that they seem to be doing all right, but that it will take them several days to finish. You also have several groups of men working at other locations.
   The MOST efficient way for you to make sure that the men continue doing the new job properly is to
   A. stay on that job with the men until it is finished just in case trouble develops
   B. visit the men every half hour until the job is done
   C. stay away from their job that day and visit the men the next day to ask them if they had any problems
   D. visit the men a few times each day until they finish the new job

7. Assume that one of your new employees is older than you are. You also think that he may be hard to get along with because he is older than you.
   The BEST way for you to avoid any problems with the older worker is for you to
   A. lay down the law immediately and tell the man he better not cause you any trouble
   B. treat the man just the way you would any other worker
   C. always ask the older worker for advice in the presence of all the men
   D. ignore the man entirely until he realizes that you are the boss

8. Assume that you have tried a new method suggested by one of your employees and find that it is easier and cheaper than the method you had been using.
   The PROPER thing for you to do NEXT is to
   A. say nothing to anyone but train your men to use the new method
   B. train your men to use the new method and tell your crew that you got the idea from one of the men
   C. continue using the old method because a supervisor should not use suggestions of his men
   D. have your crew learn the new method and take credit for the idea since you are the boss

9. Suppose you are a supervisor and your superior tells you that the way your men are doing a certain procedure is wrong and that you should re-train our men as soon as possible.
   When you begin to re-train the men, the FIRST thing you should do is to
   A. tell your men that a wrong procedure had been used and that a new method must be learned as a result
   B. train your employees in the new method with no explanation since you are the boss

C. tell the crew that your superior has just decided that everyone should learn a new method
D. tell the crew that your superior says your method is wrong but that you don't agree with this

10. It is BAD practice to criticize a man in front of the other men because
    A. people will think you are too strict
    B. it is annoying to anyone who walks by
    C. it is embarrassing to the man concerned
    D. it will antagonize the other men

10.____

11. A supervisor decides not to put his two best men on a work detail because he knows that they won't like it.
    For the supervisor to make the work assignment this way is a
    A. *good* idea because it is only fair to give your best men a break once in a while
    B. *bad* idea because you should treat all of your me fairly and not show favoritism
    C. *good* idea because you save the strength of these men for another job
    D. *bad* idea because more of the men should be exempted from the assignment

11.____

12. Suppose you are a supervisor and you find it inconvenient to obey an established procedure set by your agency. You think another procedure would be better.
    The BEST thing to do first about this procedure that you don't like is for you to
    A. obey the procedure even if you don't to and suggest your idea to your own supervisor
    B. disregard the procedure because a supervisor is supposed to have some privileges
    C. follow the procedure some of the time but ignore it when the men are not watching
    D. organize a group of other supervisors to get the procedure changed

12.____

13. A supervisor estimated that it would take his crew one workday per week to do a certain job each week. However, after a month he noticed that the job averaged two and a half days a week and this delayed other jobs that had to be done.
    The FIRST thing that the supervisor should do in this case is to
    A. call him men together and warn them that they will get a poor work evaluation if they do not work harder
    B. talk to each man personally, asking him to work harder on the job
    C. go back and study the maintenance job by himself to see if more men should be assigned to the job
    D. write his boss a report describing in detail how much time it is taking the men to do the job

13.____

14. An employee complains to you that some of the work assignments are too difficult to do alone.
 Which of the following is the BEST way for you to handle this complaint?
 A. Go with him to see exactly what he does and why he finds it so difficult
 B. Politely tell the man that he has to do the job or be brought up on charges
 C. Tell the man to send his complaint to the head of your agency
 D. Sympathize with the man and give him easier jobs

15. The BEST way for a supervisor to keep control of his work assignments is to
 A. ask the men to report to him immediately when their jobs are finished
 B. walk around the buildings once a week and get a first-hand view of what is being done
 C. keep his ears open for problems and complaints, but leave the men aloe to do the work
 D. write up a work schedule and check it periodically against the actual work done

16. A supervisor made a work schedule for his men. At the bottom of it, he wrote, *No changes or exceptions will be made in this schedule for any reason.*
 For the supervisor to have made this statement is
 A. *good*, because the men will respect the supervisor for his attitude
 B. *bad*, because there are emergencies and special situations that occur
 C. *good*, because each man will know exactly what is expected of him
 D. *bad*, because the men should expect that no changes will ever be made in the work schedule without written permission

17. Which one of the following would NOT be a result of a well-planned work schedule?
 The schedule
 A. makes efficient use of the time of the staff
 B. acts as a checklist for an important job that might be left out
 C. will give an idea of the work to a substitute supervisor
 D. shows at a glance who the best men are

18. A new piece of equipment you have ordered is delivered. You are familiar with it, but the men under you who will use it do not know the equipment.
 Of the following methods, which is the BEST to take in explaining to them how to operate this equipment?
 A. Ask the men to watch other crews using the equipment
 B. Show one reliable man how to operate the equipment and ask him to teach the other men
 C. Ask the men to read the instructions in the manual for the equipment
 D. Call the men together and show them how to operate the equipment

19. One supervisor assigns work to his men by calling his crew together each week and describing what has to be done that week. He then tells them to arrange individual assignments among themselves and to work as a team during the week.

5 (#1)

This method of scheduling work is a
- A. *good* idea because this guarantees that the men will work together
- B. *bad* idea because responsibility for doing the job is poorly fixed
- C. *good* idea because the men will finish the job in less time, working together
- D. *bad* idea because the supervisor should always stay with his men

20. Suppose that an employee came to his supervisor with a problem concerning his assignment.
For the supervisor to listen to his problem is a
- A. *good* idea because a supervisor should always take time off to talk when one of his men wants to talk
- B. *bad* idea because the supervisor should not be bothered during the work day
- C. *good* idea because it is the job of the supervisor to deal with problems of job assignment
- D. *bad* idea because the employee could start annoying the supervisor with all sorts of problems

20.____

21. Suppose that on the previous afternoon you were looking for an experienced employee in order to give him an emergency job and he was missing from his job location. The next morning, he tells you that he got sick suddenly and had to go home, but could not tell you since you were not around. He has never done this before.
What should you do?
- A. Tell the man he is excused and that in such circumstances he did the wisest thing
- B. Bring the man up on charges because whatever he says he could still have notified you
- C. Have the man examined by a doctor to see if he really was sick the day before
- D. Explain to the mean that he should make every effort to tell you or to get a message to you if he must leave

21.____

22. An employee had a grievance and went to his supervisor about it. The employee was not satisfied with the way the supervisor tried to help him and told him so. Yet, the supervisor had done everything he could under the circumstances.
The PROPER action for the supervisor to take at this time is to
- A. politely tell the employee that there is nothing more for the supervisor to do about the problem
- B. let the employee know how he can bring his complaint to a higher authority
- C. tell the employee that he must solve the problem on his own since he did not want to follow the supervisor's advice
- D. suggest to the employee that he ask for another supervisor for assistance

22.____

23. In which of the following situations is it BEST to give your men spoken rather than written orders?
    A. You want your men to have a record of the instructions.
    B. Spoken instructions are less likely to be forgotten.
    C. An emergency situation has arisen in which there is no time to write up instructions.
    D. There are instructions on time and leave regulations which are complicated.

24. One of your employees tells you that a week ago he had a small accident on the job but he did not bother telling you because he was able to continue working.
    For the employee not to have told his supervisor about the accident was
    A. *good*, because the accident was a small one
    B. *bad*, because all accidents should be reported, no matter how small
    C. *good*, because the supervisor should be bothered only for important matters
    D. *bad*, because having an accident is one way to get excused for the day

25. For a supervisor to deal with each of his subordinate in exactly the same manner is
    A. *poor*, because each man presents a different problem and there is no one way of handling all problems
    B. *good*, because once a problem is handled with one man, he can handle another man with the same problem
    C. *poor*, because the men will resent it if they are not handled each in a better way than others
    D. *good*, because this assures fair and impartial treatment of each subordinate

KEY (CORRECT ANSWERS)

1.	B	11.	B
2.	D	12.	A
3.	D	13.	C
4.	C	14.	A
5.	C	15.	D
6.	D	16.	B
7.	B	17.	D
8.	B	18.	D
9.	A	19.	B
10.	C	20.	C

21. D
22. B
23. C
24. B
25. A

TEST 2

DIRECTIONS: Each question or incomplete statement is followed by several suggested answers or completions. Select the one that BEST answers the question or completes the statement. *PRINT THE LETTER OF THE CORRECT ANSWER IN THE SPACE AT THE RIGHT.*

1. Jim Johnson has been on your staff for over four years. He has always been a conscientious and productive worker. About a month ago, his wife died; and since that time, his work performance has been very poor.
   As his supervisor, which one of the following is the BEST way for you to deal with this situation?
   A. Allow Jim as much time as he needs to overcome his grief and hope that his work performance improves
   B. Meet with Jim to discuss ways to improve his performance
   C. Tell Jim directly that you are more concerned with his work performance than with his personal problem
   D. Prepare disciplinary action on Jim as soon as possible

2. You are responsible for the overall operation of a storehouse which is divided into two sections. Each section has its own supervisor. You have decided to make several complex changes in the storekeeping procedures which will affect both sections.
   Of the following, the BEST way to make sure that these changes are understood by the two supervisors is for you to
   A. meet with both supervisors to discuss the changes
   B. issue a memorandum to each supervisor explaining the changes
   C. post the changes where the supervisors are sure to see them
   D. instruct one supervisor to explain the changes to the other supervisor

3. You have called a meeting of all your subordinates to tell them what has to be done on a new project in which they will all be involved. Several times during the meeting, you ask if there are any questions about what you have told them.
   Of the following, to ask the subordinates whether there are any questions during the meeting can BEST be described as
   A. *inadvisable*, because it interferes with their learning about the new project
   B. *advisable*, because you will find out what they don't understand and have a chance to clear up any problems they may have
   C. *inadvisable*, because it makes the meeting too long and causes the subordinates to lose interest in the new project
   D. *advisable*, because it gives you a chance to learn which of your subordinates are paying attention to what you say

4. As a supervisor, you are responsible for seeing to it that absenteeism does not become a problem among your subordinates.
   Which one of the following is NOT an acceptable way of controlling the problem of excessive absences?

A. Distribute a written statement to your staff on the policies regarding absenteeism in your organization
B. Arrange for workers who have the fewest absences to talk to those workers who have the most absences
C. Let your subordinates know that a record is being kept of all absences
D. Arrange for counseling of those employees who are frequently absent

5. One of your supervisors has been an excellent worker for the past two years. There are no promotion opportunities for this worker in the foreseeable future. Due to the city's present budget crisis, a salary increase is not possible.
Under the circumstances, which one of the following actions on your part would be MOST likely to continue to motivate this worker?
    A. Tell the worker that times are bad all over and jobs are hard to find
    B. Give the worker less work and easier assignments
    C. Tell the worker to try to look for a better paying job elsewhere
    D. Seek the worker's advice often and show that the suggestions provided are appreciated

5._____

6. As a supervisor in a warehouse, it is important that you use your available work force to its fullest potential.
Which one of the following actions on your part is MOST likely to increase the effectiveness of your work force?
    A. Assigning more workers to a job than the number actually needed
    B. Eliminating all job training to allow more time for work output
    C. Using your best workers on jobs that average workers can do
    D. Making sure that all materials and equipment used are maintained in good working order

6._____

7. You learn that your storage area will soon be undergoing changes which will affect the work of your subordinates. You decide not to tell your subordinates about what is to happen.
Of the following, your action can BEST be described as
    A. *wise*, because your subordinates will learn of the changes for themselves
    B. *unwise*, because your subordinates should be advised about what is to happen
    C. *wise*, because it is better for your subordinates to continue working without being disturbed by such news
    D. *unwise*, because the work of your subordinates will gradually slow down

7._____

8. In making plans for the operation of your unit, you are MOST likely to see these plans carried out successfully if you
    A. allow your staff to participate in developing these plans
    B. do not spend any time on the minor details of these plans
    C. base these plans on the past experiences of others
    D. allow these plans to interact with outside activities in other units

8._____

9. As a supervisor in charge of the total operation of a food supply warehouse, you find vandalism to be a potentially serious problem. On occasion, trespassers have gained entrance into the facility by climbing over an unprotected 8-foot fence surrounding the warehouse whose dimensions measure 100 feet by 100 feet.
Assuming that all of the following would be equally effective ways in preventing these breaches in security in the situation described above, which one would be LEAST costly?
    A. Using two trained guard dogs to roam freely throughout the facility at night
    B. Hiring a security guard to patrol the facility after working hours
    C. Installing tape razor wire on top of the fence surrounding the facility
    D. Installing an electronic burglar alarm system requiring the installation of a new fence

10. The area for which you have program responsibility has undergone recent changes. Your staff is now required to perform many new tasks, and morale is low.
The LEAST effective way for you to improve long-term staff morale would be to
    A. develop support groups to discuss problems
    B. involve staff in job development
    C. maintain a comfortable social environment within the group
    D. adequately plan and give assignments in a timely manner

11. As a supervisor in a large office, one of your subordinate supervisors stops you in the middle of the office and complains loudly that he is being treated unfairly. The rest of the staff ceases work and listens to the complaint.
The MOST appropriate action for you to take in this situation is to
    A. ignore this unprofessional behavior and continue on your way
    B. tell the supervisor that his behavior is unprofessional and he should learn how to conduct himself
    C. explain to the supervisor why you believe he is not being treated unfairly
    D. ask the supervisor to come to your office at a specific time to discuss the matter

12. You are told that one of your subordinates is distributing literature which attempts to recruit individuals to join a particular organization. Several workers complain that their rights are being violated.
Of the following, the BEST action for you to take FIRST is to
    A. ignore the situation because no harm is being done
    B. discuss the matter further with your supervisor
    C. ask the worker to stop distributing the literature
    D. tell the workers that they do not have to read the material

13. You have been assigned to develop a short training course for a recently issued procedure.
In designing this course, which of the following statements is the LEAST important for you to consider?

A. The learning experience must be interesting and meaningful in terms of the staff member's job.
B. The method of teaching must be strictly followed in order to develop successful learning experiences.
C. The course content should incorporate the rules and regulations of the agency.
D. The procedure should be consistent with the agency's objectives.

14. As a supervisor, there are several newly-promoted employees under your supervision. Each of these employees is subject to a probationary period PRIMARILY to
    A. assess the employee's performance to see if the employee should be retained or removed from the position
    B. give the employee the option to return to his former employment if the employee is unhappy in the new position
    C. give the employee an opportunity to learn the duties and responsibilities of the position
    D. judge the employee's potential for upward mobility in the future

14.____

15. An employee under your supervision rushes into your office to tell you he has just received a telephone bomb threat.
    As the administrative supervisor, the FIRST thing you should do is
    A. evacuate staff from the floor
    B. call the police and building security
    C. advise your administrator
    D. do a preliminary search

15.____

16. After reviewing the Absence Control form for a unit under your supervision, you find that one of your staff members has a fifth undocumented sick leave within a six-month period.
    In this situation, the FIRST action you should take is to
    A. discuss the seriousness of the matter with the staff member when he returns to work and fully document the details of the discussion
    B. review the case with the location director and warn the staff member that future use of sick leave will be punished
    C. submit the proper disciplinary forms to ensure that the staff member is penalized for excessive absences
    D. request that the timekeeper put the staff member on doctor's note restriction

16.____

17. A subordinate supervisor recently assigned to your office begins his first conference with you by saying that he has learned something that another supervisor is doing that you should know about.
    After hearing this statement, of the following, the BEST approach for you to take is to
    A. explain to the supervisor that the conference is to discuss his work and not that of his co-workers
    B. tell the supervisor that you do not encourage a spy system among the staff you supervise

17.____

C. tell the supervisor that you will listen to his report only if the other supervisor is present
D. allow the supervisor to continue talking until you have enough information to make a decision on how best to respond

18. Assume that you are a supervisor recently assigned to a new unit. You notice that, for the past few days, one of the employees in your unit whose work is about average has been stopping work at about four o'clock and has been spending the rest of the afternoon relaxing at his desk.
The BEST of the following actions for you to take in this situation is to
    A. assign more work to this employee since it is apparent that he does not have enough work to keep him busy
    B. observe the employee's conduct more closely for about ten days before taking any more positive action
    C. discuss the matter with the employee, pointing out to him how he can use the extra hour daily to raise the level of his job performance
    D. question the previous supervisor in charge of the unit in order to determine whether he had sanctioned such conduct when he supervised that unit

18.____

19. A new supervisor was assigned to your program four months ago. Although he tries hard, he has been unable to meet certain standards because he still has a lot to learn. As his supervisor, you are required to submit performance evaluations within a few days.
How would you rate this employee on the tasks where he fails to meet standards because of lack of experience?
    A. Satisfactory   B. Conditional
    C. Unsatisfactory   D. Unratable

19.____

20. You find that there is an important procedural error in a memo which you distributed to your staff several days ago.
The BEST approach for you to take at this time is to
    A. send a corrected memo to the staff, indicating what prior error was made
    B. send a corrected memo to the staff without mentioning the prior error
    C. tell the staff about the error at the next monthly staff meeting
    D. place the corrected memo on the office bulletin board

20.____

21. Your superior asks you, a supervisor, about the status of the response to a letter from a public official concerning a client's case. When you ask the subordinate who was assigned to prepare the response to give you the letter, the subordinate denies that it was given to him. You are certain that the subordinate has the letter, but is withholding it because the response has not yet been prepared.
Of the following, in order to secure the letter from the subordinate, you should FIRST
    A. accuse the subordinate of lying and demand that the letter be given to you immediately
    B. say that you would consider it a personal favor if the subordinate would find the letter

21.____

C. continue to question the subordinate until he admits to having been given the letter
D. offer a face-saving solution, such as asking the subordinate to look again for the letter

22. As a supervisor, you have been assigned to write a few paragraphs to be included in the agency's annual report, describing a public service agency department this year as compared to last year.
    Which of the following elements basic to the agency is LEAST likely to have changed since last year?
    A. Mission   B. Structure   C. Technology   D. Personnel

23. As a supervisor, you have been informed that a grievance has been filed against you, accusing you of assigning a subordinate to out-of-title tasks.
    Of the following, the BEST approach for you to take is to
    A. waive the grievance so that it will proceed to a Step II hearing
    B. immediately change the subordinate's assignment to avoid future problems
    C. respond to the grievance, giving appropriate reasons for the assignment
    D. review the job description to ensure that the subordinate's tasks are not out-of-title

24. Which of the following is NOT a correct statement about agency group training programs in a public service agency?
    A. Training sessions continue for an indefinite period of time.
    B. Group training sessions are planned for designated personnel.
    C. Training groups are organized formally through administrative planning.
    D. Group training is task-centered and aimed toward accomplishing specific educational goals.

25. As a supervisor, you have submitted a memo to your superior requesting a conference to discuss the performance of a manager under your supervision. The memo states that the manager has a good working relationship with her staff; however, she tends to interpret agency policy too liberally and shows poor administrative skills by missing some deadlines and not keeping proper controls.
    Which of the following steps should NOT be taken in order to prepare for this conference with your superior?
    A. Collect and review all your notes regarding the manager's prior performance.
    B. Outline your agenda so that you will have sufficient time to discuss the situation.
    C. Tell the manager that you will be discussing her performance with your superior.
    D. Clearly define objectives which will focus on improving the manager's performance.

KEY (CORRECT ANSWERS)

1.	B	11.	D
2.	A	12.	C
3.	B	13.	B
4.	B	14.	A
5.	D	15.	B
6.	D	16.	A
7.	B	17.	D
8.	A	18.	C
9.	C	19.	B
10.	C	20.	A

21.	D
22.	A
23.	C
24.	A
25.	C

EXAMINATION SECTION
TEST 1

DIRECTIONS: Each question or incomplete statement is followed by several suggested answers or completions. Select the one that BEST answers the question or completes the statement. *PRINT THE LETTER OF THE CORRECT ANSWER IN THE SPACE AT THE RIGHT.*

1. A *basic* method of operation that a *good* supervisor should follow is to

   A. check the work of subordinates constantly to make sure they are not making exceptions to the rules
   B. train subordinates so they can handle problems that come up regularly themselves and come to him only with special cases
   C. delegate to subordinates only those duties which he cannot do himself
   D. issue directions to subordinates only on special matters

2. To do a *good* job of performance evaluation, it is BEST for a supervisor to

   A. compare the employee's performance to that of another employee doing similar work
   B. give greatest weight to instances of unusually good or unusually poor performance
   C. leave out any consideration of the employee's personal traits
   D. measure the employee's performance against standard performance requirements

3. Of the following, the MOST important reason for a supervisor to have private face to face discussions with subordinates about their performance is to

   A. help employees improve their work
   B. give special praise to employees who perform well
   C. encourage the employees to compete for higher performance ratings
   D. discipline employees who perform poorly

4. Of the following, the CHIEF purpose of a probationary period for a new employee is to allow time for

   A. finding out whether the selection processes are satisfactory
   B. the employee to make adjustments in his home circumstances made necessary by the job
   C. the employee to decide whether he wants a permanent appointment
   D. determining the fitness of the employee to continue in the job

5. When a subordinate resigns his job, it is MOST important to conduct an exit interview in order to

   A. try to get the employee to remain on the job
   B. learn the true reasons for the employee's resignation
   C. see that the employee leaves with a good opinion of the agency
   D. ask the employee if he would consider a transfer

6. Chronic lateness of employees is generally LEAST likely to be due to

   A. distance of job location from home   B. poor personnel administration
   C. unexpressed employee grievances   D. low morale

33

7. Of the following, the LEAST effective stimulus for motivating employees toward inproved performance over a long-range period is

   A. their sense of achievement
   B. their feeling of recognition
   C. opportunity for their self-development
   D. an increase in salary

8. Suppose that NOT ONE of a group of employees has turned in an idea to the employees suggestion system during the past year.
   The *most probable* reason for this situation is that the

   A. money awards given for suggestions used are not high enough to make employees interested
   B. employees in this group are not able to develop any good ideas
   C. supervisor of these employees is not doing enough to encourage them to take part in the program
   D. methods and procedures of operation do not need improvement

9. A subordinate tells you that he is having trouble concentrating on his work due to a personal problem at home.
   Of the following, it would be BEST for you to

   A. refer him to a community service agency
   B. listen quietly to the story because he may just need a sympathetic ear
   C. tell him that you cannot help him because the problem is not job related
   D. ask him questions about the nature of the problem and tell him how you would handle it

10. For you as a supervisor to give each of your subordinates *exactly* the same type of supervision is

    A. *advisable,* because doing this insures fair and impartial treatment of each individual
    B. *not advisable,* because individuals like to think that they are receiving better treatment than others
    C. *advisable,* because once a supervisor learns how to deal with a subordinate who brings a problem to him, he can handle another subordinate with this problem in the same way
    D. *not advisable,* because each person is different and there is no one supervisory procedure for dealing with individuals that applies in every case

11. A senior employee under your supervision tells you that he is reluctant to speak to one of his subordinates about his poor work habits, because this worker is "strong-willed" and he does not want to antagonize him.
    For you to offer to speak to the subordinate about this matter yourself would be

    A. *advisable,* since you are in a position of greater authority
    B. *inadvisable,* since handling this problem is a basic supervisory responsibility of the senior employee
    C. *advisable,* since the senior employee must work more closely with the worker than you do
    D. *inadvisable,* since you should not risk antagonizing the employee yourself

12. Some of your subordinates have been coming to you with complaints you feel are unimportant. For you to hear their stories out is

    A. *poor practice,* you should spend your time on more important matters
    B. *good practice,* this will increase your popularity with your subordinates
    C. *poor practice,* subordinates should learn to come to you only with major grievances
    D. *good practice,* it may prevent minor complaints from developing into major grievances

13. Assume that an agency has an established procedure for handling employee grievances. An employee in this agency, comes to his immediate supervisor with a grievance. The supervisor investigates the matter and makes a decision.
    However, the employee is not satisfied with the decision made by the supervisor. The BEST action for the supervisor to take is to

    A. tell the employee he will review the matter further
    B. remind the employee that he is the supervisor and the employee must act in accordance with his decision
    C. explain to the employee how he can carry his complaint forward to the next step in the grievance procedure
    D. tell the employee he will consult with his own superiors on the matter

14. Subordinate employees and senior employees often must make quick decisions while in the field. The supervisor can BEST help subordinates meet such situations by

    A. training them in the appropriate action to take for every problem that may come up
    B. limiting the areas in which they are permitted to make decisions
    C. making certain they understand clearly the basic policies of the bureau and the department
    D. delegating authority to make such decisions to only a few subordinates on each level

15. Studies have shown that the CHIEF cause of failure to achieve success as a supervisor is

    A. an unwillingness to delegate authority to subordinates
    B. the establishment of high performance standards for subordinates
    C. the use of discipline that is too strict
    D. showing too much leniency to poor workers

16. When a supervisor delegates to a subordinate certain work that he normally does himself, it is MOST important that he give the subordinate

    A. responsibility for also setting the standards for the work to be done
    B. sufficient authority to be able to carry out the assignment
    C. written, step-by-step instructions for doing the work
    D. an explanation of one part of the task at a time

17. It is particularly important that disciplinary actions be equitable as between individuals. This statement *implies* that

    A. punishment applied in disciplinary actions should be lenient
    B. proposed disciplinary actions should be reviewed by higher authority
    C. subordinates should have an opportunity to present their stories before penalties are applied
    D. penalties for violations of the rules should be standardized and consistently applied

18. You discover that from time to time a number of false rumors circulate among your subordinates.
    Of the following, the BEST way for you to handle this situation is to

    A. ignore the rumors since rumors circulate in every office and can never be eliminated
    B. attempt to find those responsible for the rumors and reprimand them
    C. make sure that your employees are informed as soon as possible about all matters that affect them
    D. inform your superior about the rumors and let him deal with the matter

19. Supervisors who allow the "halo effect" to influence their evaluations of subordinates are *most likely* to

    A. give more lenient ratings to older employees who have longer service
    B. let one highly favorable or unfavorable trait unduly affect their judgment of an employee
    C. evaluate all employees on one trait before considering a second
    D. give high evaluations in order to avoid antagonizing their subordinates

20. For a supervisor to keep records of reprimands to subordinates about infractions of the rules is

    A. *good practice,* because these records are valuable to support disciplinary actions recommended or taken
    B. *poor practice,* because such records are evidence of the supervisor's inability to maintain discipline
    C. *good practice,* because such records indicate that the supervisor is doing a good job
    D. *poor practice,* because the best way to correct subordinates is to give them more training

21. When a new departmental policy has been established, it would be MOST advisable for you, as a supervisor, to

    A. distribute a memo which states the new policy and instruct your subordinates to read it
    B. explain specifically to your subordinates how the policy is going to affect them
    C. make sure your subordinates understand that you are not responsible for setting the policy
    D. tell your subordinates whether you agree or disagree with the policy

22. As a supervisor, you receive several complaints about the rude conduct of a subordinate. The FIRST action you should take is to

   A. request his transfer to another office
   B. prepare a charge sheet for disciplinary action
   C. assign a senior employee to work with him for a week
   D. interview the employee to determine possible reason, and warn that correction is necessary

23. A supervisor is *most likely* to get subordinates to work cooperatively toward accomplishing bureau goals if he

   A. creates an atmosphere that contributes to their feeling of security
   B. backs up subordinates even when they occasionally disobey regulations
   C. shows interest in subordinates by helping them solve their personal problems
   D. uses an authoritarian or "bossy" approach to supervision

24. A supervisor is holding a staff meeting with his senior employees to try to find an acceptable solution to a problem that has come up.
    Of the following, the CHIEF role of the supervisor at this meeting should be to

   A. see that every member of the group contributes at least one suggestions
   B. act as chairman of the meeting, but take no other active part to avoid influencing the senior employees
   C. keep the participants from wandering off into discussions of irrelevant matters
   D. make certain the participants hear his views on the matter at the beginning of the meeting

25. An employee shows you a certificate that he has just received for completing two years of study in conversational Spanish. As his supervisor, it would be BEST for you to

   A. put a note about this accomplishment in his personnel folder
   B. assign him to areas in which people of Spanish origin live
   C. congratulate him on this accomplishment, but tell him frankly that you doubt this is likely to have any direct bearing on his work
   D. encourage him to continue his studies and become thoroughly fluent in speaking the language

KEY (CORRECT ANSWERS)

1. B
2. D
3. A
4. D
5. B

6. A
7. D
8. C
9. B
10. D

11. B
12. D
13. C
14. C
15. A

16. B
17. D
18. C
19. B
20. A

21. B
22. D
23. A
24. C
25. A

TEST 2

DIRECTIONS: Each question or incomplete statement is followed by several suggested answers or completions. Select the one that BEST answers the question or completes the statement. *PRINT THE LETTER OF THE CORRECT ANSWER IN THE SPACE AT THE RIGHT.*

1. Of the following, the factor affecting employee morale which the immediate supervisor is LEAST able to control is

    A. handling of grievances
    B. fair and impartial treatment of subordinates
    C. general presonnel rules and regulations
    D. accident prevention

    1.____

2. When one of your workers does outstanding work, you should

    A. explain to your other employees that you expect the same kind of work of them
    B. praise him for his work so that he will know it is appreciated
    C. say nothing, because other employees may think you are showing favoritism
    D. show him how his work can be improved still more so that he will not sit back

    2.____

3. For you as a supervisor to consider a suggestion from a probationary worker for improving a procedure would be

    A. *poor practice,* because this employee is too new on the job to know much about it
    B. *good practice,* because you may be able to share credit for the suggestion
    C. *poor practice,* because it may hurt the morale of the older employees
    D. *good practice,* because the suggestion may be worthwhile

    3.____

4. If you find you must criticize the work of one of your workers, it would be BEST for you to

    A. mention the good points in his work as well as the faults
    B. caution him that he will receive an unsatisfactory performance report unless his work improves
    C. compare his work to that of the other agents you supervise
    D. apologize for making the criticism

    4.____

5. As a senior employee which one of the following matters would it be BEST for you to talk over with your supervisor before you take final action?

    A. One of the workers you supervise continues to disregard your instructions repeatedly in spite of repeated warnings
    B. One of your workers tells you he wants to discuss a personal problem
    C. A probationary employee tells you he does not understand a procedure
    D. One of your workers tells you he disagrees with the way you rate his work

    5.____

6. If one of your subordinates asks you a question about a department rule and you do not know the answer, you should tell him that

    A. he should try to get the information himself
    B. you do not have the answer, but you will get it for him as soon as you can
    C. he should ask you the question again a week from now
    D. he should put the question in writing

    6.____

7. If, as a supervisor, you realize that you have been unfair in criticizing one of your subordinates, the BEST action for you to take is to

   A. say nothing, but overlook some error made by this employee in the future
   B. be frank and tell the employee that you are sorry for the mistake you made
   C. let the employee know in some indirect way without admitting your mistake, that you realize he was not at fault
   D. say nothing, but be more careful about criticizing subordinates in the future

8. Of the following, the MOST important reason for a supervisor to write an accident report as soon as possible after an accident has happened is to

   A. make sure that important facts about the accident are not forgotten
   B. avoid delay in getting compensation for the injured person
   C. get adequate medical treatment for the injured person
   D. keep department accident statistics up to date

9. In any matter which may require disciplinary action, the FIRST responsibility of the supervisor is to

   A. decide what penalty should be applied for the offense
   B. refer the matter to a higher authority for complete investigation
   C. place the interests of the department above those of the employee
   D. investigate the matter fully to get all the facts

10. Suppose you find it necessary to criticize one of the subordinates you supervise. You should

    A. send an official letter to his home
    B. speak to him about the matter privately
    C. speak to him at a staff meeting
    D. ask another worker who is friendly with him to talk to him about the matter

11. Some of your subordinates have been coming to you with complaints you feel are unimportant. For you to hear their stories out is

    A. *poor practice,* you should spend your time on more important matters
    B. *good practice,* this will increase your popularity with your subordinates
    C. *poor practice,* subordinates should learn to come to you only with major grievances
    D. *good practice,* it may prevent minor complaints from developing into major grievances

12. Suppose that NOT ONE of a group of employees has turned in an idea to the employees' suggestion system during the past year. The *most probable* reason for this situation is that the

    A. supervisor of these employees is not doing enough to encourage them to take part in this program
    B. employees in this group are not able to develop any good ideas
    C. money awards given for suggestions used are not high enough to make employees interested
    D. methods and procedures of operation do not need improvement

13. For you as a supervisor to give each of your subordinates *exactly* the same type of supervision is

    A. *advisable,* because doing this insures fair and impartial treatment of each individual
    B. *not advisable,* because each person is different and there is no one supervisory procedure for dealing with individuals that applies in every case
    C. *advisable,* because once a supervisor learns how to deal with a subordinate who brings a problem to him, he can handle another subordinate with this problem in the same way
    D. *not advisable,* because individuals like to think that they are receiving better treatment than others

14. In evaluating personnel, a supervisor should keep in mind that the MOST important objective of performance evaluations is to

    A. encourage employees to compete for higher performance ratings
    B. give recognition to employees who perform well
    C. help employees improve their work
    D. discipline employees who perform poorly

15. A subordinate tells you that he is having trouble concentrating on his work due to a personal problem at home. Of the following, it would be BEST for you to

    A. refer him to a community service agency
    B. listen quietly to the story because he may just need a sympathetic ear
    C. tell him that you cannot help him because the problem is not job-related
    D. ask him some questions about the nature of the problem and tell him how you would handle it

16. To do a good job of performance evaluation, it is BEST for a supervisor to

    A. measure the employee's performance against standard performance requirements
    B. compare the employee's performance to that of another employee doing similar work
    C. leave out any consideration of the employee's personal traits
    D. give greatest weight to instances of unusually good or unusually poor performance

17. It is particularly important that disciplinary actions be equitable as between individuals. This statement *implies* that

    A. punishment applied in disciplinary actions should be lenient
    B. proposed disciplinary actions should be reviewed by higher authority
    C. subordinates should have an opportunity to present their stories before penalties are applied
    D. penalties for violations of the rules should be standardized and consistently applied

18. Assume that an agency has an established procedure for handling employee grievances. An employee in this agency comes to his immediate supervisor with a grievance. The supervisor investigates the matter and makes a decision. However, the employee is not satisfied with the decision made by the supervisor.
    The BEST action for the supervisor to take is to

A. tell the employee he will review the matter further
B. remind the employee that he is the supervisor and the employee must act in accordance with his decision
C. explain to the employee how he can carry his complaint forward to the next step in the grievance procedure
D. tell the employee he will consult with his own superiors on the matter

19. Of the following, the CHIEF purpose of a probationary period for a new employee is to allow time for

   A. finding out whether the selection processes are satisfactory
   B. determining the fitness of the employee to continue in the job
   C. the employee to decide whether he wants a permanent appointment
   D. the employee to make adjustments in his home circumstances made necessary by the job

20. Of the following, the subject that would be MOST important to include in a "break-in" program for new employees is

   A. explanation of rules, regulations and policies of the agency
   B. Instruction in the agency's history and programs
   C. explanation of the importance of the new employees' own particular job
   D. explanation of the duties and responsibilities of the employee

21. Suppose a new employee under your supervision seems slow to learn and is making mistakes in performing his duties. Your FIRST action should be to

   A. pass this information on to the bureau director
   B. reprimand the worker so he will not repeat these mistakes
   C. find out whether this worker understands your instructions
   D. note these facts for future reference when writing up the monthly performance evaluation

22. In training new employees to do a certain job it would be LEAST desirable for you to

   A. demonstrate how the job is done, step by step
   B. encourage the workers to ask questions if they aren't clear about any point
   C. tell them about the various mistakes other agents have made in doing this job
   D. have the workers do the job, explaining to you what they are doing and why

23. One of the workers under your supervision is resentful when you ask her to remove her jangling bracelets before she starts her tour of duty.
Of the following, the BEST explanation you can give her for the rule against wearing such jewelry while on duty is that

   A. the jewelry may create a safety hazard
   B. employees must give up certain personal liberties if they want to keep their jobs
   C. workers cannot perform their duties as efficiently if they wear distracting jewelry
   D. citizens may receive an unfavorable impression of the department

5 (#2)

24. Of the following, the LEAST important reason for having a department handbook and a bureau standard operating procedure is to

    A. help in training new employees
    B. provide a source of reference for department and bureau rules and procedures
    C. prevent errors in work by providing clear guidelines
    D. make the supervisor's job easy

25. On inspecting your squad prior to their tour of duty, you note an employee improperly and unacceptably dressed.
    The FIRST action you should take is to

    A. call the employee aside and insist on immediate correction if possible
    B. notify the district commander right away
    C. have the employee submit a memorandum explaining the reason for the improper uniform
    D. permit the employee to proceed on duty but warn him not to let this happen again

KEY (CORRECT ANSWERS)

1.	C	11.	D
2.	B	12.	A
3.	D	13.	B
4.	A	14.	C
5.	A	15.	B
6.	B	16.	A
7.	B	17.	D
8.	A	18.	C
9.	D	19.	B
10.	B	20.	D

21. C
22. C
23. D
24. D
25. A

EXAMINATION SECTION
TEST 1

DIRECTIONS: Each question or incomplete statement is followed by several suggested answers or completions. Select the one that BEST answers the question or completes the statement. *PRINT THE LETTER OF THE CORRECT ANSWER IN THE SPACE AT THE RIGHT.*

1. At times there may be a conflict between employees' needs and agency goals. A supervisor's MAIN role in motivating employees in such circumstances is to try to
    A. develop good work habits among the employees whom he supervises
    B. emphasize the importance of material rewards such as merit increases
    C. keep careful records of employees' performance for possible disciplinary action
    D. reconcile employees' objectives with those of the public agency

1.____

2. Organizations cannot function effectively without policies.
However, when an organization imposes excessively detailed policy restrictions, it is MOST likely to lead to
    A. conflicts among individual employees
    B. a lack of adequate supervision
    C. a reduction of employee initiative
    D. a reliance on punitive discipline

2.____

3. The PRIMARY responsibility for establishing good employee relations in the public service usually rests with
    A. employees   B. management
    C. civil service organizations   D. employee organizations

3.____

4. At times, certain off-the-job conduct of public employees may be of concern to management. This concern stems from the fact that
    A. agency programs could be harmed by adverse publicity if employees' conduct is considered detrimental by the public
    B. fairness to all concerned is usually the major consideration in disciplinary cases
    C. public employees must meet higher standards than employees working in private industry
    D. public employees have high ethical standards and may participate in social action programs

4.____

5. At one time or another, most employees ask for, or expect, special treatment. For a supervisor faced with this problem, the one of the following which is the MOST valid guideline is:
    A. According to the rules, a supervisor must give identical treatment to all his subordinates, regardless of the circumstances.

5.____

B. Although all employees have equal rights, it is sometimes necessary to give an employee special treatment to meet an individual need.
C. It would damage morale if any employee were to receive special treatment, regardless of circumstances.
D. Since each employee has different needs, there is little reason to maintain general rules.

6. Mental health problems exist in many parts of our society and may also be found in the work setting.
   The BASIC role of the supervisor in relation to the mental health problems of his subordinates is to
   A. restrict himself solely to the taking of disciplinary measures, if warranted, and follow up carefully
   B. avoid involvement in personal matters
   C. identify mental health problems as early as possible
   D. resolve mental health problems through personal counseling

7. Supervisory expectation of high levels of employee performance, where such performance is possible, is MOST likely to lead to employees'
   A. expecting frequent praise and encouragement
   B. gaining a greater sense of satisfaction
   C. needing less detailed instructions than previously
   D. reducing their quantitative output

8. In public agencies, as elsewhere, supervisors sometimes compete with one another to increase their units' productivity.
   Of the following, the MAJOR disadvantage of such competition, from the general viewpoint of providing good public service, is that
   A. while individual employee effort will increase, unit productivity will decrease
   B. employees will be discouraged from sincere interest in their work
   C. the supervisors' competition may hinder the achievement of agency goals
   D. total payroll costs will increase as the activities of each unit increase

9. If employees are motivated primarily by material compensation, the amount of effort an individual employee will put into performing his work effectively will depend MAINLY upon how he perceives
   A. cooperation to be tied to successful effort
   B. the association between good work and increased compensation
   C. the public status of his particular position
   D. the supervisor's behavior in work situations

10. Cash awards to individual employees are sometimes used to encourage useful suggestions. However, some management experts believe that awards should involve some form of employee recognition other than cash.
    Which of the following reasons BEST supports opposition to using cash as a reward for worthwhile suggestions?

A. Cash awards cause employees to expend excessive time in making suggestions.
   B. Taxpayer opposition to dash awards has increased following generous salary increases for public employees in recent years.
   C. Public funds expended on awards leads to a poor image of public employees.
   D. The use of cash awards raises the problem of deciding the monetary value of suggestions.

11. The BEST general rule for a supervisor to follow in giving praise and criticism is to
    A. criticize and praise publicly
    B. criticize publicly and praise privately
    C. praise and criticize privately
    D. praise publicly and criticize privately

12. An important step in designing an error-control policy is to determine the maximum number of errors that can be considered acceptable for the entire organization.
    Of the following, the MOST important factor in making such a decision is the
    A. number of clerical staff available to check for errors
    B. frequency of errors by supervisors
    C. human and material costs of errors
    D. number of errors that will become known to the public

13. When a supervisor tries to correct a situation where errors have been widespread, he should concentrate his efforts, and those of the employees involved, on
    A. avoiding future mistakes   B. fixing appropriate blame
    C. preparing a written report   D. determining fair penalties

14. When delegating work to a subordinate, a supervisor should ALWAYS tell the subordinate
    A. each step in the procedure for doing the work
    B. how much time to expend
    C. what is to be accomplished
    D. whether reports are necessary

15. The responsibilities of all employees should be clearly defined and understood. In addition, in order for employees to successfully fulfill their responsibilities, they should also GENERALLY be given
    A. written directives   B. close supervision
    C. corresponding authority   D. daily instructions

16. The one of the following types of training in which positive transfer of training to the actual work situation is MOST likely to take place is _____ training.
    A. conference   B. demonstration
    C. classroom   D. on-the-job

17. The type of training or instruction in which the subject matter is presented in small units called frames is known as
    A. programmed instruction
    B. reinforcement
    C. remediation
    D. skills training

17.____

18. In order to bring about maximum learning in a training situation, a supervisor acting as a trainer should attempt to create a setting in which
    A. all trainees experience a large amount of failure as an incentive
    B. all trainees experience a small amount of failure as an incentive
    C. each trainee experiences approximately the same amounts of success and failure
    D. each trainee experiences as much success and as little failure as possible

18.____

19. Assume that, in a training course given by an agency, the instructor conducts a brief quiz, on paper, toward the close of each session.
    From the point of view of maximizing learning, it would be BEST for the instructor to
    A. wait until the last session to provide the correct answers
    B. give the correct answers aloud immediately after each quiz
    C. permit trainees to take the questions home with them so that they can look up the answers
    D. wait until the next session to provide the correct answers

19.____

20. A supervisor, in the course of evaluating employees, should ALWAYS determine whether
    A. employees realize that their work is under scrutiny
    B. the ratings will be included in permanent records
    C. employees meet standards of performance
    D. his statements on the rating form are similar to those made by the previous supervisor

20.____

21. All of the following are legitimate objectives of employee performance reporting systems EXCEPT
    A. serving as a check on personnel policies such as job qualification requirements and placement techniques
    B. determining who is the least efficient worker among a large number of employees
    C. improving employee performance by identifying strong and weak points in individual performance
    D. developing standards of satisfactory performance

21.____

22. Studies of existing employee performance evaluation schemes have revealed a common tendency to construct guides in order to measure <u>inferred</u> traits.
    Of the following, the BEST example of an inferred trait is
    A. appearance   B. loyalty   C. accuracy   D. promptness

22.____

5 (#1)

23. Which of the following is MOST likely to be a positive influence in promoting common agreement at a staff conference?
    A. A mature, tolerant group of participants
    B. A strong chairman with firm opinions
    C. The normal differences of human personalities
    D. The urge to forcefully support one's views

23.____

24. Before holding a problem-solving conference, the conference leader sent to each invitee an announcement on which he listed the names of all invitees. His action in listing the names was
    A. *wise*, mainly because all invitees will know who has been invited, and can, if necessary, plan a proper approach
    B. *unwise*, mainly because certain invitees could form factions prior to the conference
    C. *unwise*, mainly because invitees might come to the conference in a belligerent mood if they had had interpersonal conflicts with other invitees
    D. *wise*, mainly because invitees who are antagonistic to each other could decide not to attend

24.____

25. Methods analysis is a detailed study of existing or proposed work methods for the purpose of improving agency operations.
    Of the following, it is MOST accurate to say that this type of study
    A. can sometimes be made informally by the experienced supervisor who can identify problems and suggest solutions
    B. is not suitable for studying the operations of a public agency
    C. will be successfully accomplished only if an outside organization reviews agency operations
    D. usually costs more to complete than is justified by the potential economies to be realized

25.____

KEY (CORRECT ANSWERS)

1.	D	11.	D
2.	C	12.	C
3.	B	13.	A
4.	A	14.	C
5.	B	15.	C
6.	C	16.	D
7.	B	17.	A
8.	C	18.	D
9.	B	19.	B
10.	D	20.	C

21.
22. B
23. A
24. A
25. A

TEST 2

DIRECTIONS: Each question or incomplete statement is followed by several suggested answers or completions. Select the one that BEST answers the question or completes the statement. *PRINT THE LETTER OF THE CORRECT ANSWER IN THE SPACE AT THE RIGHT.*

1. Present-day managerial practices advocate that adequate hierarchical levels of communication be maintained among all levels of management.
   Of the following, the BEST way to accomplish this is with
   A. intradepartmental memoranda only
   B. interdepartmental memoranda only
   C. periodic staff meetings, interdepartmental and intradepartmental memoranda
   D. interdepartmental and intradepartmental memoranda

   1._____

2. It is generally agreed upon that it is important to have effective communications in the unit so that everyone knows exactly what is expected of him.
   Of the following, the communications system which can assist in fulfilling this objective BEST is one which consists of
   A. written policies and procedures for administrative functions and verbal policies and procedures for professional functions
   B. written policies and procedures for professional and administrative functions
   C. verbal policies and procedures for professional and administrative functions
   D. verbal policies and procedures for professional functions

   2._____

3. If a department manager wishes to build an effective department, he MOST generally must
   A. be able to hire and fire as he feels necessary
   B. consider the total aspects of his job, his influence and the effects of his decisions
   C. have access to reasonable amounts of personnel and money with which to build his programs
   D. attend as many professional conferences as possible so that he can keep up-to-date with all the latest advances in the field

   3._____

4. Of the following, the factor which generally contributes MOST effectively to the performance of the unit is that the supervisor
   A. personally inspect the work of all employees
   B. fill orders at a faster rate than his subordinates
   C. have an exact knowledge of theory
   D. implement a program of professional development for his staff

   4._____

5. Administrative policies relate MOST closely to
   A. control of commodities and personnel
   B. general policies emanating from the central office
   C. fiscal management of the department only
   D. handling and dispensing of funds

   5._____

6. Part of being a good supervisor is to be able to develop an attitude towards employees which will motivate them to do their best on the job.
The GOOD supervisor, therefore, should
   A. take an interest in subordinates, but not develop an all-consuming attitude in this area
   B. remain in an aloof position when dealing with employees
   C. be as close to subordinates as possible on the job
   D. take a complete interest in all the activities of subordinates, both on and off the job

6.____

7. The practice of a supervisor assigning an experienced employee to train new employees instead of training them himself is GENERALLY considered
   A. *undesirable*; the more experienced employee will resent being taken away from his regular job
   B. *desirable*; the supervisor can then devote more time to his regular duties
   C. *undesirable*; the more experienced employee is not working at the proper level to train new employees
   D. *desirable*; the more experienced employee is probably a better trainer than the supervisor

7.____

8. It is generally agreed that on-the-job training is MOST effective when new employees are
   A. provided with study manuals, standard operating procedures and other written materials to be studied for at least two weeks before the employees attempt to do the job
   B. shown how to do the job in detail, and then instructed to do the work under close supervision
   C. trained by an experienced worker for at least a week to make certain that the employees can do the job
   D. given work immediately which is checked at the end of each day

8.____

9. Employees sometimes form small informal groups, commonly called cliques. With regard to the effect of such groups on processing of the workload, the attitude a supervisor should take towards these cliques is that of
   A. *acceptance*, since they take the employees' minds off their work without wasting too much time
   B. *rejection*, since those workers inside the clique tend to do less work than the outsiders
   C. *acceptance*, since the supervisor is usually included in the clique
   D. *rejection*, since they are usually disliked by higher management

9.____

10. Of the following, the BEST statement regarding rules and regulations in a unit is that they
    A. are "necessary evils" to be tolerated by those at and above the first supervisory level only
    B. are stated in broad, indefinite terms so as to allow maximum amount of leeway in complying with them

10.____

C. must be understood by all employees in the unit
D. are primarily for management's needs since insurance regulations mandate them

11. It is sometimes considered desirable for a supervisor to survey the opinions of his employees before taking action on decisions affecting them.
Of the following the greatest DISADVANTAGE of following this approach is that the employees might
    A. use this opportunity to complain rather than to make constructive suggestions
    B. lose respect for their supervisor whom they feel cannot make his own decisions
    C. regard this as an attempt by the supervisor to get ideas for which he can later claim credit
    D. be resentful if their suggestions are not adopted

11.____

12. Of the following, the MOST important reason for keeping statements of duties of employees up-to-date is to
    A. serve as a basis of information for other governmental jurisdictions
    B. enable the department of personnel to develop job-related examinations
    C. differentiate between levels within the occupational groups
    D. enable each employee to know what his duties are

12.____

13. Of the following, the BEST way to evaluate the progress of a new subordinate is to
    A. compare the output of the new employee from week to week as to quantity and quality
    B. obtain the opinions of the new employee's co-workers
    C. test the new employee periodically to see how much he has learned
    D. hold frequent discussions with the employee focusing on his work

13.____

14. Of the following, a supervisor is LEAST likely to contribute to good morale in the unit if he
    A. encourages employees to increase their knowledge and proficiency in their work on their own time
    B. reprimands subordinates uniformly when infractions are committed
    C. refuses to accept explanations for mistakes regardless of who has made them or how serious they are
    D. compliments subordinates for superior work performance in the presence of their peers

14.____

15. The practice of promoting supervisors from within a given unit only, rather than from within the entire agency, may BEST be described as
    A. *desirable*, because the type of work in each unit generally is substantially different from all other units
    B. *undesirable*, since it will severely reduce the number of eligible from which to select a supervisor

15.____

C. *desirable*, since it enables each employee to know in advance the precise extent of promotion opportunities in his unit
D. *undesirable*, because it creates numerous administrative and budgetary difficulties

16. Of the following, the BEST way for a supervisor to make assignments GENERALLY is to
    A. give the easier assignments to employees with greater seniority
    B. give the difficult assignments to the employees with greater seniority
    C. make assignments according to the ability of each employee
    D. rotate the assignments among the employees

17. Assume that a supervisor makes a proposal through appropriate channels which would delegate final authority and responsibility to a subordinate employee for a major control function within the agency.
    According to current management theory, this proposal should be
    A. *adopted*, since this would enable the supervisor to devote more time to non-routine tasks
    B. *rejected*, since final responsibility for this high-level assignment may not properly be delegated to a subordinate employee
    C. *adopted*, since the assignment of increased responsibility to subordinate employees is a vital part of their development and training
    D. *rejected*, since the morale of the subordinate employees not selected for this assignment would be adversely affected

18. If it becomes necessary for a supervisor to improve the performance of a subordinate to assure the achievement of results according to plans, the BEST course of action, of the following, generally would be to
    A. emphasize the subordinate's strengths and try to motivate the employee to improve on those factors
    B. emphasize the subordinate's weak areas of performance and try to bring them up to an acceptable standard
    C. issue a memorandum to all employees warning that if performance does not improve, disciplinary measures will be taken
    D. transfer the subordinate to another section engaged in different work

19. A supervisor who specifies each phase of a job in detail supervises closely and permits very little discretion in performance of tasks GENERALLY
    A. provides motivation for his staff to produce more work
    B. finds that his subordinate make fewer mistakes than those with minimal supervision
    C. finds that his subordinates have little or no incentive to work any harder than necessary
    D. provides superior training opportunities for his employees

5 (#2)

20. Assume that you supervise two employees who do not get along well with each other. Their relationship has been continuously deteriorating. You decide to take steps to solve this problem by first determining the reason for their inability to get along with each other.
    This course of action is
    A. *desirable*, because their work is probably adversely affected by their differences
    B. *undesirable*, because your inquiries might be misinterpreted by the employees and cause resentment
    C. *desirable*, because you could then learn who is at fault for causing the deteriorating relationship and take appropriate disciplinary measures
    D. *undesirable*, because it is best to let them work their differences out between themselves

21. Routine procedures that have worked well in the past should be reviewed periodically by a supervisor MAINLY because
    A. they may have become outdated or in need of revision
    B. employees may dislike the procedures even though they have proven successful in the past
    C. these reviews are the main part of a supervisor's job
    D. this practice serves to give the supervisor an idea of how productive his subordinates are

22. Assume that an employee tells his supervisor about a grievance he has against a co-worker. The supervisor assures the employee that he will immediately take action to eliminate the grievance.
    The supervisor's attitude should be considered
    A. *correct*, because a good supervisor is one who can come to a quick decision
    B. *incorrect*, because the supervisor should have told the employee that he will investigate the grievance and then determine a future course of action
    C. *correct*, because the employee's morale will be higher, resulting in greater productivity
    D. *incorrect*, because the supervisor should remain uninvolved and let the employees settle grievances between themselves

23. If an employee's work output is low and of poor quality due to faulty work habits, the MOST constructive of the following ways for a supervisor to correct this situation *generally* is to
    A. discipline the employee
    B. transfer the employee to another unit
    C. provide additional training
    D. check the employee's work continuously

24. Assume that it becomes necessary for a supervisor to ask his staff to work overtime.
    Which one of the following techniques is MOST likely to win their willing cooperation to do this?

A. Point out that this is part of their job specification entitled "performs related work"
B. Explain the reason it is necessary for the employees to work overtime
C. Promise the employees special consideration regarding future leave matters
D. Warn that if the employees do not work overtime, they will face possible disciplinary action

25. If an employee's work performance has recently fallen below established minimum standards for quality and quantity, the threat of demotion or other disciplinary measures as an attempt to improve this employee's performance would probably be the MOST acceptable and effective course of action
    A. *only* after other more constructive measures have failed
    B. *if* applied uniformly to all employees as soon as performance falls below standard
    C. *only* if the employee understands that the threat will not actually be carried out
    D. *if* the employee is promised that, as soon as his work performance improves, he will be reinstated to his previous status

25.____

KEY (CORRECT ANSWERS)

1.	C	11.	D
2.	B	12.	D
3.	B	13.	A
4.	D	14.	C
5.	A	15.	B
6.	A	16.	C
7.	B	17.	B
8.	B	18.	B
9.	A	19.	C
10.	C	20.	A

21. A
22. B
23. C
24. B
25. A

TEST 3

DIRECTIONS: Each question or incomplete statement is followed by several suggested answers or completions. Select the one that BEST answers the question or completes the statement. *PRINT THE LETTER OF THE CORRECT ANSWER IN THE SPACE AT THE RIGHT.*

1. If, as a supervisor, it becomes necessary for you to assign an employee to supervise your unit during your vacation, it would generally be BEST to select the employee who
    A. is the best technician on the staff
    B. can get the work out smoothly, without friction
    C. has the most seniority
    D. is the most popular with the group

    1.____

2. Assume that, as a supervisor, your own work has accumulated to the point where you decide that it is desirable for you to delegate in order to meet your deadlines.
    The one of the following tasks which would be MOST appropriate to delegate to a subordinate is
    A. checking the work of the employees for accuracy
    B. attending a staff conference at which implementation of a new departmental policy will be discussed
    C. preparing a final report including a recommendation on purchase of expensive new laboratory equipment
    D. preparing final budget estimates for next year's budget

    2.____

3. Of the following actions, the one LEAST appropriate for you to take during an initial interview with a new employee is to
    A. find out about the experience and education of the new employee
    B. attempt to determine for what job in your unit the employee would best be suited
    C. tell the employee about his duties and responsibilities
    D. ascertain whether the employee will make good promotion material

    3.____

4. If it becomes necessary to reprimand a subordinate employee, the BEST of the following ways to do this is to
    A. ask the employee to stay after working hours and then reprimand him
    B. reprimand the employee immediately after the infraction has been committed
    C. take the employee aside and speak to him privately during regular working hours
    D. write a short memo to the employee warning that strict adherence to departmental policy and procedures is required of all employees

    4.____

5. If you, as a supervisor, believe that one of your subordinate employees has a serious problem, such as alcoholism or an emotional disturbance, which is adversely affecting his work, the BEST way to handle this situation *initially* would be to

    5.____

A. urge him to seek proper professional help before he is dismissed from his job
B. ignore it and let the employee work out the problem himself
C. suggest that the employee take an extended leave of absence until he can again function effectively
D. frankly tell the employee that unless his work improves, you will take disciplinary measures against him

6. Of the following, the BEST way to develop a subordinate's potential is to
    A. give him a fair chance to learn by doing
    B. assign him more than his share of work
    C. criticize only his work
    D. urge him to do his work rapidly

6.____

7. During a survey, an employee from another agency asks you to assist him on a job which would require a full day of your time.
    Of the following, the BEST immediate action for you to take is to
    A. refuse to assist him
    B. ask for compensation before doing it
    C. assist him promptly
    D. notify his department head

7.____

8. Of the following, the BEST way to handle an overly talkative subordinate is to
    A. have your superior talk to him about it
    B. have a subordinate talk to him about it
    C. talk to him about it in a group conference
    D. talk to him about it in private

8.____

9. While you are making a survey, a citizen questions you about the work you are doing.
    Of the following, the BEST thing to do is to
    A. answer the questions tactfully
    B. refuse to answer any questions
    C. advise him to write a letter to the main office
    D. answer the questions in double-talk

9.____

10. Respect for a supervisor is MOST likely to increase if he is
    A. morose   B. sporadic   C. vindictive   D. zealous

10.____

11. A subordinate who continuously bypasses his immediate supervisor for technical information should be
    A. reprimanded by his immediate supervisor
    B. ignored by his immediate supervisor
    C. given more difficult work to do
    D. given less difficult work to do

11.____

12. Complicated instructions should NOT be written
    A. accurately   B. lucidly   C. factually   D. verbosely

12.____

13. Of the following, the MOST important reason for checking a report is to
    A. check accuracy
    B. eliminate unnecessary sections
    C. catch mistakes
    D. check for delineation

14. Two subordinates under your supervision dislike each other to the extent that production is cut down.
    Your BEST action as a supervisor is to
    A. ignore the matter and hope for the best
    B. transfer the more aggressive man
    C. cut down on the workload
    D. talk to them together about the matter

15. One of the following characteristics which a supervisor should NOT display while explaining a job to a subordinate is
    A. enthusiasm   B. confidence   C. apathy   D. determination

16. Of the following, for BEST production of work, it should be assigned according to a person's
    A. attitude toward the work
    B. ability to do the work
    C. salary
    D. seniority

17. You receive an anonymous written complaint from a citizen about a subordinate who used abusive language.
    Of the following, your BEST course of action is to
    A. ignore the letter
    B. report it to your supervisor
    C. discuss the complaint with the subordinate privately
    D. keep the subordinate in the office

18. A supervisor should recognize that the way to get the BEST results from his instructions and assignments to the staff is to use
    A. a suggestive approach after he has decided exactly what is to be done and how
    B. the willing and cooperative staff members and avoid the hard-to-handle people
    C. care to select the persons most capable of carrying out the assignments
    D. an authoritative, non-nonsense tone when issuing instructions or giving assignments

19. As the supervisor of a unit, you find that you are spending too much of your time on routine tasks and not enough on coordinating the work of the staff or preparing necessary reports.
    Of the following, it would be MOST advisable for you to
    A. discard a great portion of the routine jobs done in the unit
    B. give some of the routine jobs to other members of the staff
    C. postpone the routine jobs and concentrate on coordinating the work of the staff
    D. delegate the job of coordinating the work to the most capable member of the staff

20. At times a supervisor may be called upon to train new employees. Suppose that you are giving such training in several sessions to be held on different days. During the first session, a trainee interrupts several times to ask questions at key points in your discussion.
Of the following, the BEST way to handle this trainee is to
    A. advise him to pay closer attention so he can avoid asking too many questions
    B. tell him to listen without interrupting and he'll hear his questions answered
    C. answer his questions to show him that you know your field, but make a mental note that this trainee is a troublemaker
    D. answer each question fully and make certain he understands the answers

21. Employee errors can be reduced to a minimum by effective supervision and by training.
Which of the following approaches used by a supervisor would usually be MOST effective in handling an employee who has made an avoidable and serious error for the first time?
    A. Tell the worker how other employees avoid making errors
    B. Analyze with the employee the situation leading to the error and then take whatever administrative or training steps are needed to avoid such errors
    C. Use this error as the basis for a staff meeting at which the employee's error is disclosed and discussed in an effort to improve the performance
    D. Urge the employee to modify his behavior in light of his mistake

22. Suppose that a particular staff member, formerly one of your most regular workers, has recently fallen into the habit of arriving a bit late to work several times a week. You feel that such a habit can grow consistently worse and spread to other staff members unless it is checked.
Of the following, the BEST action for you to take, as the supervisor in charge of the unit, is to
    A. go immediately to your own supervisor, present the facts, and have this employee disciplined
    B. speak privately to this tardy employee, advise him of the need to improve his punctuality, and inform him that he'll be disciplined if late again
    C. talk to the co-worker with whom this late employee is most friendly, and ask the friend to help him solve his tardiness problem
    D. speak privately with this employee, and try to discover and deal with the reasons for the latenesses

23. A supervisor may make an assignment in the form of a request, a command, or a call for volunteers.
It is LEAST desirable to make an assignment in the form of a request when
    A. an employee does not like the particular kind of assignment to be given
    B. the assignment requires working past the regular closing day
    C. an emergency has come up
    D. the assignment is not particularly pleasant for anybody

24. When you give a certain task that you normally perform yourself to one of your employees, it is MOST important that you
    A. lead the employee to believe that he has been chosen above others to perform this job
    B. describe the job as important even though it is merely a routine task
    C. explain the job that needs to be accomplished, but always let the employee decide how to do it
    D. tell the employee why you are delegating the job to him and explain exactly what he is to do

25. A supervisor when instructing new trainees in the routine of his unit should include a description of the department's overall objectives and programs in order to
    A. insure that individual work assignments will be completed satisfactorily
    B. create a favorable impression of his supervisory capabilities
    C. develop a better understanding of the purposes behind work assignments
    D. produce an immediate feeling of group cooperation

KEY (CORRECT ANSWERS)

1.	B	11.	A
2.	A	12.	D
3.	D	13.	C
4.	C	14.	D
5.	A	15.	C
6.	A	16.	B
7.	A	17.	C
8.	D	18.	C
9.	A	19.	B
10.	D	20.	D

21.	B
22.	D
23.	A
24.	D
25.	C

TEST 4

DIRECTIONS: Each question or incomplete statement is followed by several suggested answers or completions. Select the one that BEST answers the question or completes the statement. *PRINT THE LETTER OF THE CORRECT ANSWER IN THE SPACE AT THE RIGHT.*

1. An integral part of every supervisor's job is getting his ideas or instructions across to his staff.
   The extent of his success, if he has a reasonably competent staff, is PRIMARILY dependent on the
   A. interest of the employee
   B. intelligence of the employee
   C. reasoning behind the ideas or instructions
   D. presentation of the ideas or instructions

   1.____

2. Generally, what is the FIRST action the supervisor should take when an employee approaches him with a complaint?
   A. Review the employee's recent performance with him
   B. Use the complaint as a basis to discuss improvement of procedures
   C. Find out from the employee the details of the complaint
   D. Advise the employee to take his complaint to the head of the department

   2.____

3. Of the following, which is NOT usually considered one of the purposes of counseling an employee after an evaluation of his performance?
   A. Explaining the performance standards used by the supervisor
   B. Discussing necessary discipline action to be taken
   C. Emphasizing the employee's strengths and weaknesses
   D. Planning better utilization of the employee's strengths

   3.____

4. Assume that a supervisor, when reviewing a decision reached by one of his subordinates, finds the decision incorrect.
   Under these circumstances, it would be MOST desirable for the supervisor to
   A. correct the decision and inform the subordinate of this at a staff meeting
   B. correct the decision and suggest a more detailed analysis in the future
   C. help the employee find the reason for the correct decision
   D. refrain from assigning this type of a problem to the employee

   4.____

5. An IMPORTANT characteristic of a good supervisor is his ability to
   A. be a stern disciplinarian   B. put off the settling of grievances
   C. solve problems   D. find fault in individuals

   5.____

6. A new supervisor will BEST obtain the respect of the men assigned to him if he
   A. makes decisions rapidly and sticks to the, regardless of whether they are right or wrong
   B. makes decisions rapidly and then changes them just as rapidly if the decisions are wrong
   C. does not make any decisions unless he is absolutely sure that they are right
   D. makes his decisions after considering carefully all available information

   6.____

2 (#4)

7. A newly appointed worker is operating at a level of performance below that of the other employees.
   In this situation, a supervisor should FIRST
   A. lower the acceptable standard for the new man
   B. find out why the new man cannot do as well as the others
   C. advise the new worker he will be dropped from the payroll at the end of the probationary period
   D. assign another new worker to assist the first man

   7.____

8. Assume that you have to instruct a new man on a specific departmental operation. The new man seems unsure of what you have said.
   Of the following, the BEST way for you to determine whether the man has understood you is to
   A. have the man explain the operation to you in his own words
   B. repeat your explanation to him slowly
   C. repeat your explanation to him, using simpler wording
   D. emphasize the important parts of the operation to him

   8.____

9. A supervisor realizes that he has taken an instantaneous dislike to a new worker assigned to him.
   The BEST course of action for the supervisor to take in this case is to
   A. be especially observant of the new worker's actions
   B. request that the new worker be reassigned
   C. make a special effort to be fair to the new worker
   D. ask to be transferred himself

   9.____

10. A supervisor gives detailed instructions to his men as to how a certain type of job is to be done.
    One ADVANTAGE of this practice is that this will
    A. result in a more flexible operation
    B. standardize operations
    C. encourage new men to learn
    D. encourage initiative to learn

    10.____

11. Of the following the one that would MOST likely be the result of poor planning is:
    A. Omissions are discovered after the work is completed
    B. During the course of normal inspection, a meter is found to be inaccessible
    C. An inspector completes his assignments for that day ahead of schedule
    D. A problem arises during an inspection and prevents an inspector from completing his day's assignments

    11.____

12. Of the following, the BEST way for a supervisor to maintain good employee morale is for the supervisor to
    A. avoid correcting the employee when he makes mistakes
    B. continually praise the employee's work even when it is of average quality
    C. show that he is willing to assist in solving the employee's problems
    D. accept the employee's excuses for failure even though the excuses are not valid

    12.____

13. A supervisor takes time to explain to his men why a departmental order has been issued.
    This practice is
    A. *good*, mainly because without this explanation the men will not be able to carry out the order
    B. *bad*, mainly because time will be wasted for no useful purpose
    C. *good*, because understanding the reasons behind an order will lead to more effective carrying out of the order
    D. *bad*, because men will then question every order that they receive

14. Of the following, the MOST important responsibility of a supervisor in charge of a section is to
    A. establish close personal relationships with each of his subordinates in the section
    B. insure that each subordinate in the section knows the full range of his duties and responsibilities
    C. maintain friendly relations with his immediate supervisor
    D. protect his subordinate from criticism from any source

15. The BEST way to get a good work output from employees is to
    A. hold over them the threat of disciplinary action or removal
    B. maintain a steady, unrelenting pressure on them
    C. show them that you can do anything they can do faster and better
    D. win their respect and liking, so they want to work for you

KEY (CORRECT ANSWERS)

1.	A	6.	D	11.	A
2.	C	7.	B	12.	C
3.	A	8.	A	13.	C
4.	C	9.	C	14.	B
5.	C	10.	B	15.	D

EXAMINATION SECTION
TEST 1

DIRECTIONS: Below are 10 groups of statements and conclusions, numbered 1 through 10. For each group of statements, select the one conclusion lettered A, B, C, which is fully supported by and is based SOLELY on the statements. *PRINT THE LETTER OF THE CORRECT ANSWER IN THE SPACE AT THE RIGHT.*

1. He is either approved or disapproved for this examination. But, he is not approved. Therefore, he is

    A. qualified
    B. disapproved
    C. a taxpayer

    1._____

2. In planning the itinerary for Mr. Kane, his secretary told him: Route 20 runs parallel to Route 6. Route 6 runs parallel to Route 18.
Mr. Kane concluded that,
Therefore, Route

    A. 20 is north of Route 6
    B. 18 intersects Route 20
    C. 20 is parallel to Route 18

    2._____

3. Either the valedictorian is more intelligent than the salutatorian, or as intelligent, or less intelligent.
But the valedictorian is not more intelligent, nor is she less intelligent.
Therefore, the valedictorian is

    A. less intelligent than the salutatorian
    B. as intelligent as the salutatorian
    C. more intelligent than the salutatorian

    3._____

4. If the date for the examination is changed, it will be held July 28, or it will be postponed until October 15.
The date is not changed.
Therefore, the examination

    A. will probably be held July 28
    B. date is uncertain
    C. will be held July 28, or it will be postponed until October 15

    4._____

5. Joan transcribes faster than Nancy.
Nancy transcribes faster than Anne.
Therefore,

    A. Nancy transcribes faster than Joan
    B. Joan transcribes faster than Anne
    C. Nancy has had longer experience than Anne in taking dictation

    5._____

6. The files in Division D contain either pending matter, completed case records, or dead material.
They do not contain pending matter.
Therefore, they contain

    6._____

A. completed case records
B. completed case records and dead material
C. either completed case records or dead material

7. Either stenographer B in pool C types faster than stenographer A in pool D, or she types at the same rate as stenographer A, or she types slower than stenographer A. But, she does not type faster than stenographer A, nor does she type slower than stenographer Therefore, stenographer

   A. B does not type as fast as stenographer A
   B. B is more efficient than stenographer A
   C. A types as fast as stenographer B

8. Miss Andre can be eligible for retirement when she has been in city service 35 years, or if she is 55 years of age. She is fifty-four years old and has been in city service 36 years. Therefore, she

   A. is not eligible for retirement now
   B. is eligible for retirement now
   C. will be eligible for retirement only if she stays in city service for another year

9. If K is L, O is P; if M is N, Q is R.
   Either K is L, or M is N.
   Therefore,

   A. K is P or M is R
   B. either O is P or Q is R
   C. the conclusion is uncertain

10. If the employee is in error, the supervisor's refusal to listen to his side is unreasonable. If he is not in error, the supervisor's refusal is unjust. But the employee is in error or he is not.
    Therefore, the supervisor's refusal

    A. may be considered later
    B. is either unreasonable or it is unjust
    C. is justifiable

KEY (CORRECT ANSWERS)

1.	B	6.	C
2.	C	7.	C
3.	B	8.	B
4.	B	9.	B
5.	B	10.	B

TEST 2

Questions 1-5

DIRECTIONS: Below are 5 groups of statements and conclusions, numbered 1 through 5. For each group of statements, select the one conclusion lettered A, B, C, which is fully supported by and is based SOLELY on the statements. *PRINT THE LETTER OF THE CORRECT ANSWER IN THE SPACE AT THE RIGHT.*

1. Three desks are placed in a straight row just inside the door in our office. Desk 1 is farther from the door than Desk 2. Desk 3 is farther from the door than Desk 1. Which desk is in the middle position from the door? Desk

    A. 1   B. 2   C. 3

2. The problem is either correct or incorrect or is unsolvable.
   The problem is not correct.
   Therefore, the

    A. problem is incorrect
    B. problem is either incorrect or is unsolvable
    C. conclusion is uncertain

3. Village E is situated between City F and Village G.
   City F is situated between Village G and Town H.
   Therefore, Village E is

    A. not situated between Village G and Town H
    B. situated between City F and Town H
    C. situated nearer to City F than to Town H

4. Jurisdiction No. 1 is between Jurisdictions No. 2 and No. 3.
   Jurisdiction No. 2 is between Jurisdictions No. 3 and No. 4.
   Therefore, Jurisdiction No. 1 is

    A. not between Jurisdictions No. 3 and No. 4
    B. between Jurisdictions No. 2 and No. 4
    C. nearer to Jurisdiction No. 2 than to No. 4

5. Five candidates (A, B, C, D, and E) are seated in the same room. D is between A and B; E is between A and D; C is the same distance from A and E, and D is the same distance from A and B.
   Therefore,

    A. E is nearer to B than to A
    B. C is nearer to E than to D
    C. B is nearer to E than to D

Questions 6-10.

DIRECTIONS: Each question or incomplete statement is followed by several suggested answers or completions. Select the one that BEST answers the question or completes the statement. *PRINT THE LETTER OF THE CORRECT ANSWER IN THE SPACE AT THE RIGHT.*

6. If John is older than Mary and Mary is younger than Jane, then

    A. twice Mary's age is less than the sum of the ages of John and Jane
    B. the sum of the ages of John and Mary exceeds the age of Jane
    C. the ages of John and Jane are equal
    D. three times Mary's age equals the sum of the ages of John and Jane

7. John is older than Mary, Henry is older than Mary.
   It follows, therefore, that

    A. John and Henry are the same age
    B. the sum of the ages of John and Mary exceeds the age of Henry
    C. Mary's age is less than half of the sum of John's and Henry's ages
    D. none of the preceding three statements is true

8. The average of 9 numbers is 70.
   It follows that

    A. the sum of the numbers is 630
    B. the median of the numbers is 70
    C. the median of the numbers cannot be 70
    D. no two of the numbers can be equal

9. John is twice as old as Mary.
   The only statement about their ages which is NOT true is

    A. in five years, John will be twice as old as Mary
    B. in five years, the sum of their ages will be 10 more than the present sum of their ages
    C. Mary's present age is one-third of the sum of their present ages
    D. two years ago, the difference between their ages was the same as it will be two years hence

10. A is taller than B; C is 2 inches shorter than B.
    The one statement of the following four statements which is NOT necessarily true is

    A. B is taller than C
    B. A is taller than C
    C. A is taller than C by more than 2 inches
    D. B's height is the average of the heights of A and C

KEY (CORRECT ANSWERS)

1. A
2. B
3. C
4. C
5. B

6. A
7. C
8. D
9. A
10. D

TEST 3

DIRECTIONS: Each question or incomplete statement is followed by several suggested answers or completions. Select the one that BEST answers the question or completes the statement. *PRINT THE LETTER OF THE CORRECT ANSWER IN THE SPACE AT THE RIGHT.*

1. A stenographer can BEST deal with the situation which arises when her pencil breaks during dictation by   1.____

    A. asking the person dictating to lend her one
    B. being equipped at every dictation with several pencils
    C. going back to her desk to secure another one
    D. making a call to the supply room for some pencils

2. Accuracy is of greater importance than speed in filing CHIEFLY because   2.____

    A. city offices have a tremendous amount of filing to do
    B. fast workers are usually inferior workers
    C. there is considerable difficulty in locating materials which have been filed incorrectly
    D. there are many varieties of filing systems which may be used

3. Many persons dictate so rapidly that they pay little attention to matters of punctuation and English, but they expect their stenographers to correct errors.
   This statement implies MOST clearly that stenographers should be   3.____

    A. able to write acceptable original reports when required
    B. good citizens as well as good stenographers
    C. efficient clerks as well as good stenographers
    D. efficient in language usage

4. A typed letter should resemble a picture properly framed.
   This statement MOST emphasizes   4.____

    A. accuracy   B. speed
    C. convenience   D. neatness

5. Of the following, the CHIEF advantage of the use of a mechanical check is that it   5.____

    A. guards against tearing in handling the check
    B. decreases the possibility of alteration in the amount of the check
    C. tends to prevent the mislaying and loss of checks
    D. facilitates keeping checks in proper order for mailing

6. Of the following, the CHIEF advantage of the use of a dictating machine is that the   6.____

    A. stenographer must be able to take rapid dictation
    B. person dictating tends to make few errors
    C. dictator may be dictating letters while the stenographer is busy at some other task
    D. usual noise in an office is lessened

69

7. The CHIEF value of indicating enclosures beneath the identification marks on the lower left side of a letter is that it 7.____

   A. acts as a check upon the contents before mailing and upon receiving a letter
   B. helps determine the weight for mailing
   C. is useful in checking the accuracy of typed matter
   D. requires an efficient mailing clerk

8. The one of the following which is NOT an advantage of the window envelope is that it 8.____

   A. saves time since the inside address serves also as an outside address
   B. gives protection to the address from wear and tear of the mails
   C. lessens the possibility of mistakes since the address is written only once
   D. tends to be much easier to seal than the plain envelope

9. A question as to proper syllabication of a word at the end of a line may BEST be settled by consulting 9.____

   A. the person who dictated the letter
   B. a shorthand manual
   C. a dictionary
   D. a file of letters

10. Mailing a letter which contains many erasures is undesirable CHIEFLY because 10.____

    A. paper should not be wasted
    B. some stenographers are able to carry on some of the correspondence in an office without consulting their superiors
    C. correspondence should be neat
    D. erasures indicate that the dictator was not certain of what he intended to say in the letter

---

KEY (CORRECT ANSWERS)

1. B	6. C
2. C	7. A
3. D	8. D
4. D	9. C
5. B	10. C

TEST 4

DIRECTIONS: Each question or incomplete statement is followed by several suggested answers or completions. Select the one that BEST answers the question or completes the statement. *PRINT THE LETTER OF THE CORRECT ANSWER IN THE SPACE AT THE RIGHT.*

1. A charter operates for a city in somewhat the same fashion as   1.____

   A. the United States Supreme Court functions with regard to federal legislation
   B. the United States Constitution operates for the entire country
   C. the Governor functions for New York State
   D. a lease for a landlord

2. All civil employees should be especially interested in the activities of the United States Supreme Court PRIMARILY because   2.____

   A. its decisions provide certain kinds of important general rules
   B. the Supreme Court consists of nine persons appointed by the President
   C. the American Constitution is the finest document which man has ever produced
   D. the President's plan for reorganization of the court may be revived

3. Of the following, it is most frequently argued that labor problems are of concern to the civil employee PRIMARILY because   3.____

   A. the problems of labor are the same as the problems of government
   B. newspapers carry considerable information about labor problems
   C. the civil employee is a wage or salary earner
   D. a government is of the people, for the people, and by the people

4. Warfare in any part of the world should be of interest to the civil employee PRIMARILY as a result of the fact that   4.____

   A. strict American neutrality is secured by not permitting the sale of munitions to any country at war
   B. war has not been declared though warfare is raging
   C. the United States participates in the meetings of the UN
   D. facilities for transportation and communication have produced a "smaller" world

5. Cities regulate certain aspects of housing CHIEFLY because   5.____

   A. the city is the largest municipality in the country
   B. zoning is the concern of all residents of the city
   C. housing affects health
   D. the state constitution makes regulation optional

6. In general, it is PROBABLY true that the functions which a city administers are those   6.____

   A. most necessary to the preservation of the well-being of its residents
   B. of little or no interest to private business
   C. forbidden to the state
   D. not capable of being financed by private business

7. There is no more convincing mark of a cultured speaker or writer than accuracy of statement.
   This statement stresses the importance of

   A. new ideas
   B. facts
   C. acquiring a pleasing speaking voice
   D. poise

8. When a department is called, the voice which answers the telephone is, to the person calling, the department itself.
   This statement implies *most clearly* that

   A. only one person should answer the telephone in each office
   B. a clerk with a pleasing, courteous telephone manner is an asset to an office
   C. an efficient clerk will terminate all telephone conversations as quickly as possible
   D. making personal telephone calls is looked upon with disfavor in some offices

9. Probably the CHIEF advantage of filling higher vacancies by promotion is that this procedure

   A. stimulates the worker to improve his work and general knowledge and technique
   B. provides an easy check on the work of the individual
   C. eliminates personnel problems in a department
   D. harmonizes the work of one department with that of all other departments

10. Greatest efficiency is reached when filing method and filing clerk are harmoniously adjusted to the needs of an office.
    This statement means *most nearly* that

    A. the filing method is more important than the clerk in securing the successful handling of valuable papers
    B. almost any clerk can do office filing well
    C. a good clerk using a good filing system assures good filing
    D. every office needs a filing system

KEY (CORRECT ANSWERS)

1. B
2. A
3. C
4. D
5. C

6. A
7. B
8. B
9. A
10. C

TEST 5

DIRECTIONS: Each question or incomplete statement is followed by several suggested answers or completions. Select the one that BEST answers the question or completes the statement. *PRINT THE LETTER OF THE CORRECT ANSWER IN THE SPACE AT THE RIGHT.*

1. Your superior, Mr. Hotchkiss, is in conference and has requested that he not be disturbed.
   The condition under which you would MOST probably disturb the conference is:

   A. A Mr. Smith, whom you have not seen before, says he has important business with Mr. Hotchkiss
   B. Mrs. Hotchkiss telephones, saying there has been a serious accident at home
   C. You do not know how a certain letter should be filed and wish to ask the advice of Mr. Hotchkiss
   D. A fellow clerk wishes to ask Mr. Hotchkiss whether a particular city department handles certain matters

   1._____

2. Your superior directs you to find certain papers. You know the purpose for which the papers are to be used. In the course of your search for the papers, you come across certain material which would be very useful for the purpose to be served by the papers. You should

   A. bring the papers to your superior and ask whether he wants the other materials
   B. go to your superior immediately and ask whether he wishes both the materials and the papers or only one of the two
   C. bring to your superior the other materials, together with the papers you were directed to find
   D. bring only the other materials to your superior and point out the manner in which these materials are of greater value than the papers

   2._____

3. If a fellow employee asks you a question to which you do not know the answer, you should say,

   A. "I don't know. What's the difference?"
   B. "The answer to that question forms no part of my duties here."
   C. "My dear sir, the thing for you to do is to look the matter up yourself because it is your responsibility, not mine."
   D. "I'm sorry. I don't know."

   3._____

4. In general, it is PROBABLY true that MOST people are

   A. so self-seeking that they pay no attention to the wants, needs, or behavior of others
   B. so changeable that one never knows what his fellow employee is likely to do next
   C. not worth the trouble to bother about
   D. quite ready to help others

   4._____

5. Of the following, the one which is NOT a reason for avoiding clerical errors is that

   A. time is lost
   B. money is wasted
   C. many clerks are very intelligent
   D. serious consequences may follow

   5._____

6. Of the following, the MAIN reason for keeping a careful record of incoming mail is that

   A. some people are less industrious than others
   B. this record helps to speed up outgoing mail
   C. this record is a kind of legal evidence
   D. this information may be useful in answering questions which may arise

7. Of the following, the MAIN reason for using a calculating machine is that

   A. a lesser knowledge of arithmetic is needed
   B. a more attractive product is obtained
   C. greater speed and accuracy are obtained
   D. it is not difficult to learn how to operate a calculating machine

8. Of the following, the MAIN reason for being polite over the telephone is that

   A. persons who are speaking over the telephone cannot see each other
   B. politeness makes for pleasant business relationships
   C. it is not at all difficult or costly to be courteous
   D. one's voice is of great importance because voice reflects mood

9. Because telephone directories contain printed pages, they are called books.
   This statement assumes *most nearly* that

   A. some books do not contain printed pages
   B. not all telephone directories are books which contain printed pages
   C. material which contains printed pages is called a book
   D. all books which contain printed pages are called telephone directories

10. Mr. Cross must be using a budget because he has been able to reduce his unnecessary expenses.
    On the basis of only the material included in this statement, it may MOST accurately be said that this statement assumes that

    A. all people who use budgets lower certain types of expenses
    B. some people who do not use budgets reduce unnecessary expenses
    C. some people who use budgets do not reduce unnecessary expenses
    D. all types of expenses are reduced by the use of a budget

KEY (CORRECT ANSWERS)

1. B
2. C
3. D
4. D
5. C

6. D
7. C
8. B
9. C
10. A

REASONING AND JUDGMENT

EXAMINATION SECTION
TEST 1

DIRECTIONS: Each question or incomplete statement is followed by several suggested answers or completions. Select the one that BEST answers the question or completes the statement. *PRINT THE LETTER OF THE CORRECT ANSWER IN THE SPACE AT THE RIGHT.*

1. Lapland consists of the most northern parts of Norway, Sweden, and Finland, and the Kola Peninsula in Russia. The inhabitants, called Lapps, are very hardy people who farm and fish for a livelihood. Their meat, milk, and furs come from the reindeer, which is their only domestic animal.
   There is no country named Lapland, so we cannot ask,

   A. "Who is president of Lapland?"
   B. "What kind of education is there in Lapland?"
   C. "What is the climate in Lapland?"
   D. "Are any of the Lapps wealthy?"

   1.____

2. Induction is a method of reasoning by which general laws are inferred from the observation of a large number of individual cases. The laws thus derived are based not upon logical necessity but upon consistency among observations.
   Since any new observation conceivably could fail to follow the inductive law which it would be predicted to follow, an inductive law is never

   A. sought in scientific research
   B. as useful as a deductive law
   C. used as a basis for action
   D. more than probably true

   2.____

3. A lion, finding a hare asleep, was about to devour it when he saw a deer passing. He left the hare and chased the deer, which was so swift that it escaped him. When the lion returned to eat the hare, he found that it had been awakened by the noise and had escaped.
   This story was told to make the point that men often lose moderate gains by trying for

   A. easier ones   B. larger ones
   C. sure profit   D. great losses

   3.____

4. In Norse mythology, no god was better loved than Balder, the god of light and peace. He was slain by the trickery of Loki, a jealous god.
   When the dark winter comes to the Norseland, the people say, "All nature grieves for Balder," and when the spring comes again, they say,

   A. "Summer is here again."
   B. "Balder has never lived."
   C. "Loki will never return to earth."
   D. "The spirit of Balder has returned."

   4.____

75

5. Living organisms are able to exist at great ocean depths in spite of the tremendous pressure of the water so long as their, body spaces are not filled with air or any other gas. This is possible because the pressure is equally applied on all sides of the organism and the same pressure is maintained inside and outside. Similarly, man does not feel the effects of pressure in the atmosphere exerted on him at 14.7 pounds per square inch, but he cannot withstand the great pressure of water below depths of 100 feet because his body contains spaces filled with _____ pressure.

   A. water at low
   B. air at the same
   C. water at high
   D. air at low

6. The oak tree has long been a symbol of strength and bravery. Mindful of this symbolism, the Romans, who were a hardy people, decorated their war heroes with crowns of _____ leaves.

   A. maple   B. olive   C. laurel   D. oak

7. In aviation, the ceiling is the distance from the ground to the bottom of the clouds when the sky is more than half-covered. When there is heavy fog on the ground, the ceiling is said to be zero. When the sky is clear or there are only scattered clouds, the ceiling is unlimited. An airplane pilot must know what the ceiling is before takeoff so that he can determine the proper flight

   A. altitude   B. direction   C. instruments   D. speed

8. In THE RIGHTS OF MAN, Thomas Paine wrote, *"Every age and generation must be as free to act for itself in all oases as the ages and generations which preceded it. The vanity and presumption of governing beyond the grave is the most ridiculous and insolent of all tyrannies. Man has no property in man; neither has any generation a property in the generations which are to follow."*
   According to this, citizens of the United States should respect the Constitution because they believe it is right and not because it is

   A. debatable   B. old   C. English   D. misunderstood

9. Before newspapers were common, a man called a town crier was appointed to make public announcements. The town crier was an important person in England and in the British North American colonies, but he disappeared when newspapers became more widely distributed. Nowadays we often hear news before we read it in the paper. We hear it from an electronic town crier -

   A. the theater
   B. a radio or a television set
   C. a town meeting
   D. a phonograph

10. The opal is a gem that reflects a number of beautiful colors. For a long time, opals were unpopular because of a superstition that it was bad luck to wear them unless they were one's birthstone.
    Few people believe this superstition anymore, and opals have become more

    A. transparent   B. colorful   C. popular   D. beautiful

11. Newton's third law of motion states that for every action there is an equal and opposite reaction. When a gun is fired, the force that pushes the bullet forward is equal to the force with which the gun recoils.
Space vehicles, having left the earth's atmosphere, can maneuver by firing small rockets in the direction

    A. of the earth
    B. in which they wish to go
    C. opposite to their destination
    D. at right angles to their destination

12. When the purchasing power of the dollar steadily declines over a period of time, we speak of *inflation.* The reverse situation, in which a dollar buys more than formerly, is called deflation.
Inflation and deflation, then, are defined by changes in the relation between

    A. borrowing and lending B. money and goods
    C. supply and demand   D. decrease and increase

13. The seed gatherers were a group of Indians who lived in the arid region between the Rocky Mountains and the Sierra Nevada. They were called seed gatherers because of the way in which they got most of their food. Seeds and berries suitable to eat grew in different regions at different times of the year.
For this reason, the seed gatherers

    A. were skilled archers   B. changed homes often
    C. fished in the sea   D. made fancy baskets

14. The men of the Coast Guard rescue many people from disasters at sea. Their work is often dangerous because they sometimes have to go out on a rescue mission under very bad conditions.
The men have excellent equipment, and they are well-trained, but their duties involve great

    A. speed   B. preparation   C. risks   D. thrills

15. A crocodile can snap a wooden plank in two with its powerful jaws. But a man can hold the jaws of a crocodile together with very little effort.
The crocodile exerts the greatest amount of power when

    A. snapping at wood   B. opening its mouth
    C. C. lashing its tail   D. closing its jaws

16. All of Alaska is farther west than the westernmost part of the continental United States. Juneau, the capital of Alaska, is in the same time zone as California, although its longitude should place it in the Yukon time zone. Some of the Aleutian Islands, a part of Alaska, are on one side of the 180 meridian and some are on the other, but the date line does not follow the 180 meridian and does not cut the Aleutians.
The result is that although there are four time zones in the United States, they are all

    A. on the same side of the date line
    B. on standard time
    C. really west of Greenwich
    D. in the Western Hemisphere

17. In Greek mythology, a chimera was a fire-breathing female monster with the head of a lion, the body of a goat, and the tail of a dragon. Of course, there really was no such animal, but the idea was so fantastic that we use the name chimera now for any

    A. deliberate falsehood
    B. figment of the imagination
    C. strange animal
    D. hybrid animal

17.____

18. The German shepherd is intelligent, alert, loyal, highly trainable, and has a good disposition. It is frequently used as a guide dog for the blind.
    It is sometimes called *German police dog* because so many of this breed have been trained for

    A. seeing eye dogs
    C. army scouts
    B. police work
    D. rescue work

18.____

19. Unless an adequate supply of protein is included in a person's diet, loss of weight and even death may result. The problem of determining the amount of protein needed is important in rationing food in war or in famine. The minimal requirement of protein to maintain the body in health is less when the protein consumed is animal protein than when it is vegetable protein.
    In some parts of the world, protein deficiency is a problem because the diet of the people is almost completely made up of

    A. animal proteins
    C. solids
    B. fish
    D. cereals

19.____

20. Emerson said, "Character is adroitness to keep the old and trodden 'round, and power and courage to make new roads to new and better goals."
    This means that the person of high character is both

    A. conformist and creator
    C. student and laborer
    B. friendly and aloof
    D. popular and unpopular

20.____

KEY (CORRECT ANSWERS)

1.	A	11.	C
2.	D	12.	B
3.	B	13.	B
4.	D	14.	C
5.	D	15.	D
6.	D	16.	A
7.	A	17.	B
8.	B	18.	B
9.	B	19.	D
10.	C	20.	A

TEST 2

DIRECTIONS: Each question or incomplete statement is followed by several suggested answers or completions. Select the one that BEST answers the question or completes the statement. *PRINT THE LETTER OF THE CORRECT ANSWER IN THE SPACE AT THE RIGHT.*

1. The small Boston terrier has a dark coat with white chest, neck, and feet. Many people are drawn to this dog because of its neat appearance and large brown eyes. The Boston terrier is a popular pet because it likes people and

    A. grows so large
    B. bites postmen
    C. is hard to train
    D. makes friends easily

1.____

2. The gradations of the moral faculties in the higher animals and man are so imperceptible that to deny to the first a certain sense of responsibility and consciousness would certainly be an exaggeration of the difference between animals and man.
When animals fight with one another, when they associate for a common purpose, when they warn one another of danger, when they come to the rescue of another, when they display pain and joy, they manifest impulses of the same kind as are considered among the

    A. most general in the animal kingdom
    B. animal instincts of man
    C. divine provisions for man
    D. moral attributes of man

2.____

3. In ancient times, a country guaranteed its treaty promises by giving hostages to the other party. The hostages were often important people in their own country. They were held as prisoners and could be killed if their country failed to keep its treaty promises.
Today, most countries rely on the good faith of other countries and on public opinion to ensure that they will keep their treaties, and the hostage system

    A. is strictly observed
    B. is no longer used
    C. protects treaty makers
    D. has grown in effectiveness

3.____

4. The Pekingese was held in great esteem by Chinese royalty. The dog was bred to accentuate marks that were related in various ways to the upper classes of society. A white spot on the forehead of a Pekingese was admired, for this mark was associated with the Buddha.
A mark round the dog's body resembling a sash was quite admirable, for during the time when the Pekingese breed was so much admired,

    A. sashes were used to hold the outer garments together
    B. only high-ranking officials could wear sashes
    C. it was difficult to breed a dog with a sash mark
    D. sash marks signified royal blood

4.____

79

5. A recent U.S. study showed that of 100 high school seniors who received national academic scholarships, nine out of ten read at least one book a month, while of 100 high school seniors accepted by various colleges but not awarded scholarships, only six out of ten read at least one book a month.
This shows that those who read more are MOST likely to

   A. waste time
   B. achieve more
   C. become librarians
   D. spend less money

6. Turbines in motor vehicles cannot be operated on gasoline containing lead. Diesel fuel, on which turbines can be operated, is available only on major turnpikes and on roads that trucks use.
Thus, if regular cars are to utilize turbines,

   A. highways must be rerouted
   B. the turbines must be small
   C. diesel fuel distribution must be expanded
   D. filling stations must stop selling regular gasoline

7. A gun collector of my acquaintance owns an old rifle that sold for about $35 twenty years ago and would now bring a price of $400 to $450. But it isn't always easy to make money on antiques. Experts warn that people who have never dabbled in antiques should study the market carefully, choose a few specialties, read every available book in those fields, and consult reliable dealers before buying. They say that few pieces will be acquired cheaply by the

   A. inexperienced seller
   B. gun collector
   C. novice collector
   D. country tourist

8. Dinosaurs were the largest land animals ever known. They were sixty to ninety feet long. These figures are not guesses; they are based on measurements of bones that have been

   A. found   B. painted   C. reproduced   D. molded

9. Painting goes back at least as far as the time of cavemen. Wall paintings have been found inside some of their caves. It is believed that these pictures were not drawn primarily for decoration because most of them are

   A. pictures of animals rather than of people
   B. far back in the cave away from all light
   C. unrelated to the cavemen's lives
   D. intricate drawings that have beauty

10. The ermine, a native of northern countries, is a weasel with valuable fur. In the summer the fur is brown, but as the weather gets cooler, the fur gets lighter until it is pure white during the coldest part of the year. Since most people prefer the white ermine pelts, most ermine trapping is done

    A. with specialized traps
    B. in early fall
    C. after the snow disappears
    D. during the winter

11. The pilot of an airplane is dependent upon the plane's radio for communication from the ground concerning takeoff, landing, the movements of other planes, and the weather. The safety of the passengers in the plane is dependent upon this communication. In case the radio is out of order, a pilot may use other signals, such as lights, but the radio is very important.
    Even small planes are usually equipped with.

    A. radios B. landing gear C. horns D. pilots

12. Although more men than women play golf, women have played the game for many years. Mary, Queen of Scots, who lived in the sixteenth century, may have been the first woman golfer. She used the term *cadet* (pupil) for the boy who carried her clubs around the course.
    This term is still used today, but the spelling has been changed to

    A. Scotsman B. cadet C. caddy D. golfer

13. According to Emerson, "A man is a center for nature, running out threads of relation through everything, fluid and solid, material and elemental... How few materials are yet used by our arts! It would seem as if each waited like the enchanted princes in fairy tales, for a destined human deliverer. All that is yet inanimate will one day speak and reason. Unpublished nature will have its whole secret told."
    If Emerson were to come to life in the twentieth century, he would

    A. lose his faith in fairy tales
    B. not be surprised by man's advancement in outer space
    C. feel compelled to use more materials in his arts
    D. be frightened by this industrial age

14. At one time, California had to ship its products around Cape Horn, which is at the southern tip of South America, to get them to the eastern part of the United States. This route was long, but the land routes were worse because of the mountains, deserts, and plains. It is not surprising that California planned a big celebration in 1914 to emphasize the importance of the opening of

    A. the Panama Canal   B. eastern harbors
    C. European routes   D. Chinese trade

15. Gordius, mythical king of Phrygia, tied an intricate knot in the thong that held the pole of his chariot to the yoke. An oracle had declared that he who untied the knot should be master of Asia. Many tried and failed. Alexander the Great looked at the knot and quickly cut it with his sword. We use the expression *to cut the Gordian knot* to mean to

    A. do the impossible
    B. use your head instead of your hands
    C. solve a difficult problem by bold action
    D. become an oracle

16. Many millions of dollars worth of gold, silver, and jewels have gone down with ships in numerous ship disasters. These treasures lie at the bottom of almost every major body of water in the world.
    It is not surprising that divers spend a great deal of time and money looking for

    A. treasure islands   B. sunken treasure
    C. scientific data   D. new oceans

17. The following quotation is from Thomas Hobbes: *"Nature has made men so equal in the faculties of body and mind* as that though there be found one man sometimes manifestly stronger in body, or of quicker mind than another, yet when all is reckoned together, the difference between man and man is not so considerable as that one man can thereupon claim to himself any benefit to which another

    A. has already attained."
    B. is capable of attaining."
    C. may not reach as well as he."
    D. would deny him."

18. The Louvre in Paris has the restoration of a stone found in 1868 at Dhiban in what was ancient Moab. The stone is believed to have been carved by a scribe about 800 B.C. and is of interest to scholars of ancient languages. When the French tried to buy the stone, the Arabs broke it into many pieces, hoping to get more money for it.
    The French bought some of the larger pieces and were able to make the restoration of the entire stone because a French embassy official at Constantinople (now Istanbul) had

    A. made a paper cast of the stone
    B. hidden the original from the Turks
    C. had the writing deciphered
    D. handled the financial arrangements

19. There are many primitive countries in the world that have never taken a census, an official count of the population. Population figures from these countries are

    A. accurate   B. too high   C. estimates   D. lost

20. The National Audubon Society reported that their 1962 census of bald eagles in the United States, excluding Alaska, was 3807, as compared to 3642 in 1961. Of 118 dead eagles reported to the society in 1962, 91 had been shot. There is great concern that the bald eagle, which is the national bird, may completely disappear.
    The Audubon Society urges a nationwide campaign to educate the public not to _____ eagles.

    A. protect   B. feed   C. harm   D. count

KEY (CORRECT ANSWERS)

1.	D	11.	A
2.	D	12.	C
3.	B	13.	B
4.	B	14.	A
5.	B	15.	C
6.	C	16.	B
7.	C	17.	C
8.	A	18.	A
9.	B	19.	C
10.	D	20.	C

TEST 3

DIRECTIONS: Each question or incomplete statement is followed by several suggested answers or completions. Select the one that BEST answers the question or completes the statement. *PRINT THE LETTER OF THE CORRECT ANSWER IN THE SPACE AT THE RIGHT.*

1. A library may be very large, but if it is in disorder, it is not as useful as one that is small but

    A. disordered
    B. closed to the public
    C. nearby
    D. well arranged

2. It is no great wonder if in the long process of time, while fortune takes her course hither and thither, numerous coincidences should spontaneously occur.
If the number of subjects to be wrought upon be infinite, it is all the more easy for fortune, with such an abundance of material, to

    A. effect this similarity of results
    B. fill all men with wonder
    C. prevent spontaneous coincidences
    D. effect a man's success

3. Clearinghouses are useful in reducing the volume of concrete interbank transactions. Each member bank sends to the clearinghouse a record of the money it has paid out on checks drawn on each other member.
When the lists are compared, equal reciprocal debts are

    A. reduced   B. collected   C. recorded   D. canceled

4. Many citizens of other nations deposit their money in banks in Switzerland. The Swiss banks carefully protect the identities of their depositors, a matter of some importance to certain depositors. An agent trying to determine if someone has money in a particular Swiss bank sometimes tries to make a deposit in the name of that person.
Since the acceptance of such a deposit would imply that the account did exist, Swiss banks will not

    A. cash large checks for depositors
    B. accept deposits that have been mailed in
    C. allow foreigners to open checking accounts
    D. accept deposits from unidentified persons

5. Very few states have done anything to ensure that untrained people are not allowed to carry guns. Safe gun loading can be taught, and if people had to pass a test before they could obtain a hunting license, the number of shooting accidents would probably

    A. pass laws   B. fail   C. increase   D. decrease

6. In a Dutch auction, so called because it originated in the Netherlands, the auctioneer offers an object for sale at a price above its value. He gradually reduces the price until someone accepts it. In a regular auction, the auctioneer asks for an opening bid, which is always low. Then the auctioneer tries to get people to make higher bids and sells when no one will raise the bid.
These two methods, though opposite in procedure, may both reach a sale at the highest price

    A. anyone is willing to pay
    B. that is fair to the buyer
    C. that the object is worth
    D. the seller can demand

7. Optical glass is used in cameras, telescopes, eyeglasses, and many kinds of scientific equipment. The glass is almost flawless; it must be made with great care and only from the finest materials.
For these reasons, optical glass is

   A. expensive   B. scientific   C. brittle   D. unavailable

8. It was quite understandable that it was the policy of the old priest-nobles of Egypt and India to divert their peoples from becoming familiar with the seas and to represent the occupation of a seaman as incompatible with the purity of the highest caste.
The sea deserved to be hated by those who wished to maintain the old aristocracies, inasmuch as

   A. the sea has been the mightiest instrument in the leveling of mankind
   B. the life of a sailor was quite dangerous
   C. many of the sailors lost their lives while on voyages
   D. the priest-nobles were trying to further the spread of education

9. Six cities of ancient Palestine were set aside as places of refuge for people who had killed any person unawares. In these cities, the accused could receive a fair trial. If he was found guilty of intentional murder, he was returned for punishment to the place from which he had escaped.
But if the killing was found to be accidental or not willful, the accused was allowed to remain safely in

   A. his boyhood home   B. a country of exile
   C. the city of refuge   D. the original prison

10. The average density of a cubic foot of earth is about 5.5 times that of a cubic foot of water. This is determined by dividing the earth mass by its volume. However, rocks on the earth's surface have an average density of approximately 2.7.
Therefore, in order to offset the lighter weight of the surface materials, the interior of the earth MUST have a density

   A. of 5.5   B. greater than 5.5
   C. less than 5.5   D. less than 2.7

11. Our opinions and actions are influenced to a great extent by words - the words we read and the words we hear. Yet we do not carefully attend to the subtle implications, good or bad, conveyed by these words through association.
Some words are slippery: they gloss over the actual attributes of the thing to which they refer. For example, the supporters of a favored point of view are *progressive* while those who hold an opinion less to our liking are *radical.*
The words that are chosen imply

   A. only one interpretation   B. precisely what they state
   C. no subtle connotation   D. more than they state

12. When the Mormons who settled in the Valley of the Great Salt Lake applied for statehood in 1849, they wanted the name of the state to be Deseret. Deseret is the Mormon word for honeybee, which the Mormons had taken as a symbol of the work they all had to do to make the desert productive. They were refused statehood and remained the Territory of Utah until 1896, when Utah became the forty-fifth state. The state seal has a beehive on it, and the official motto of the state is *Industry.* These are tributes to Utah's

    A. acceptance as a state
    B. principal occupation
    C. Ute Indians
    D. early Mormon settlers

13. Pythagoras, an ancient Greek, discovered the true nature of the harmonic series by observing the vibration of a single taut string stretched over a resonator. When a movable bridge was placed at the string's midpoint, the string vibrated in two segments at twice the speed at which it vibrated without a bridge. When moved to a third of the string's length, the string would vibrate in three segments at three times the speed. This phenomenon was repeated with each successive position of the bridge. Thus, Pythagoras was able to express the pitch relationships of the harmonic series in terms of

    A. mathematical ratios
    B. string lengths
    C. musical notation
    D. chemical formulas

14. Not only were the Romans undemocratic, but at no period of its history did Rome love equality. In the Republic, rank was determined by wealth. The census was the basis of the social system. Every citizen had to declare his fortune before a magistrate, and his grade was then assigned him.
    Poverty and wealth established the

    A. legal differences between men
    B. democratic system of the Republic
    C. need for a strong judicial system
    D. social equality among men

15. A surveyor's chain has 100 links, each 792 inches long. The chain is a unit of measurement that for most purposes would be very awkward, but it is particularly useful in surveying land because ten square chains made on acre. The original measuring instrument was actually made of chains. A surveyor's chain has 100 links, each 792 inches long. The chain is a unit of measurement that for most purposes would be very awkward, but it is particularly useful in surveying land because ten square chains made on acre.
    The original measuring instrument was actually made of chains.

    A. numerical   B. accurate   C. awkward   D. easy

16. Millions of people in the world spend as much as one-third of their days by hauling water. Their diets are determined by a water shortage that restricts the variety of their agricultural products.
    If the scientists of the United States can increase the water supply of arid regions by removing the salt from sea-water, they will gain

    A. new travel opportunities abroad
    B. new export articles
    C. the gratitude of millions
    D. great profits from friends

17. *"A friend stands at the door,*
    In either tight-closed hand
    Hiding rich gifts, three hundred
    And three score."
    These lines are from a poem titled

    A. EASTER MORNING B. CHRISTMAS EVE
    C. NEW YEAR'S EVE D. THANKSGIVING DAY

18. Our repugnance to death increases in proportion to our consciousness of having lived in vain - to the

    A. usefulness of our lives
    B. keenness of our disappointments
    C. intensity of our physical suffering
    D. greatness of our vanity

19. The ripeness or unripeness of the occasion must ever be well weighed; and generally it is good to commit the beginnings of all great actions to Argus with his hundred eyes, and the ends to Briareus with his hundred hands; first to watch, and then to

    A. consider   B. decide   C. begin   D. speed

20. Benjamin Franklin said, *"We may perhaps learn to deprive large masses of their Gravity, and give them absolute Levity for the sake of easy Transport. Agriculture may diminish its Labour and double its Produce; all Diseases may by sure means be prevented or cured, not excepting even that of old Age, and our Lives lengthened at pleasure even beyond the antediluvian Standard. O that moral science were in as fair a way of*

    A. Acceptance   B. Cure   C. Religion   D. Study

KEY (CORRECT ANSWERS)

1.	D	11.	D
2.	A	12.	D
3.	D	13.	A
4.	D	14.	A
5.	D	15.	D
6.	A	16.	C
7.	A	17.	C
8.	C	18.	B
9.	C	19.	D
10.	B	20.	D

EVALUATING CONCLUSIONS IN LIGHT OF KNOWN FACTS

An ability needed in many state jobs is the ability to decide if a conclusion is true, based on a set of facts. (These questions can also be called "Logic".) First read the facts (or premises) that are given, and then look at the conclusion. Assume the facts are true, and decide if the conclusion is:

1. Necessarily true.
2. Probably, but not necessarily true.
3. Indeterminable, cannot be determined.
4. Probably, but not necessarily false.
5. Necessarily false.

These five answer choices (above) are the same for each inference question.

1. FACTS: If the Commission approves the new proposal, the agency will move to a new location immediately. If the agency moves, five new supervisors will be appointed immediately. The Commission approved the new proposal.

    CONCLUSION: No new supervisors were appointed.

    1. Necessarily true.
    2. Probably, but not necessarily true.
    3. Indeterminable, cannot be determined.
    4. Probably, but not necessarily false.
    5. Necessarily false.

2. FACTS: If the director retires, John Jackson, the associate director, will not be transferred to another agency. Jackson will be promoted to director if he is not transferred. The director retired.

    CONCLUSION: Jackson will be promoted to director.

    1. Necessarily true.
    2. Probably, but not necessarily true.
    3. Indeterminable, cannot be determined.
    4. Probably, but not necessarily false.
    5. Necessarily false.

3. FACTS: If the maximum allowable income for food stamp recipients is increased, the number of food stamp recipients will increase. If the number of food stamp recipients increases, more funds must be allocated to the food stamp program, which will require a tax increase. Taxes cannot be raised without the approval of Congress. Congress probably will not approve a tax increase.

   CONCLUSION: The maximum allowable income for food stamp recipients will increase.

   1. Necessarily true.
   2. Probably, but not necessarily true.
   3. Indeterminable, cannot be determined.
   4. Probably, but not necessarily false.
   5. Necessarily false.

4. FACTS: If prices are raised and sales remain constant, profits will increase. Prices were raised and sales levels will probably be maintained.

   CONCLUSION: Profits will increase.

   1. Necessarily true.
   2. Probably, but not necessarily true.
   3. Indeterminable, cannot be determined.
   4. Probably, but not necessarily false.
   5. Necessarily false.

5. FACTS: Some employees in the personnel department are technicians. Most of the technicians working in the personnel department are test development specialists. Lisa Jones works in the personnel department.

   CONCLUSION: Lisa Jones is a technician.

   1. Necessarily true.
   2. Probably, but not necessarily true.
   3. Indeterminable, cannot be determined.
   4. Probably, but not necessarily false.
   5. Necessarily false.

INFERENCE QUESTION ANSWERS AND EXPLANATIONS

1. The correct answer is number 5 (necessarily false). The new proposal was approved. According to the facts, approval means that the agency will move, and moving to a new location means that five new supervisors will be appointed.

2. The correct answer is number 1 (necessarily true). According to the facts, the director retired, which means that Jackson will not be transferred and, therefore, will be promoted to director.

3. The correct answer is number 4 (probably, but not necessarily false). Since Congress probably will not approve a tax increase, the maximum allowable income for food stamp recipients probably will not increase.

4. The correct answer is number 2 (probably, but not necessarily true). According to the facts, profits will increase if prices are raised and sales remain constant. It is known that prices were raised. Although sales level will probably be maintained, this is not certain.

5. The correct answer is number 3 (indeterminable, cannot be determined). The facts give no indication of the proportion of employees who are technicians. Therefore, no conclusion can be drawn with respect to the probability that any one employee is a technician.

LOGICAL REASONING
EVALUATING CONCLUSIONS IN LIGHT OF KNOWN FACTS

EXAMINATION SECTION
TEST 1

DIRECTIONS: For the following questions, select the letter before the statement below which BEST expresses the relationship between the facts and the conclusion. Mark your answer:
    A. The facts prove the conclusion; or
    B. The facts disprove the conclusion; or
    C. The facts neither prove nor disprove the conclusion.
PRINT THE LETTER OF THE CORRECT ANSWER IN THE SPACE AT THE RIGHT.

1. FACTS: Andy types half as fast as Bill. Bill types twice as slow as Charlie. Bill types 60 words a minute.

    CONCLUSION: Charlie types 30 words a minute.

2. FACTS: If Albert gets traded to the Cubs, Chris will have to be traded to the Padres. Albert will avoid being traded only if he hits a home run in his turn at bat.
If Chris goes to the Padres, Dave will be traded to the Dodgers. Albert strikes out in this crucial at-bat.

    CONCLUSION: Dave gets traded to the Dodgers.

3. FACTS: All beads are forms of jewelry. All jewelry is expensive. Everyone loves expensive beads.

    CONCLUSION: All beads are expensive.

4. FACTS: No shrimp are mussels. Mussels are bivalves. All mussels have shells.

    CONCLUSION: Therefore, no shrimp have shells.

5. FACTS: On their latest diet, Abby, Bea, Celia, and Donna lost a combined total of 260 pounds. Abby lost twice as much as Celia. Celia lost half as much as the woman who lost the most. Donna lost 80 pounds.

    CONCLUSION: Abby lost 100 pounds; Bea, 30; Celia, 50; and Donna, 80.

6. FACTS: Ann's office is two floors above Brenda's.
Brenda's office is one floor below the only woman in the building whose birthday is today. Sally's office is on the third floor. Ann's office is on the fourth floor.

    CONCLUSION: Today is Ann's birthday.

7. FACTS: Douglas Ave. is perpendicular to Bates St. Bates St. is parallel to Adams Ave. Douglas Ave. is parallel to Charles St. Evans Ave. is parallel to the streets that are perpendicular to Bates St.

    CONCLUSION: Evans Ave. is perpendicular to Douglas Ave.

91

8. FACTS: There's one out, and Bill is the runner on third base. If Arnie hits the ball hard, Bill will run, but so slowly that he will be out at home plate. The team captain, on second base, will not run unless Arnie hits the ball hard. The captain runs.

   CONCLUSION: Bill is safe.

   8.____

9. FACTS: Some members of this genus are members of that species. All members of that species are butterflies. Some butterflies are different from others.

   CONCLUSION: Some members of this genus are butterflies.

   9.____

10. FACTS: Some woodwinds are clarinets. Flutes are not clarinets. All clarinets are beautiful things.

    CONCLUSION: Therefore, all beautiful things are woodwinds.

    10.____

11. FACTS: Using a grid exactly like the one below, Joe Genius filled in the numbers 1 through 9 in the boxes. Each horizontal, vertical, and diagonal row added up to 15. A different number went in each box.

    CONCLUSION: The number Joe put in the middle box was 6.

    11.____

12. FACTS: Max, Nick, Pete, and Ollie all bought different colored suits: grey, green, blue, and brown, but not necessarily respectively. Max paid less for his green suit than Nick paid for his suit. Ollie paid twice what Pete paid. Pete paid the same as the man who bought the grey suit. Ollie bought the brown suit.

    CONCLUSION: Ollie paid the most.

    12.____

13. FACTS: Four people (Alice, Bob, Carol, and Dave) are sitting at a square table, discussing their favorite sports. Bob sits directly across from the jogger. Carol sits to the right of the basketball player. Alice sits across from Dave. The golfer sits to the left of the tennis player. A man sits on Dave's right.

    CONCLUSION: Dave plays golf.

    13.____

14. FACTS: An employer decided to offer a job to everyone who scored higher than 50 on an exam. Alice scored 20. Betty scored lower than Carol, but more than twice as high as Alice.

    CONCLUSION: Of the three women, only Carol was offered the job.

    14.____

15. FACTS: If Camille's squirrel has rabies and the squirrel bites Casey's cat, the squirrel will have to be caught and the cat will get rabies. If the cat has had rabies shots within the last two years, the cat will not get rabies. Casey's cat did not get rabies.

    CONCLUSION: Casey's cat has had rabies shots within the last two years.

    15.____

16. FACTS: Sally will file a grievance only if Bill fires her. If Laura tells Frank the whole story, Frank will tell it to Bill. If Bill hears the whole story, he will not fire Sally. Laura tells Fred the whole story.

    CONCLUSION: Sally files a grievance.

    16.____

17. FACTS: If Alice leaves work early, Barb has to work late, and Barb wants to go to the game tonight. The singing of the National Anthem always precedes the game. Carl calls Alice and asks her out to dinner. Due to a thunderstorm, the singing of the National Anthem gets delayed. If Alice goes out to dinner with Carl, she will have to leave work early so she can go home and turn off her crockpot. Alice accepts Carl's invitation.

    CONCLUSION: Barb misses the first inning of the game.

    17.____

18. FACTS: Earl thinks of any whole number from 1 through 10. Because she is using the most efficient system, Eva absolutely guarantees Earl that she can correctly guess the number he's thinking of in five questions or less. Eva asks Earl a series of *yes/no* questions and guesses the number in five questions or less every time. Earl and Eva agree to play the game again in the exact same way, except that he will think of a whole number from 1 through 6.

    CONCLUSION: Using the same system, four is the absolute highest number of *yes/no* questions that Eva will need to ask in order to guess the number that Earl is thinking of this time.

    18.____

19. FACTS: Lois will cook dinner today only if Ted, Robbie, and Jennifer are all home by 6 P.M. Robbie will come home by 6 P.M. only if band practice ends early. If Ted plays Softball after work, he will take Jennifer with him, and they will not be home by 6 P.M. Band practice ends early today.

    CONCLUSION: Lois cooks dinner today.

    19.____

20. FACTS: Three card players each start with $10. Each round they play has two losers and one winner. The losers in each round have to give the winner $2 apiece. Chuck wins the first and third rounds; Bruce wins the second. At the end of the third round, Artie proposes that they change the rules so that the losers each have to give the winner half their accumulated money. They agree, play one more round, and Artie wins it.

    CONCLUSION: At the end of the fourth round, Chuck has less money than Artie.

    20.____

21. FACTS: No part-time workers at this plant get paid vacations. All cleaners at this plant are part-time workers. Joe gets a paid vacation.

    CONCLUSION: All cleaners at this plant get paid vacations.

    21.____

22. FACTS: If Myles breaks the lamp, Lucy will scream. If Tom finds Rachel spraying Windex into the cat's dish, he'll scream. If Geoffrey doesn't hear from the French soon, he'll scream. Tom screams.

    22.____

CONCLUSION: Myles broke the lamp.

23. FACTS: If Tina goes to the store, Ike will go with her. If Ike goes to the store, he will buy doughnuts. If Dick cleans the house, Sally will go to the store. If Sally goes to the store, Tina will go with her. Dick cleans the house.

    CONCLUSION: Ike buys doughnuts.

    23.____

24. FACTS: If Joe passes the test, Jill won't apply for the job. If Jill applies for the job, she'll get it. If Jill doesn't apply for the job, Jeanne will be annoyed. Joe passes the test.

    CONCLUSION: Jeanne gets annoyed.

    24.____

25. FACTS: Mary, Debbie, May, and Joan are the only people waiting for the photocopier to be fixed. When it's fixed, Debbie has to use it first because she's doing work for the boss. Joan has to use it right after the person who's been waiting the longest. The person who has the most work to copy gets to use the machine second. May has been waiting the longest. The person who has been waiting longest is not the person who has the most work to copy.

    CONCLUSION: Joan gets to use the photocopier third.

    25.____

KEY (CORRECT ANSWERS)

1. B
2. A
3. A
4. C
5. C

6. B
7. B
8. B
9. A
10. C

11. B
12. A
13. A
14. C
15. C

16. C
17. C
18. A
19. C
20. A

21. B
22. C
23. A
24. A
25. B

SOLUTIONS

1. **CORRECT ANSWER: B**
   This is an easy problem if you read it carefully. The third sentence says that Bill types 60 words a minute; the second sentence says that Bill types twice as slow as Charlie. If Bill types twice as slow as Charlie, then Charlie types twice as fast as Bill, or 2 x 60. This means that Charlie types 120 words a minute, not 30 words a minute. These two sentences alone are all you need to disprove the conclusion; the first sentence is just a decoy. If you had *fallen for it* and misread the paragraph, you would most likely have chosen A. You probably would have skimmed the second sentence and assumed that it said *twice as fast*, just because the first sentence said *half as fast*.

2. **CORRECT ANSWER: A**
   This question may look more difficult than it is because the facts are thrown together haphazardly. Many of these logic questions present the *facts* in a very strange fashion. No one would ever talk like this in real life - at least not if they wanted to be understood. The point, of course, is to see how well you can sift through these things, avoid the pitfalls, and find the *truth* of the matter. If you approach a question carefully and attack it systematically, you will usually find that it is not really all that difficult. In this case, by studying the facts, you can see that Albert gets traded. He needs a home run to avoid being traded (sentence 2), but he strikes out in his at-bat (sentence 4). You can assume that this is the at-bat that determines his future because of the way the fourth sentence is worded. It uses the words, *this crucial at-bat*. Knowing the sad truth that he's been traded, you can then trace the chain of events: Chris goes to the Padres (sentence 1), which means that Dave goes to the Dodgers (sentence 3). So the conclusion is, indeed, proved by the facts given to us.

3. **CORRECT ANSWER: A**
   This is a classic form of logic problem, and, like question 2, it doesn't correspond to reality. We all know perfectly well that some beads are cheap, but that has NO bearing on this problem. You often have to let go of your common sense and experience when doing problems like these. Just stick to the facts as they are stated in the problem. The first two sentences are given as facts, and they are enough to prove the conclusion that *all beads are expensive*. In any problem where you are told that a given fact is all-inclusive, such as that *all A are B,* you can just substitute A for B in any other factual sentence in the problem. What is true of B is true of A. Therefore, when you come across another all-inclusive *truth,* such as *all B are C,* you know that *all A are C* must be true too.
   Here are two examples. Although only one corresponds to reality as we know it, they both follow the logic formula we've outlined above, and so both are *true* according to logic.

   All dogs (A) are mammals (B).
   All mammals (B) have backbones (C).
   All dogs (A) have backbones (C).

   All apples (A) are bananas (B).
   All bananas (B) have yellow skins (C).
   All apples (A) have yellow skins (C).

6 (#1)

Note that this does not work in reverse. All bananas aren't necessarily apples, all things with yellow skins aren't necessarily bananas or apples, and all mammals aren't necessarily dogs. Don't worry if this is confusing to you. The key here is to know the formula and not think about it too much in terms of reality.

In this problem, the A is the beads, the B is the jewelry, and the C is expensive.

4. CORRECT ANSWER: C
This looks a lot like the previous question, but, in fact, the sentences show no relationship between shrimp and shells. You can eliminate the second sentence because it has nothing at all to do with the conclusion. Of the two remaining sentences, one says that mussels have shells, the other says that no shrimp are mussels. This doesn't tell us that no shrimp have shells because it is not really telling us anything about how these two animals compare with each other on this issue. It's as if we said, *all boys like sports* and *no boys are girls*. These statements don't tell us whether girls like sports. They tell us that boys and girls are different, but we don't know how different they are. Are they completely different, or do they have things in common? Is liking sports one of the ways they differ or one of the ways they are alike?

For this reason, there is also nothing in the question to show that shrimp do have shells. Here we have another case where common sense can get you into trouble. You may want to choose answer B, simply because you know that the conclusion is false. But you are not being asked whether the conclusion is true or false; you are being asked whether it is proved true or false by the facts as given. If sentence 3 had said, *only mussels have shells,* then the facts would prove the conclusion, even if that doesn't correspond to reality. But as it is, the facts neither prove nor disprove the conclusion.

5. CORRECT ANSWER: C
This is a tricky one. You may have added all the pounds in the conclusion, and been relieved to find that they totaled the 260 pounds mentioned in the first sentence. You would have been tricked into picking A because the numbers checked out. But it doesn't matter that the numbers match because the problem here is to decide whether the facts prove that those are the exact number of pounds each woman lost. And the facts show that, without knowing Bea's weight loss, we're sure of only one figure - Donna's 80-pound weight loss. This is shown below:

NAME	AMOUNT LOST
Abby	2 x Celia
Bea	?
Celia	1/2 of Abby
Donna	80

You may have tried to work the problem by assuming that Donna's 80 pounds was the highest amount lost because that clue is contained in the problem. If Donna's 80 pounds were the greatest weight loss, Celia would have lost 40 pounds because sentence 3 says that Celia lost half of the greatest amount lost. But this creates a problem because it would mean that Abby also lost 80. Sentence 2 says Abby lost twice what Celia lost. And Abby COULDN'T have lost 80 pounds because that would mean that two women (Abby and Donna) lost the most. This is impossible because sentence 3 says Celia lost half as much as the woman (not <u>women</u>) who lost the most. So the greatest amount lost must have been more than 80 pounds, and Abby must have been the one who lost it. All we know, then, is the following: Donna lost 80 pounds, the greatest amount lost was more than 80 pounds, Celia's amount was half the greatest amount, and Abby lost more than 80 pounds. As long as all these conditions are met, Bea's loss might be any amount that makes up the difference between 260 and the others' total weight loss. For example, the losses could have been:

Abby	84		Abby	90		Abby	94
Bea	54	OR	Bea	45	OR	Bea	39
Celia	42		Celia	45		Celia	47
Donna	80		Donna	80		Donna	80
	260			260			260

Or many other possible combinations. The facts simply don't give us enough information to either prove or disprove that the amounts given in the conclusion are the actual amounts each woman lost. That's why the correct answer is C.

6. **CORRECT ANSWER: B**
To see why B is the correct answer, it is helpful to draw a diagram of the floors. We know that Ann is on Four (sentence 4) and that Sally is on Three (sentence 3). If Ann is two floors above Brenda (sentence 1), Brenda must be on Two. Now we can draw:

```
Ann -------------- (4)
Sally ------------ (3)
Brenda ----------- (2)
```

So, if Brenda is one floor below the birthday-girl (sentence 2), today must be Sally's birthday, not Ann's.

7. **CORRECT ANSWER: B**
Here, you need to know what <u>perpendicular</u> and <u>parallel</u> mean. If you do, a simple diagram should show you that the facts disprove the conclusion. Perpendicular streets are those at right angles to one another, like the two lines in a plus sign (+). Parallel streets are those that run in the same direction, never touching - like the two l's in the word <u>all</u>. The first three facts tell us that the streets look like this:

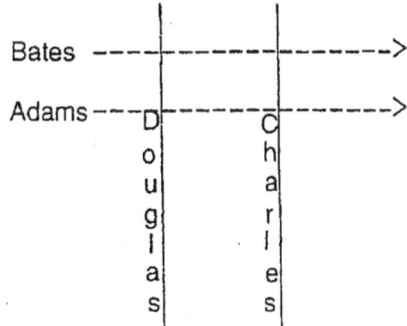

If Evans is parallel to the streets that are perpendicular to Bates (sentence 4), then Evans itself must be perpendicular to Bates. The completed diagram now looks like this:

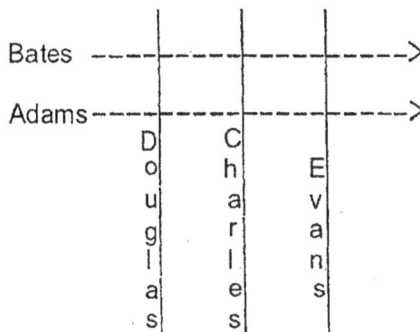

This diagram graphically shows that Evans is NOT perpendicular to Douglas, but parallel to it. The facts, then, disprove the conclusion.

8. CORRECT ANSWER: B
   If you start from the last fact given in this problem and work backwards, you will be able to find the cause of each event. This will enable you to either prove or disprove the conclusion. In this case, since the last fact says that the captain ran, that must have been because Arnie hit the ball hard (sentence 3). Even though Arnie hit the ball hard, Bill is out because Bill is so slow that he will be out at home plate (sentence 2). This disproves the conclusion, which says he is safe.

9. CORRECT ANSWER: A
   This is an easy problem if you translate the facts into a picture. First of all, ignore sentence 3, which has nothing to do with the problem. Now, draw a circle to represent all the members of this genus (sentence 1). Next, draw a smaller circle to represent the members of that species (sentence 1). You may know that a species is a subgroup of a genus, just as *semi-precious* is a subgroup of gems, or hardwoods is a subgroup of trees. For this reason, the *species* circle should be contained entirely within the *genus* circle. The problem doesn't tell you this about genus and species, but you don't need to know it to answer the question correctly. You could simply place the smaller circle partially in and partially out of the larger circle. No matter which way you portray the relationship, some members of the genus will belong to that species. You can see this in the diagrams below. Since all members of that species are butterflies (sentence 2), the *species* circle also represents butterflies.

Not all members of this genus are butterflies; this is demonstrated by the fact that there is plenty of room inside the *genus* circle for other, non-butterfly critters. But the picture clearly shows that some members of the genus are butterflies, as the conclusion states.

10. **CORRECT ANSWER: C**
The facts prove only that some woodwinds (those that are clarinets) are beautiful things; they do not prove that all beautiful things are woodwinds. If you draw circles to represent *beautiful things* and *clarinets,* the latter would have to be a smaller circle inside the former, since all clarinets are beautiful things (sentence 3).

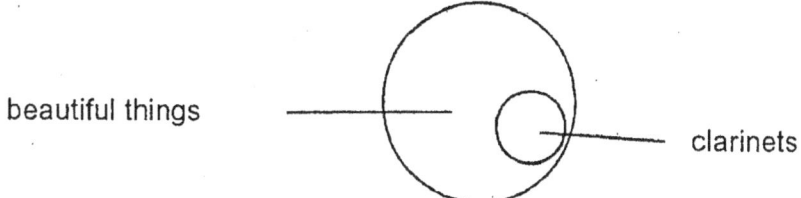

But where does the *woodwind* circle go? All the facts tell us is that some of its members are clarinets. We don't know whether it's bigger, smaller, or the same size as the circle of *beautiful things*. It could look like the following:

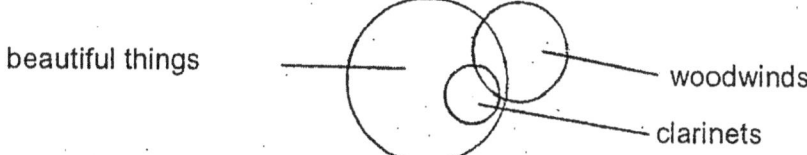

That way, there could be plenty of beautiful things that are not woodwinds, some beautiful things that are woodwinds and clarinets, and some woodwinds that are beautiful things but not clarinets. And the conclusion would be false.
OR, the *woodwinds* circle could be identical to the *beautiful things* circle:

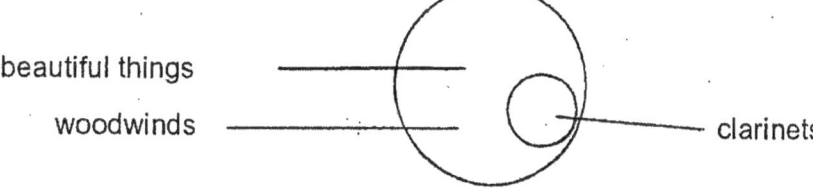

making the conclusion true.
You may have circled answer B, simply because the conclusion is obviously a false statement. But remember, the question is not whether the conclusion is true or false; it's whether it is proved or disproved by the facts given. In this case, it is neither proved nor disproved by the facts. Sentence 2, incidentally, is irrelevant, since the rest of the problem has nothing to do with flutes.

11. **CORRECT ANSWER: B**

You could use a trial-and-error approach to this problem, but it would be very time-consuming. As you worked with this problem, you may have realized that, since the number in the middle box gets added to every other number, you can solve the problem more easily by putting 6 into the diagram and adding the larger numbers to it to see if it's workable. After placing 6 in the center, you can see there is nowhere to put 9. The horizontal, vertical, and diagonal rows must add up to 15, but wherever you try to put 9, you will have a row that adds up to more than 15. Since 9 + 6 = 15 and 0 is not one of the options, there is no number that can be put in the third box in the row.

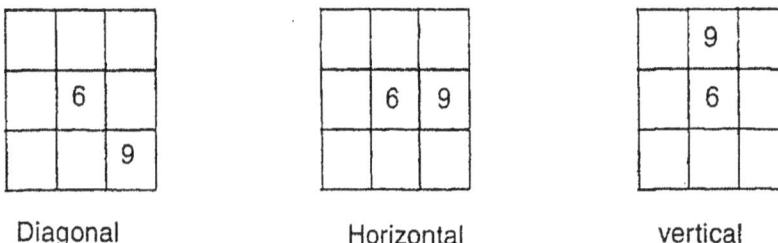

Diagonal　　　　　Horizontal　　　　　vertical

So, 6 cannot be the number in the middle box; it's too big. The facts disprove the conclusion.

12. **CORRECT ANSWER: A**

The first sentence in this problem says that these men bought various colored suits, but not necessarily <u>respectively</u>. This means that the first man (Max) didn't necessarily buy the first color suit (grey), the second man (Nick) didn't necessarily buy the second color suit (green), and so on. <u>Respectively</u> means *in the same order*.

At first glance, this problem looks impossible, but it can be simplified by drawing a chart to show what we *know* about each person:

NAME	PAID	FOR THIS COLOR SUIT
Max	less than Nick	green
Nick	same as Pete	grey (not green, brown or blue)
Pete	same as Nick	blue (not grey, green or brown)
Ollie	2x Nick; 2x Pete	brown

Sentence 2 says Max's suit is green, and sentence 5 says Ollie's is brown, but how do we know Pete's is blue? Well, sentence 4 indicates that someone other than Pete bought the grey one. That means Nick got the grey one. Since the grey, green, and brown suits are all accounted for, the blue one must be Pete's.

Now, all we need to know is who paid the most! Ollie paid twice what Pete paid (sentence 3). This means that he also paid twice what Nick paid because Pete paid the same as the man who bought the grey suit (sentence 4) - and Nick bought the grey suit. So the highest-payer can't be Nick or Pete; it must either be Ollie or Max. But sentence 2 says Max paid <u>less</u> than Nick. So the highest-payer must be Ollie, as proved by the facts given.

13. CORRECT ANSWER: A

The man sitting on Dave's right (sentence 6) has to be Bob because he's the only other man in the group. Alice sits across from Dave (sentence 4). This means that Carol must be sitting across from Bob. From this information, you can draw a diagram of the table and the people seated at it:

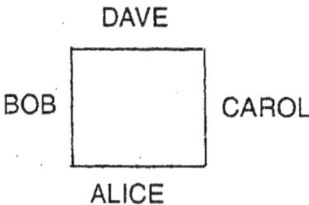

Now all you need to know is whether Dave plays golf. It may help keep everything straight if you put the name of the sport next to the name of the proper person as you figure out each one. Here, we have abbreviated each sport using a lower-case initial (*j* for jogging, *g* for golf, and so on). Since Carol sits to the right of the basketball player (sentence 3), Alice must play basketball. (Remember, it's not Carol's right; it's the basketball player's right. This confuses some people.) Since Bob sits across from the jogger (sentence 2), Carol must jog. After adding this information, your diagram would look like this:

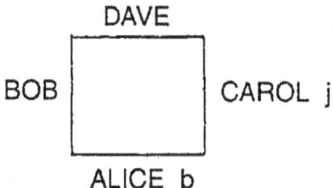

At this point, all you need to know is: Does Bob golf and Dave play tennis, or is it the other way around? A quick trial-and-error produces the answer. Sentence 5 says the golfer sits to the left of the tennis player. If Dave played tennis, would this be true? No. So, it must be Bob who's the tennis player, and Dave who's the golfer. The conclusion is thus proved by the facts. If you have spatial problems, you might want to twist the diagram around to see this more clearly.

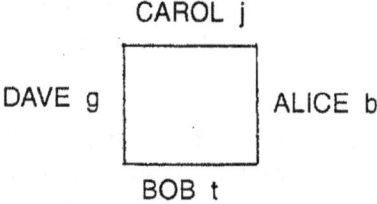

14. CORRECT ANSWER: C

To visualize this problem it is helpful to draw a small chart, showing what we know about each woman's score.

NAME	SCORE
Carol	higher than Betty

Betty	higher than 40 (according to sentence 3 she scored more than twice as high as Alice
Alice	20

From this chart, we can see that Carol's score could have been any number higher than 41. It could have been 50, or 65, or 92–in which case she would have scored high enough to be hired. But it also could have been 42, or 43, or 47 –in which case she would not have scored high enough. So, we can't prove that Carol was offered the job, but we can't prove that she wasn't either. In addition, we can't prove that Carol was the only one who was offered the job. We know Alice didn't get an offer (with a score of 20), but we don't know about Betty. She could have gotten anything above 40. So, the facts here neither prove nor disprove the conclusion.

15. CORRECT ANSWER: C
    This is a sneaky little question. If you read it quickly, you might have thought it was easy. The cat didn't get rabies (sentence 3), so the cat had had its rabies shots within the last two years (sentence 2). But perhaps the cat didn't get rabies because the squirrel never bit it, or perhaps the squirrel never had rabies to begin with. The first sentence says, *If Camille's squirrel has rabies"* and *(if)* the squirrel bites Casey's cat...the cat will get rabies. (The second *if* is implied by the structure of the sentence.) Nothing in this paragraph ever tells us that the squirrel had rabies or that the squirrel bit the cat. As we said - sneaky. Since you don't know why the cat didn't get rabies, you can't prove that it was spared because it had had its shots, and you can't disprove it either. Therefore, C is the only possible answer.

16. CORRECT ANSWER: C
    This is another sneaky question. (The exams haven't used this kind of trick lately, but we wanted to give you practice – just in case.) If you didn't read the problem carefully, you might have chosen B. You would have thought that Laura told Frank (sentence 4), who told Bill (sentence 2), who chose not to fire Sally (sentence 3). Since Sally didn't get fired, she didn't file a grievance (sentence 1). The only problem is that Laura told Fred, not Frank, and we have no way of knowing how Fred fits into this crew. He could have told Frank, thereby setting in motion the cycle above and preventing Sally from getting fired. In that case, the conclusion would be false. Or he could have not told anyone, Sally would have gotten fired, she would have filed a grievance, and the conclusion would have been true. You just don't know, so C is the only option.

17. CORRECT ANSWER: C
    Obviously, if the *pre-game* song gets delayed, the game will also be delayed, but we don't know for how long. We also don't know how late Barb had to work. (We know that she did have to work late, because of sentences 1, 5, and 6.) For all we know, the game may have been delayed for an hour due to the storm, and Barb may have had to work only a half hour later than usual–thereby not missing any of the game at all. In questions of this type, it is always good to work backwards from the conclusion and try to see if there is a cause of that conclusion contained in the facts. In this case, although we can find a cause for Barb's having to work late (Alice's acceptance of Carl's invitation), we can find nothing that would necessarily cause Barb to miss the first inning of the game.

18. CORRECT ANSWER: A
The conclusion seems likely because it only takes Eva five tries to guess a number from 1 through 10. The most efficient way to guess is to eliminate half of all possible numbers with each guess. When the number is from 1 through 10, the first question should be, *Is the number you're thinking of 6 or more?* The answer to that question, whether it's yes or no, will eliminate five numbers - half of all the numbers Earl could possibly be thinking of. Let's say Earl said yes. The second question would be, *Is it 8 or more?* That answer will eliminate two or three of the five remaining possible numbers. No matter what range of numbers Earl wants to use, whether it be 1 through 50, 1 through 100, or whatever, Eva could use this method until she narrows the answers down to one possible number. (We can assume that she uses this method because sentence 2 says she is using the most efficient method.)

For the range 1 through 6, then, you can see that four is the highest number of guesses she will need using this system. The most she can be sure of eliminating with one guess is 3 numbers. *(Is the number you're thinking of 4 or more?)* At that point, she may need as many as three more guesses to eliminate the two remaining wrong numbers one by one and then to *guess* the right number. Since this is four guesses, the facts prove the conclusion.

19. CORRECT ANSWER: C
Here is a case in which it is clear that certain facts are missing. You know from sentences 4 and 2 that Robbie is home in time for Lois to make dinner, but what about Ted and Jennifer? Nowhere in the facts does it say whether or not Ted played softball after work. Since sentence 1 says Lois will cook only if all three are home by 6 P.M., we simply don't have enough information to either prove or disprove the conclusion.

20. CORRECT ANSWER: A
Unless you are excellent in math, just about the only way to figure this one out is to set up a grid showing the amount of money each player has after each round. After setting up such a grid, the answer can be found quite easily.

	ARTIE $10	BRUCE $10	CHUCK $10
AFTER ROUND #1	$8	$8	$14
#2	$6	$12	$12
#3	$4	$10	$16
#4	$17	$5	$8

Chuck won the first round (sentence 4). Since everyone started with $10 (sentence 1), you can see that after Round #1, each loser would be out $2 (sentences 2 and 3), bringing their totals down to $8 each. Chuck, on the other hand, would be up to $14, having collected $2 from each of the two losers. The second line of the grid shows the situation after Round #2, which was won by Bruce (sentence 4). The third line shows the situation after Round #3, when Chuck is way ahead (sentence 4). Likewise, the fourth line shows the situation after Round #4, when the rules had been changed and Artie won (sentences 5 and 6). Since each of the other two had to give him half their money (sentence 5), he collected $5 from Bruce and $8 from Chuck. His total of $17 was $9 more than

Chuck had at that point. So, the conclusion that Artie ended up with more money than Chuck is proven by the facts given.

21. CORRECT ANSWER: B
The facts prove just the opposite of the conclusion. If all cleaners work part-time (sentence 2), and no part-timers get paid vacations (sentence 1), then no cleaners can get paid vacations. Where *facts* are given in the form, *No A are B, and all C are A,* you can simply substitute C for A, and that will prove that no C are B. (This is much like question 3, except the first fact is all-exclusive rather than all-inclusive. It excludes rather than includes all of something. See the explanation to question 3, if this is not clear.) In this case, *A* is the part-timers, *B* represents recipients of paid vacations, and *C* is cleaners. The facts disprove the conclusion. Since we don't know what Joe's occupation is, sentence 3 is irrelevant to this problem.

22. CORRECT ANSWER: C
In this case, no amount of *following the trail* of facts will lead you to the conclusion given because there is no trail. No fact implies, or leads to, any other; they are simply a collection of statements with no relationship to one another. The facts neither prove nor disprove the conclusion.

23. CORRECT ANSWER: A
Unlike question 22, this question lends itself to *following the trail* of facts. As we've noticed earlier, a good place to begin the trail is with the last fact. It follows from sentence 5 (Dick cleans the house) that Sally goes to the store (sentence 3), which means that Tina also goes to the store (sentence 4). This, in turn, means that Ike goes (sentence 1), and buys the doughnuts (sentence 2). The facts here prove the conclusion.

24. CORRECT ANSWER: A
To decide whether the facts prove the conclusion, you must understand what each fact means. The fact that Joe passed the test (sentence 4) means that Jill didn't apply for the job (sentence 1). Knowing this, all you have to do is reread sentence 3 to see that Jeanne does, indeed, get annoyed. Sentence 2 is not needed to solve this problem, although it may explain why Jeanne got annoyed.

25. CORRECT ANSWER: B
It is helpful to make a list of who's using the machine when, and to fill in the facts you're given. Then you can gradually deduce more information, until you can see whether the conclusion is proved, disproved, or neither. Sentence 2 says Debbie goes first, so your list, at the start, would look something like this:

> First - Debbie
> Second - ?
> Third - ?
> Last - ?

It is clear from sentences 3 and 5 that Joan immediately follows May. This also means that Joan cannot be second, May cannot be last, and Mary cannot be third. You may then wish to enter the possibilities to your list:

> First - Debbie
> Second - May or Mary

15 (#1)

>Third - May or Joan
>Last - Joan or Mary

Now, all we need to know is: Does May go second? If so, the conclusion is proved by the facts; if not, it's disproved. We know from sentence 4 that the person with the most work goes second. That person can't be May, however, because May has been waiting longest (sentence 5), and the longest-waiter is not the person with the most work (sentence 6). So, Debbie is first, Mary is second, May is third, Joan is fourth, and the conclusion is disproved.

>First - Debbie
>Second - Mary
>Third - May
>Last - Joan

EVALUATING CONCLUSIONS IN LIGHT OF KNOWN FACTS
EXAMINATION SECTION
TEST 1

DIRECTIONS: Each question or incomplete statement is followed by several suggested answers or completions. Select the one that BEST answers the question or completes the statement. *PRINT THE LETTER OF THE CORRECT ANSWER IN THE SPACE AT THE RIGHT.*

Questions 1-9.

DIRECTIONS: In Questions 1 through 9, you will read a set of facts and a conclusion drawn from them. The conclusion may be valid or invalid, based on the facts—it's your task to determine the validity of the conclusion.

For each question, select the letter before the statement that BEST expresses the relationship between the given facts and the conclusion that has been drawn from them. Your choices are:
  A. The facts prove the conclusion;
  B. The facts disprove the conclusion; or
  C. The facts neither prove nor disprove the conclusion.

1. FACTS: If the supervisor retires, James, the assistant supervisor, will not be transferred to another department. James will be promoted to supervisor if he is not transferred. The supervisor retired.

   CONCLUSION: James will be promoted to supervisor.
   A. The facts prove the conclusion.
   B. The facts disprove the conclusion.
   C. The facts neither prove nor disprove the conclusion.

2. FACTS: In the town of Luray, every player on the softball team works at Luray National Bank. In addition, every player on the Luray softball team wear glasses.

   CONCLUSIONS: At least some of the people who work at Luray National Bank wear glasses.
   A. The facts prove the conclusion.
   B. The facts disprove the conclusion.
   C. The facts neither prove nor disprove the conclusion.

3. FACTS: The only time Henry and June go out to dinner is on an evening when they have childbirth classes. Their childbirth classes meet on Tuesdays and Thursdays.

2 (#1)

CONCLUSION: Henry and June never go out to dinner on Friday or Saturday.
  A. The facts prove the conclusion.
  B. The facts disprove the conclusion.
  C. The facts neither prove nor disprove the conclusion.

4. FACTS: Every player on the field hockey team has at least one bruise. Everyone on the field hockey team also has scarred knees.

   CONCLUSION: Most people with both bruises and scarred knees are field hockey players.
   A. The facts prove the conclusion.
   B. The facts disprove the conclusion.
   C. The facts neither prove nor disprove the conclusion.

   4.____

5. FACTS: In the chess tournament, Lance will win his match against Jane if Jane wins her match against Mathias. If Lance wins his match against Jane, Christine will not win her match against Jane.

   CONCLUSION: Christine will not win her match against Jane if Jane wins her match against Mathias.
   A. The facts prove the conclusion.
   B. The facts disprove the conclusion.
   C. The facts neither prove nor disprove the conclusion.

   5.____

6. FACTS: No green lights on the machine are indicators for the belt drive status. Not all of the lights on the machine's upper panel are green. Some lights on the machine's lower panel are green.

   CONCLUSION: The green lights on the machine's lower panel may be indicators for the belt drive status.
   A. The facts prove the conclusion.
   B. The facts disprove the conclusion.
   C. The facts neither prove nor disprove the conclusion.

   6.____

7. FACTS: At a small, one-room country school, there are eight students: Amy, Ben, Carla, Dan, Elliot, Francine, Greg, and Hannah. Each student is in either the 6th, 7th, or 8th grade. Either two or three students are in each grade. Amy, Dan, and Francine are all in different grades. Ben and Elliot are both in the 7th grade. Hannah and Carl are in the same grade.

   CONCLUSION: Exactly three students are in the 7th grade.
   A. The facts prove the conclusion.
   B. The facts disprove the conclusion.
   C. The facts neither prove nor disprove the conclusion.

   7.____

8. FACTS: Two married couples are having lunch together. Two of the four people are German and two are Russian, but in each couple the nationality of the spouse is not necessarily the same as the other's. One person in the group is a teacher, the other a lawyer, one an engineer, and the other a writer. The teacher is a Russian man. The writer is Russian, and her husband is an engineer. One of the people, Mr. Stern, is German.

   CONCLUSION: Mr. Stern's wife is a writer.
   A. The facts prove the conclusion.
   B. The facts disprove the conclusion.
   C. The facts neither prove nor disprove the conclusion.

   8.____

9. FACTS: The flume ride at the county fair is open only to children who are at least 36 inches tall. Lisa is 30 inches tall. John is shorter than Henry, but more than 10 inches taller than Lisa.

   CONCLUSION: Lisa is the only one who can't ride the flume ride.
   A. The facts prove the conclusion.
   B. The facts disprove the conclusion.
   C. The facts neither prove nor disprove the conclusion.

   9.____

Questions 10-17.

DIRECTIONS: Questions 10 through 17 are based on the following reading passage. It is not your knowledge of the particular topic that is being tested, but your ability to reason based on what you have read. The passage is likely to detail several proposed courses of action and factors affecting these proposals. The reading passage is followed by a conclusion or outcome based on the facts in the passage, or a description of a decision taken regarding the situation. The conclusion is followed by a number of statements that have a possible connection to the conclusion. For each statement, you are to determine whether:
   A. The statement proves the conclusion.
   B. The statement supports the conclusion but does not prove it.
   C. The statement disproves the conclusion.
   D. The statement weakens the conclusion but does not disprove it.
   E. The statement has no relevance to the conclusion.

Remember that the conclusion after the passage is to be accepted as the outcome of what actually happened, and that you are being asked to evaluate the impact each statement would have had on the conclusion.

PASSAGE:

The Grand Army of Foreign Wars, a national veteran's organization, is struggling to maintain its National Home, where the widowed spouses and orphans of deceased members are housed together in a small village-like community. The Home is open to spouses and children who are bereaved for any reason, regardless of whether the member's death was related to military service, but a new global conflict has led to a dramatic surge in the number of members' deaths: many veterans who re-enlisted for the conflict have been killed in action.

The Grand Army of Foreign Wars is considering several options for handling the increased number of applications for housing at the National Home, which has been traditionally supported by membership due. At its national convention, it will choose only one of the following:

The first idea is a one-time $50 tax on all members, above and beyond the dues they pay already. Since the organization has more than a million member, this tax should be sufficient for the construction and maintenance of new housing for applicants on the existing grounds of the National Home. The idea is opposed, however, by some older members who live on fixed incomes. These members object in principle to the taxation of Grand Army members. The Grand Army has never imposed a tax on its members.

The second idea is to launch a national fundraising drive the public relations campaign that will attract donations for the National Home. Several national celebrities are members of the organization, and other celebrities could be attracted to the cause. Many Grand Army members are wary of this approach, however: in the past, the net receipts of some fundraising efforts have been relatively insignificant, given the costs of staging them.

A third approach, suggested by many of the younger members, is to have new applicants share some of the costs of construction and maintenance. The spouses and children would pay an up-front "enrollment" fee, based on a sliding scale proportionate to their income and assets, and then a monthly fee adjusted similarly to contribute to maintenance costs. Many older members are strongly opposed to this idea, as it is in direct contradiction to the principles on which the organization was founded more than a century ago.

The fourth option is simply to maintain the status quo, focus the organization's efforts on supporting the families who already live at the National Home, and wait to accept new applicants based on attrition.

CONCLUSION: At its annual national convention, the Grand Army of Foreign Wars votes to impose a one-time tax of $10 on each member for the purpose of expanding and supporting the National Home to welcome a larger number of applicants. The tax is considered to be the solution most likely to produce the funds needed to accommodate the growing number of applicants.

10. Actuarial studies have shown that because the Grand Army's membership consists mostly of older veterans from earlier wars, the organization's membership will suffer a precipitous decline in numbers in about five years.
    A. The statement proves the conclusion.
    B. The statement supports the conclusion but does not prove it.
    C. The statement disproves the conclusion.
    D. The statement weakens the conclusion but does not disprove it.
    E. The statement has no relevance to the conclusion.

11. After passage of the funding measure, a splinter group of older members appeals for the "sliding scale" provision to be applied to the tax, so that some members may be allowed to contribute less based on their income.
    A. The statement proves the conclusion.
    B. The statement supports the conclusion but does not prove it.
    C. The statement disproves the conclusion.
    D. The statement weakens the conclusion but does not disprove it.
    E. The statement has no relevance to the conclusion.

5 (#1)

12. The original charter of the Grand Army of Foreign Wars specifically states that the organization will not levy taxes or duties on its members beyond its modest annual dues. It takes a super-majority of attending delegates at the national convention to make alterations to the charter.
    A. The statement proves the conclusion.
    B. The statement supports the conclusion but does not prove it.
    C. The statement disproves the conclusion.
    D. The statement weakens the conclusion but does not disprove it.
    E. The statement has no relevance to the conclusion.

12.____

13. Six months before Grand Army of Foreign Wars' national convention, the Internal Revenue Service rules that because it is an organization that engages in political lobbying, the Grand Army must no longer enjoy its own federal tax-exempt status.
    A. The statement proves the conclusion.
    B. The statement supports the conclusion but does not prove it.
    C. The statement disproves the conclusion.
    D. The statement weakens the conclusion but does not disprove it.
    E. The statement has no relevance to the conclusion.

13.____

14. Two months before the national convention, Dirk Rockwell, arguably the country's most famous film actor, announces in a nationally televised interview that he has been saddened to learn of the plight of the National Home, and that he is going to make it his own personal crusade to see that it is able to house and support a greater number of widowed spouses and orphans in the future.
    A. The statement proves the conclusion.
    B. The statement supports the conclusion but does not prove it.
    C. The statement disproves the conclusion.
    D. The statement weakens the conclusion but does not disprove it.
    E. The statement has no relevance to the conclusion.

14.____

15. The Grand Army's final estimate is that the cost of expanding the National Home to accommodate the increased number of applicants will be about $61 million.
    A. The statement proves the conclusion.
    B. The statement supports the conclusion but does not prove it.
    C. The statement disproves the conclusion.
    D. The statement weakens the conclusion but does not disprove it.
    E. The statement has no relevance to the conclusion.

15.____

16. Just before the national convention, the Federal Department of Veterans Affairs announces steep cuts in the benefits package that is currently offered to the widowed spouses and orphans of veterans.
    A. The statement proves the conclusion.
    B. The statement supports the conclusion but does not prove it.
    C. The statement disproves the conclusion.
    D. The statement weakens the conclusion but does not disprove it.
    E. The statement has no relevance to the conclusion.

16.____

17. After the national convention, the Grand Army of Foreign Wars begins charging a modest "start-up" fee to all families who apply for residence at the national home.
    A. The statement proves the conclusion.
    B. The statement supports the conclusion but does not prove it.
    C. The statement disproves the conclusion.
    D. The statement weakens the conclusion but does not disprove it.
    E. The statement has no relevance to the conclusion.

17._____

Questions 18-25.

DIRECTIONS: Questions 18 through 25 each provide four factual statements and a conclusion based on these statements. After reading the entire question, you will decide whether:
   A. The conclusion is proved by statements I-IV;
   B. The conclusion is disproved by statements I-IV.
   C. The facts are not sufficient to prove or disprove the conclusion.

18. FACTUAL STATEMENTS:
    I. In the Field Day high jump competition, Martha jumped higher than Frank.
    II. Carl jumped higher than Ignacio.
    III. Ignacio jumped higher than Frank.
    IV. Dan jumped higher than Carl.

    CONCLUSION: Frank finished last in the high jump competition.
    A. The conclusion is proved by statements I-IV;
    B. The conclusion is disproved by statements I-IV.
    C. The facts are not sufficient to prove or disprove the conclusion.

18._____

19. FACTUAL STATEMENTS:
    I. The door to the hammer mill chamber is locked if light 6 is red.
    II. The door to the hammer mill chamber is locked only when the mill is operating.
    III. If the mill is not operating, light 6 is blue.
    IV. Light 6 is blue.

    CONCLUSION: The door to the hammer mill chamber is locked.
    A. The conclusion is proved by statements I-IV;
    B. The conclusion is disproved by statements I-IV.
    C. The facts are not sufficient to prove or disprove the conclusion.

19._____

20. FACTUAL STATEMENTS:
    I. Ziegfried, the lion tamer at the circus, has demanded ten additional minutes of performance time during each show.
    II. If Ziegfried is allowed his ten additional minutes per show, he will attempt to teach Kimba the tiger to shoot a basketball.
    III. If Kimba learns how to shoot a basketball, then Ziegfried was not given his ten additional minutes.
    IV. Ziegfried was given his ten additional minutes.

20._____

7 (#1)

CONCLUSION: Despite Ziegfried's efforts, Kimba did not learn how to shoot a basketball.
   A. The conclusion is proved by statements I-IV;
   B. The conclusion is disproved by statements I-IV.
   C. The facts are not sufficient to prove or disprove the conclusion.

21. FACTUAL STATEMENTS: 21.____
   I. If Stan goes to counseling, Sara won't divorce him.
   II. If Sara divorces Stan, she'll move back to Texas.
   III. If Sara doesn't divorce Stan, Irene will be disappointed.
   IV. Stan goes to counseling.

   CONCLUSION: Irene will be disappointed.
   A. The conclusion is proved by statements I-IV;
   B. The conclusion is disproved by statements I-IV.
   C. The facts are not sufficient to prove or disprove the conclusion.

22. FACTUAL STATEMENTS: 22.____
   I. If Delia is promoted to district manager, Claudia will have to be promoted to team leader.
   II. Delia will be promoted to district manager unless she misses her fourth-quarter sales quota.
   III. If Claudia is promoted to team leader, Thomas will be promoted to assistant team leader.
   IV. Delia meets her fourth-quarter sales quota.

   CONCLUSION: Thomas is promoted to assistant team leader.
   A. The conclusion is proved by statements I-IV;
   B. The conclusion is disproved by statements I-IV.
   C. The facts are not sufficient to prove or disprove the conclusion.

23. FACTUAL STATEMENTS: 23.____
   I. Clone D is identical to Clone B.
   II. Clone B is not identical to Clone A.
   III. Clone D is not identical to Clone C.
   IV. Clone E is not identical to the clones that are identical to Clone B.

   CONCLUSION: Clone E is identical to Clone D.
   A. The conclusion is proved by statements I-IV;
   B. The conclusion is disproved by statements I-IV.
   C. The facts are not sufficient to prove or disprove the conclusion.

24. FACTUAL STATEMENTS: 24.____
   I. In the Stafford Tower, each floor is occupied by a single business.
   II. Big G Staffing is on a floor between CyberGraphics and MainEvent.
   III. Gasco is on the floor directly below CyberGraphics and three floors above Treehorn Audio.
   IV. MainEvent is five floors below EZ Tax and four floors below Treehorn Audio.

8 (#1)

CONCLUSION: EZ Tax is on a floor between Gasco and MainEvent.
  A. The conclusion is proved by statements I-IV;
  B. The conclusion is disproved by statements I-IV.
  C. The facts are not sufficient to prove or disprove the conclusion.

25. FACTUAL STATEMENTS: 25.____
  I. Only county roads lead to Nicodemus.
  II. All the roads from Hill City to Graham County are federal highways.
  III. Some of the roads from Plainville lead to Nicodemus.
  IV. Some of the roads running from Hill City lead to Strong City.

CONCLUSION: Some of the roads from Plainville are county roads.
  A. The conclusion is proved by statements I-IV;
  B. The conclusion is disproved by statements I-IV.
  C. The facts are not sufficient to prove or disprove the conclusion.

KEY (CORRECT ANSWERS)

1.	A		11.	A
2.	A		12.	D
3.	A		13.	E
4.	C		14.	D
5.	A		15.	B
6.	B		16.	B
7.	A		17.	C
8.	A		18.	A
9.	A		19.	B
10.	E		20.	A
21.	A			
22.	A			
23.	B			
24.	A			
25.	A			

SOLUTIONS TO PROBLEMS

1. **CORRECT ANSWER: A**
   Given Statement 3, we deduce that James will not be transferred to another department. By Statement 2, we can conclude that James will be promoted.

2. **CORRECT ANSWER: A**
   Since every player on the softball team wears glasses, these individuals compose some of the people who work at the bank. Although not every person who works at the bank plays softball, those bank employees who do play softball wear glasses.

3. **CORRECT ANSWER: A**
   If Henry and June go out to dinner, we conclude that it must be on Tuesday or Thursday, which are the only two days when they have childbirth classes. This implies that if it is not Tuesday or Thursday, then this couple does not go out to dinner.

4. **CORRECT ANSWER: C**
   We can only conclude that if a person plays on the field hockey team, then he or she has both bruises and scarred knees. But there are probably a great number of people who have both bruises and scarred knees but do not play on the field hockey team. The given conclusion can neither be proven or disproven.

5. **CORRECT ANSWER: A**
   From statement 1, if Jane beats Mathias, then Lance will beat Jane. Using statement 2, we can then conclude that Christine will not win her match against Jane.

6. **CORRECT ANSWER: B**
   Statement 1 tells us that no green light can be an indicator of the belt drive status. Thus, the given conclusion must be false.

7. **CORRECT ANSWER: A**
   We already know that Ben and Elliot are in the 7th grade. Even though Hannah and Carl are in the same grade, it cannot be the 7th grade because we would then have at least four students in this 7th grade. This would contradict the third statement, which states that either two or three students are in each grade. Since Amy, Dan, and Francine are in different grade, exactly one of them must be in the 7th grade. Thus, Ben, Elliot, and exactly one of Amy, Dan, and Francine are the three students in the 7th grade.

8. **CORRECT ANSWER: A**
   One man is a teacher, who is Russian. We know that the writer is female and is Russian. Since her husband is an engineer, he cannot be the Russian teacher. Thus, her husband is of German descent, namely Mr. Stern. This means that Mr. Stern's wife is the writer. Note that one couple consists of a male Russian teacher and a female German lawyer. The other couple consists of a male German engineer and a female Russian writer.

9. CORRECT ANSWER: A
Since John is more than 10 inches taller than Lisa, his height is at least 46 inches. Also, John is shorter than Henry, so Henry's height must be greater than 46 inches. Thus, Lisa is the only one whose height is less than 36 inches. Therefore, she is the only one who is not allowed on the flume ride.

18. CORRECT ANSWER: A
Dan jumped higher than Carl, who jumped higher than Ignacio, who jumped higher than Frank. Since Martha jumped higher than Frank, every person jumped higher than Frank. Thus, Frank finished last.

19. CORRECT ANSWER: B
If the light is red, then the door is locked. If the door is locked, then the mill is operating. Reversing the logical sequence of these statements, if the mill is not operating, then the door is not locked, which means that the light is blue. Thus, the given conclusion is disproved.

20. CORRECT ANSWER: A
Using the contrapositive of statement III, Ziegfried was given his ten additional minutes, then Kimba did not learn how to shoot a basketball. Since statement IV is factual, the conclusion is proved.

21. CORRECT ANSWER: A
From Statements IV and I, we conclude that Sara doesn't divorce Stan. Then statement III reveals that Irene will be disappointed. Thus, the conclusion is proved.

22. CORRECT ANSWER: A
Statement II can be rewritten as "Delia is promoted to district manager or she misses her sales quota." Furthermore, this statement is equivalent to "If Delia makes her sales quota, then she is promoted to district manager." From statement I, we conclude that Claudia is promoted to team leader. Finally, by statement III, Thomas is promoted to assistant team leader.

23. CORRECT ANSWER: B
By statement IV, Clone E is not identical to any clones identical to Clone B. Statement I tells us that Clones B and D are identical. Therefore, Clone E cannot be identical to Clone D. The conclusion is disproved.

24. CORRECT ANSWER: A
Based on all four statements, CyberGraphics is somewhere below MainEvent. Gasco is one floor below CyberGraphics. EZ Tax is two floors below Gasco. Treehorn Audio is one floor below EZ Tax. MainEvent is four floors below Treehorn Audio. Thus, EZ Tax is two floors below Gasco and five floors above MainEvent. The conclusion is proved.

25. CORRECT ANSWER: A
From statement III, we know that some of the roads from Plainville lead to Nicodemus. But statement I tells us that only county roads lead to Nicodemus. Therefore, some of the roads from Plainville must be county roads. The conclusion is proved.

TEST 2

DIRECTIONS: Each question or incomplete statement is followed by several suggested answers or completions. Select the one that BEST answers the question or completes the statement. *PRINT THE LETTER OF THE CORRECT ANSWER IN THE SPACE AT THE RIGHT.*

Questions 1-9.

DIRECTIONS: In Questions 1 through 9, you will read a set of facts and a conclusion drawn from them. The conclusion may be valid or invalid, based on the facts—it's your task to determine the validity of the conclusion.

For each question, select the letter before the statement that BEST expresses the relationship between the given facts and the conclusion that has been drawn from them. Your choices are:
- A. The facts prove the conclusion;
- B. The facts disprove the conclusion; or
- C. The facts neither prove nor disprove the conclusion.

1. FACTS: Some employees in the testing department are statisticians. Most of the statisticians who work in the testing department are projection specialists. Tom Wilks works in the testing department.

    CONCLUSION: Tom Wilks is a statistician.
    - A. The facts prove the conclusion.
    - B. The facts disprove the conclusion.
    - C. The facts neither prove nor disprove the conclusion.

    1.____

2. FACTS: Ten coins are split among Hank, Lawrence, and Gail. If Lawrence gives his coins to Hank, then Hank will have more coins than Gail. If Gail gives her coins to Lawrence, then Lawrence will have more coins than Hank.

    CONCLUSION: Hank has six coins.
    - A. The facts prove the conclusion.
    - B. The facts disprove the conclusion.
    - C. The facts neither prove nor disprove the conclusion.

    2.____

3. FACTS: Nobody loves everybody. Janet loves Ken. Ken loves everybody who loves Janet.

    CONCLUSION: Everybody loves Janet.
    - A. The facts prove the conclusion.
    - B. The facts disprove the conclusion.
    - C. The facts neither prove nor disprove the conclusion.

    3.____

4. FACTS: Most of the Torres family lives in East Los Angeles. Many people in East Los Angeles celebrate Cinco de Mayo. Joe is a member of the Torres family.

   CONCLUSION: Joe lives in East Los Angeles.
   A. The facts prove the conclusion.
   B. The facts disprove the conclusion.
   C. The facts neither prove nor disprove the conclusion.

4.____

5. FACTS: Five professionals each occupy one story of a five-story office building. Dr. Kane's office is above Dr. Assad's. Dr. Johnson's office is between Dr. Kane's and Dr. Conlon's. Dr. Steen's office is between Dr. Conlon's and Dr. Assad's. Dr. Johnson is on the fourth story.

   CONCLUSION: Dr. Kane occupies the top story.
   A. The facts prove the conclusion.
   B. The facts disprove the conclusion.
   C. The facts neither prove nor disprove the conclusion.

5.____

6. FACTS: To be eligible for membership in the Yukon Society, a person must be able to either tunnel through a snowbank while wearing only a T-shirt and short, or hold his breath for two minutes under water that is 50°F. Ray can only hold his breath for a minute and a half.

   CONCLUSION: Ray can still become a member of the Yukon Society by tunneling through a snowbank while wearing a T-shirt and shorts.
   A. The facts prove the conclusion.
   B. The facts disprove the conclusion.
   C. The facts neither prove nor disprove the conclusion.

6.____

7. FACTS: A mark is worth five plunks. You can exchange four sharps for a tinplot. It takes eight marks to buy a sharp.

   CONCLUSION: A sharp is the most valuable.
   A. The facts prove the conclusion.
   B. The facts disprove the conclusion.
   C. The facts neither prove nor disprove the conclusion.

7.____

8. FACTS: There are gibbons, as well as lemurs, who like to play in the trees at the monkey house. All those who like to play in the trees at the monkey house are fed lettuce and bananas.

   CONCLUSION: Lemurs and gibbons are types of monkeys.
   A. The facts prove the conclusion.
   B. The facts disprove the conclusion.
   C. The facts neither prove nor disprove the conclusion.

8.____

9. FACTS: None of the Blackfoot tribes is a Salishan Indian tribe. Salishan Indians came from the northern Pacific Coast. All Salishan Indians live each of the Continental Divide.

9._____

CONCLUSION: No Blackfoot tribes live east of the Continental Divide.
   A. The facts prove the conclusion.
   B. The facts disprove the conclusion.
   C. The facts neither prove nor disprove the conclusion.

Questions 10-17.

DIRECTIONS: Questions 10 through 17 are based on the following reading passage. It is not your knowledge of the particular topic that is being tested, but your ability to reason based on what you have read. The passage is likely to detail several proposed courses of action and factors affecting these proposals. The reading passage is followed by a conclusion or outcome based on the facts in the passage, or a description of a decision taken regarding the situation. The conclusion is followed by a number of statements that have a possible connection to the conclusion. For each statement, you are to determine whether:
   A. The statement proves the conclusion.
   B. The statement supports the conclusion but does not prove it.
   C. The statement disproves the conclusion.
   D. The statement weakens the conclusion but does not disprove it.
   E. The statement has no relevance to the conclusion.

Remember that the conclusion after the passage is to be accepted as the outcome of what actually happened, and that you are being asked to evaluate the impact each statement would have had on the conclusion.

PASSAGE:

On August 12, Beverly Willey reported that she was in the elevator late on the previous evening after leaving her office on the 16th floor of a large office building. In her report, she states that a man got on the elevator at the 11th floor, pulled her off the elevator, assaulted her, and stole her purse. Ms. Willey reported that she had seen the man in the elevators and hallways of the building before. She believes that the man works in the building. Her description of him is as follows: he is tall, unshaven, with wavy brown hair and a scar on his left cheek. He walks with a pronounced limp, often dragging his left foot behind his right.

CONCLUSION: After Beverly Willey makes her report, the police arrest a 43-year-old man, Barton Black, and charge him with her assault.

10. Barton Black is a former Marine who served in Vietnam, where he sustained shrapnel wounds to the left side of his face and suffered nerve damage in his left leg.
   A. The statement proves the conclusion.
   B. The statement supports the conclusion but does not prove it.
   C. The statement disproves the conclusion.
   D. The statement weakens the conclusion but does not disprove it.
   E. The statement has no relevance to the conclusion.

11. When they arrived at his residence to question him, detectives were greeted at the door by Barton Black, who was tall and clean-shaven.
   A. The statement proves the conclusion.
   B. The statement supports the conclusion but does not prove it.
   C. The statement disproves the conclusion.
   D. The statement weakens the conclusion but does not disprove it.
   E. The statement has no relevance to the conclusion.

12. Barton Black was booked into the county jail several days after Beverly Willey's assault.
   A. The statement proves the conclusion.
   B. The statement supports the conclusion but does not prove it.
   C. The statement disproves the conclusion.
   D. The statement weakens the conclusion but does not disprove it.
   E. The statement has no relevance to the conclusion.

13. Upon further investigation, detectives discover that Beverly Willey does not work at the office building.
   A. The statement proves the conclusion.
   B. The statement supports the conclusion but does not prove it.
   C. The statement disproves the conclusion.
   D. The statement weakens the conclusion but does not disprove it.
   E. The statement has no relevance to the conclusion.

14. Upon further investigation, detectives discover that Barton Black does not work at the office building.
   A. The statement proves the conclusion.
   B. The statement supports the conclusion but does not prove it.
   C. The statement disproves the conclusion.
   D. The statement weakens the conclusion but does not disprove it.
   E. The statement has no relevance to the conclusion.

15. In the spring of the following year, Barton Black is convicted of assaulting Beverly Willey on August 11.
   A. The statement proves the conclusion.
   B. The statement supports the conclusion but does not prove it.
   C. The statement disproves the conclusion.
   D. The statement weakens the conclusion but does not disprove it.
   E. The statement has no relevance to the conclusion.

16. During their investigation of the assault, detectives determine that Beverly Willey   16.____
    was assaulted on the 12th floor of the office building.
    A. The statement proves the conclusion.
    B. The statement supports the conclusion but does not prove it.
    C. The statement disproves the conclusion.
    D. The statement weakens the conclusion but does not disprove it.
    E. The statement has no relevance to the conclusion.

17. The day after Beverly Willey's assault, Barton Black fled the area and was never   17.____
    seen again.
    A. The statement proves the conclusion.
    B. The statement supports the conclusion but does not prove it.
    C. The statement disproves the conclusion.
    D. The statement weakens the conclusion but does not disprove it.
    E. The statement has no relevance to the conclusion.

Questions 18-25.

DIRECTIONS: Questions 18 through 25 each provide four factual statements and a conclusion based on these statements. After reading the entire question, you will decide whether:
    A. The conclusion is proved by statements I-IV;
    B. The conclusion is disproved by statements I-IV.
    C. The facts are not sufficient to prove or disprove the conclusion.

18. FACTUAL STATEMENTS: 18.____
    I. Among five spice jars on the shelf, the sage is to the right of the parsley.
    II. The pepper is to the left of the basil.
    III. The nutmeg is between the sage and the pepper.
    IV. The pepper is the second spice from the left.

    CONCLUSION: The safe is the farthest to the right.
    A. The conclusion is proved by statements I-IV;
    B. The conclusion is disproved by statements I-IV.
    C. The facts are not sufficient to prove or disprove the conclusion.

19. FACTUAL STATEMENTS: 19.____
    I. Gear X rotates in a clockwise direction if Switch C is in the OFF position.
    II. Gear X will rotate in a counter-clockwise direction is Switch C is ON.
    III. If Gear X is rotating in a clockwise direction, then Gear Y will not be rotating at all.
    IV. Switch C is ON.

    CONCLUSION: Gear X is rotating in a counter-clockwise direction.
    A. The conclusion is proved by statements I-IV;
    B. The conclusion is disproved by statements I-IV.
    C. The facts are not sufficient to prove or disprove the conclusion.

20. FACTUAL STATEMENTS:
   I. Lane will leave for the Toronto meeting today only if Terence, Rourke, and Jackson all file their marketing reports by the end of the work day.
   II. Rourke will file her report on time only if Ganz submits last quarter's data.
   III. If Terence attends the security meeting, he will attend it with Jackson, and they will not file their marketing reports by the end of the work day.

   CONCLUSION: Lane will leave for the Toronto meeting today.
   A. The conclusion is proved by statements I-IV;
   B. The conclusion is disproved by statements I-IV.
   C. The facts are not sufficient to prove or disprove the conclusion.

21. FACTUAL STATEMENTS:
   I. Bob is in second place in the Boston Marathon.
   II. Gregory is winning the Boston Marathon.
   III. There are four miles to go in the race, and Bob is gaining on Gregory at the rate of 100 yards every minute.
   IV. There are 1760 yards in a mile and Gregory's usual pace during the Boston Marathon is one mile every six minutes.

   CONCLUSION: Bob wins the Boston Marathon.
   A. The conclusion is proved by statements I-IV;
   B. The conclusion is disproved by statements I-IV.
   C. The facts are not sufficient to prove or disprove the conclusion.

22. FACTUAL STATEMENTS:
   I. Four brothers are named Earl, John, Gary, and Pete.
   II. Earl and Pete are unmarried.
   III. John is shorter than the youngest of the four.
   IV. The oldest brother is married, and is also the tallest.

   CONCLUSION: Gary is the oldest brother.
   A. The conclusion is proved by statements I-IV;
   B. The conclusion is disproved by statements I-IV.
   C. The facts are not sufficient to prove or disprove the conclusion.

23. FACTUAL STATEMENTS:
   I. Brigade X is ten miles from the demilitarized zone.
   II. If General Woundwort gives the order, Brigade X will advance to the demilitarized zone, but not quickly enough to reach the zone before the conflict begins.
   III. Brigade Y, five miles behind Brigade X, will not advance unless General Woundwort gives the order.
   IV. Brigade Y advances.

7 (#2)

CONCLUSION: Brigade X reaches the demilitarized zone before the conflict begins.
- A. The conclusion is proved by statements I-IV;
- B. The conclusion is disproved by statements I-IV.
- C. The facts are not sufficient to prove or disprove the conclusion.

24. FACTUAL STATEMENTS: 24.____
   - I. Jerry has decided to take a cab from Fullerton to Elverton.
   - II. Chubby Cab charges $5 plus $3 a mile.
   - III. Orange Cab charges $7.50 but gives free mileage for the first 5 miles.
   - IV. After the first 5 miles, Orange Cab charges $2.50 a mile.

   CONCLUSION: Orange Cab is the cheaper fare from Fullerton to Elverton.
   - A. The conclusion is proved by statements I-IV;
   - B. The conclusion is disproved by statements I-IV.
   - C. The facts are not sufficient to prove or disprove the conclusion.

25. FACTUAL STATEMENTS: 25.____
   - I. Dan is never in class when his friend Lucy is absent.
   - II. Lucy is never absent unless her mother is sick.
   - III. If Lucy is in class, Sergio is in class also.
   - IV. Sergio is never in class when Dalton is absent.

   CONCLUSION: If Lucy is absent, Dalton may be in class.
   - A. The conclusion is proved by statements I-IV;
   - B. The conclusion is disproved by statements I-IV.
   - C. The facts are not sufficient to prove or disprove the conclusion.

KEY (CORRECT ANSWERS)

1.	C		11.	E
2.	B		12.	B
3.	B		13.	D
4.	C		14.	E
5.	A		15.	A
6.	A		16.	E
7.	B		17.	C
8.	C		18.	B
9.	C		19.	A
10.	B		20.	C

21. C
22. A
23. B
24. A
25. B

SOLUTIONS TO PROBLEMS

1. **CORRECT ANSWER: C**
   Statement 1 only tells us that some employees who work in the Testing Department are statisticians. This means that we need to allow the possibility that at least one person in this department is not a statistician. Thus, if a person works in the Testing Department, we cannot conclude whether or not this individual is a statistician.

2. **CORRECT ANSWER: B**
   If Hank had six coins, then the total of Gail's collection and Lawrence's collection would be four. Thus, if Gail gave all her coins to Lawrence, Lawrence would only have four coins. Thus, it would be impossible for Lawrence to have more coins than Hank.

3. **CORRECT ANSWER: B**
   Statement 1 tells us that nobody loves everybody. If everybody loved Janet, then Statement 3 would imply that Ken loves everybody. This would contradict statement 1. The conclusion is disproved.

4. **CORRECT ANSWER: C**
   Although most of the Torres family lives in East Los Angeles, we can assume that some members of this family do not live in East Los Angeles. Thus, we cannot prove or disprove that Joe, who is a member of the Torres family, lives in East Los Angeles.

5. **CORRECT ANSWER: A**
   Since Dr. Johnson is on the 4th floor, either (a) Dr. Kane is on the 5th floor and Dr. Conlon is on the 3rd floor, or (b) Dr. Kane is on the 3rd floor and Dr. Conlon is on the 5th floor. If option (b) were correct, then since Dr. Assad would be on the 1st floor, it would be impossible for Dr. Steen's office to be between Dr. Conlon and Dr. Assad's office. Therefore, Dr. Kane's office must be on the 5th floor. The order of the doctors' offices, from 5th floor down to the 1st floor is: Dr. Kane, Dr. Johnson, Dr. Conlon, Dr. Steen, Dr. Assad.

6. **CORRECT ANSWER: A**
   Ray does not satisfy the requirement of holding his breath for two minutes under water, since he can only hold is breath for one minute in that setting. But if he tunnels through a snowbank with just a T-shirt and shorts, he will satisfy the eligibility requirement. Note that the eligibility requirement contains the key word "or." So only one of the two clauses separated by "or" need to be fulfilled.

7. **CORRECT ANSWER: B**
   Statement 2 says that four sharps is equivalent to one tinplot. This means that a tinplot is worth more than a sharp. The conclusion is disproved. We note that the order of these items, from most valuable to least valuable are: tinplot, sharp, mark, plunk.

8. **CORRECT ANSWER: C**
   We can only conclude that gibbons and lemurs are fed lettuce and bananas. We can neither prove nor disprove that these animals are types of monkeys.

9. CORRECT ANSWER: C
We know that all Salishan Indians live east of the Continental Divide. But some non-members of this tribe of Indians may also live east of the Continental Divide. Since none of the members of the Blackfoot tribe belong to the Salishan Indian tribe, we cannot draw any conclusion about the location of the Blackfoot tribe with respect to the Continental Divide.

18. CORRECT ANSWER: B
Since the pepper is second from the left and the nutmeg is between the sage and the pepper, the positions 2, 3, and 4 (from the left) are pepper, nutmeg, sage. By statement II, the basil must be in position 5, which implies that the parsley is in position 1. Therefore, the basil, not the sage, is farthest to the right. The conclusion disproved.

19. CORRECT ANSWER: A
Statement II assures us that if switch C is ON, then Gear X is rotating in a counterclockwise direction. The conclusion is proved.

20. CORRECT ANSWER: C
Based on Statement IV, followed by Statement II, we conclude that Ganz and Rourke will file their reports on time. Statement III reveals that if Terence and Jackson attend the security meeting, they will fail to file their reports on time. We have no further information if Terence and Jackson attended the security meeting, so we are not able to either confirm or deny that their reports were filed on time. This implies that we cannot know for certain that Lane will leave for his meeting in Toronto.

21. CORRECT ANSWER: C
Although Bob is in second place behind Gregory, we cannot deduce how far behind Gregory he is running. At Gregory's current pace, he will cover four miles in 24 minutes. If Bob were only 100 yards behind Gregory, he would catch up to Gregory in one minute. But if Bob were very far behind Gregory, for example 5 miles, this is the equivalent of (5)(1760) = 8800 yards. Then Bob would need 8800/100 = 88 minutes to catch up to Gregory. Thus, the given facts are not sufficient to draw a conclusion.

22. CORRECT ANSWER: A
Statement II tells us that neither Earl nor Pete could be the oldest; also, either John or Gary is married. Statement IV reveals that the oldest brother is both married and the tallest. By Statement III, John cannot be the tallest. Since John is not the tallest, he is not the oldest. Thus, the oldest brother must be Gary. The conclusion is proved.

23. CORRECT ANSWER: B
By Statements III and IV, General Woundwort must have given the order to advance. Statement II then tells us that Brigade X will advance to the demilitarized zone, but not soon enough before the conflict begins. Thus, the conclusion is disproved.

11 (#2)

24. CORRECT ANSWER: A
If the distance is 5 miles or less, then the cost for the Orange Cab is only $7.50, whereas the cost for the Chubby Cab is $5 + 3x, where x represents the number of miles traveled. For 1 to 5 miles, the cost of the Chubby Cab is between $8 and $20. This means that for a distance of 5 miles, the Orange Cab costs $7.50, whereas the Chubby Cab costs $20. After 5 miles, the cost per mile of the Chubby Cab exceeds the cost per mile of the Orange Cab. Thus, regardless of the actual distance between Fullerton and Elverton, the cost for the Orange Cab will be cheaper than that of the Chubby Cab.

25. CORRECT ANSWER: B
It looks like "Dalton" should be replaced by "Dan" in the conclusion. Then by statement I, if Lucy is absent, Dan is never in class. Thus, the conclusion is disproved.

EVALUATING CONCLUSIONS IN LIGHT OF KNOWN FACTS
EXAMINATION SECTION
TEST 1

DIRECTIONS: Each question or incomplete statement is followed by several suggested answers or completions. Select the one that BEST answers the question or completes the statement. *PRINT THE LETTER OF THE CORRECT ANSWER IN THE SPACE AT THE RIGHT.*

Questions 1-9.

DIRECTIONS: In Questions 1 through 9, you will read a set of facts and a conclusion drawn from them. The conclusion may be valid or invalid, based on the facts. It is your task to determine the validity of the conclusion.
For each question, select the letter before the statement that BEST expresses the relationship between the given facts and the conclusion that has been drawn from them. Your choices are:
   A. The facts prove the conclusion.
   B. The facts disprove the conclusion; or
   C. The facts neither prove nor disprove the conclusion.

1. FACTS: Lauren must use Highway 29 to get to work. Lauren has a meeting today at 9:00 A.M. If she misses the meeting, Lauren will probably lose a major account. Highway 29 is closed all day today for repairs.

   CONCLUSION: Lauren will not be able to get to work.

   A. The facts prove the conclusion.
   B. The facts disprove the conclusion.
   C. The facts neither prove nor disprove the conclusion.

2. FACTS: The Tumbleweed Follies, a traveling burlesque show, is looking for a new line dancer. The position requires both singing and dancing skills. If the show cannot fill the position by Friday, it will begin to look for a magician to fill the time slot currently held by the line dancers. Willa, who wants to audition for the line dancing position, can sing, but cannot dance.

   CONCLUSION: Willa is qualified to audition for the part of line dancer.

   A. The facts prove the conclusion.
   B. The facts disprove the conclusion.
   C. The facts neither prove nor disprove the conclusion.

2 (#1)

3. FACTS: Terry owns two dogs, Spike and Stan. One of the dogs is short-haired and has blue eyes. One dog as a pink nose. The blue-eyed dog never barks. One of the dogs has white fur on its paws. Sam has long hair.

   CONCLUSION: Spike never barks.

   A. The facts prove the conclusion.
   B. The facts disprove the conclusion.
   C. The facts neither prove nor disprove the conclusion.

   3.____

4. FACTS: No science teachers are members of the PTA. Some English teachers are members of the PTA. Some English teachers in the PTA also wear glasses. Every PTA member is required to sit on the dunking stool at the student carnival except for those who wear glasses, who will be exempt. Those who are exempt, however, will have to officiate the hamster races. All of the English teachers in the PTA who do not wear glasses are married.

   CONCLUSION: All the married English teachers in the PTA will set on the dunking stool at the student carnival.

   A. The facts prove the conclusion.
   B. The facts disprove the conclusion.
   C. The facts neither prove nor disprove the conclusion.

   4.____

5. FACTS: If the price of fuel is increased and sales remain constant, oil company profits will increase. The price of fuel was increased, and market experts project that sales levels are likely to be maintained.

   CONCLUSION: The price of fuel will increase.

   A. The facts prove the conclusion.
   B. The facts disprove the conclusion.
   C. The facts neither prove nor disprove the conclusion.

   5.____

6. FACTS: Some members of the gymnastics team are double-jointed, and some members of the gymnastics team ae also on the lacrosse team. Some double-jointed members of the gymnastics team are also coaches. All gymnastics team members perform floor exercises, except the coaches. All the double-jointed members of the gymnastics team who are not coaches are freshmen.

   CONCLUSION: Some double-jointed freshmen are coaches.

   A. The facts prove the conclusion.
   B. The facts disprove the conclusion.
   C. The facts neither prove nor disprove the conclusion.

   6.____

7. FACTS: Each member of the International Society speaks at least one foreign language, but no member speaks more than four foreign languages. Five members speak Spanish; three speak Mandarin; four speak French; four speak German; and five speak a foreign language other than Spanish, Mandarin, French, or German.

   CONCLUSION: The lowest possible number of members in the International Society is eight.

   A. The facts prove the conclusion.
   B. The facts disprove the conclusion.
   C. The facts neither prove nor disprove the conclusion.

   7.____

8. FACTS: Mary keeps seven cats in her apartment. Only three of the cats will eat the same kind of food. Mary wants to keep at least one extra bag of each kind of food.

   CONCLUSION: The minimum number of bags Mary will need to keep as extra is 7.

   A. The facts prove the conclusion.
   B. The facts disprove the conclusion.
   C. The facts neither prove nor disprove the conclusion.

   8.____

9. FACTS: In Ed and Marie's exercise group, everyone likes the treadmill or the stationary bicycle, or both, but Ed does not like the stationary bicycle. Marie has not expressed a preference, but spends most of her time on the stationary bicycle.

   CONCLUSION: Everyone in the group who does not like the treadmill likes the stationary bicycle.

   A. The facts prove the conclusion.
   B. The facts disprove the conclusion.
   C. The facts neither prove nor disprove the conclusion.

   9.____

Questions 10-17.

DIRECTIONS: Questions 10 through 17 are based on the following reading passage. It is not your knowledge of the particular topic that is being tested, but your ability to reason based on what you have read. The passage is likely to detail several proposed courses of action and factors affecting these proposals. The reading passage is followed by a conclusion or outcome based on the facts in the passage, or a description of a decision taken regarding the situation. The conclusion is followed by a number of statements that have a possible connection to the conclusion. For each statement, you are to determine whether:

A. The statement proves the conclusion.
B. The statement supports the conclusion but does not prove it.
C. The statement disproves the conclusion.
D. The statement weakens the conclusion but does not disprove it.
E. The statement has no relevance to the conclusion.

Remember that the conclusion after the passage is to be accepted as the outcome of what actually happened, and that you are being asked to evaluate the impact each statement would have had on the conclusion.

PASSAGE

The Owyhee Mission School District's Board of Directors is hosting a public meeting to debate the merits of the proposed abolition of all bilingual education programs within the district. The group that has made the proposal believes the programs, which teach immigrant children academic subjects in their native language until they have learned English well enough to join mainstream classes, inhibit the ability of students to acquire English quickly and succeed in school and in the larger American society. Such programs, they argue, are also a wasteful drain on the district's already scant resources.

At the meeting, several teachers and parents stand to speak out against the proposal. The purpose of an education, they say, should be to build upon, rather than dismantle, a minority child's language and culture. By teaching children in academic subjects in their native tongues, while simultaneously offering English language instruction, schools can meet the goals of learning English and progressing through academic subjects along with their peers.

Hiram Nguyen, a representative of the parents whose children are currently enrolled in bilingual education, stands at the meeting to express the parents' wishes. The parents have been polled, he says, and are overwhelmingly of the opinion that while language and culture are important to them, they are not things that will disappear from the students' lives if they are no longer taught in the classroom. The most important issue for the parents is whether their children will succeed in school and be competitive in the larger American society. If bilingual education can be demonstrated to do that, then the parents are in favor of continuing it.

At the end of the meeting, a proponent of the plan, Oscar Ramos, stands to clarify some misconceptions about the proposal. It does not call for a "sink or swim" approach, he says, but allows for an interpreter to be present in mainstream classes to explain anything a student finds too complex or confusing.

The last word of the meeting is given to Delia Cruz, a bilingual teacher at one of the district's elementary schools. A student is bound to find anything complex or confusing, she says, if it is spoken in a language he has never heard before. It is more wasteful to place children in classrooms where they don't understand anything, she says, than it is to try to teach them something useful as they are learning the English language.

CONCLUSION: After the meeting, the Owyhee Mission School District's Board of Directors votes to terminate all the district's bilingual education programs at the end of the current academic year, but to maintain the current level of funding to each of the schools that have programs cut.

5 (#1)

10. A poll conducted by the *Los Angeles Times* at approximately the same time as the Board's meeting indicated that 75% of the people were opposed to bilingual education; among Latinos, opposition was 84%.
    A. The statement proves the conclusion.
    B. The statement supports the conclusion but does not prove it.
    C. The statement disproves the conclusion.
    D. The statement weakens the conclusion but does not disprove it.
    E. The statement has no relevance to the conclusion.

10.____

11. Of all the studies connected on bilingual education programs, 64% indicate that students learned English grammar better in "sink or swim" classes without any special features than they did in bilingual education classes.
    A. The statement proves the conclusion.
    B. The statement supports the conclusion but does not prove it.
    C. The statement disproves the conclusion.
    D. The statement weakens the conclusion but does not disprove it.
    E. The statement has no relevance to the conclusion.

11.____

12. In the academic year that begins after the Board's vote, Montgomery Burns Elementary, an Owyhee Mission District school, launches a new bilingual program for the children of Somali immigrants.
    A. The statement proves the conclusion.
    B. The statement supports the conclusion but does not prove it.
    C. The statement disproves the conclusion.
    D. The statement weakens the conclusion but does not disprove it.
    E. The statement has no relevance to the conclusion.

12.____

13. In the previous academic year, under severe budget restraints, the Owyhee Mission District cut all physical education, music, and art classes, but its funding for bilingual education classes increased by 18%.
    A. The statement proves the conclusion.
    B. The statement supports the conclusion but does not prove it.
    C. The statement disproves the conclusion.
    D. The statement weakens the conclusion but does not disprove it.
    E. The statement has no relevance to the conclusion.

13.____

14. Before the Board votes, a polling consultant conducts randomly sampled assessments of immigrant students who enrolled in Owyhee District schools at a time when they did not speak any English at all. Ten years after graduating from high school, 44% of those who received bilingual education were professionals – doctors, lawyers, educators, engineers, etc. Of those who did not receive bilingual education, 38% were professionals.
    A. The statement proves the conclusion.
    B. The statement supports the conclusion but does not prove it.
    C. The statement disproves the conclusion.
    D. The statement weakens the conclusion but does not disprove it.
    E. The statement has no relevance to the conclusion.

14.____

15. Over the past several years, the scores of Owyhee District students have gradually declined, and enrollment numbers have followed as anxious parents transferred their children to other schools or applied for a state-funded voucher program.
    A. The statement proves the conclusion.
    B. The statement supports the conclusion but does not prove it.
    C. The statement disproves the conclusion.
    D. The statement weakens the conclusion but does not disprove it.
    E. The statement has no relevance to the conclusion.

    15.____

16. California and Massachusetts, two of the most liberal states in the country, have each passed ballot measures banning bilingual education in public schools.
    A. The statement proves the conclusion.
    B. The statement supports the conclusion but does not prove it.
    C. The statement disproves the conclusion.
    D. The statement weakens the conclusion but does not disprove it.
    E. The statement has no relevance to the conclusion.

    16.____

17. In the academic year that begins after the Board's vote, no Owyhee Mission Schools are conducting bilingual instruction.
    A. The statement proves the conclusion.
    B. The statement supports the conclusion but does not prove it.
    C. The statement disproves the conclusion.
    D. The statement weakens the conclusion but does not disprove it.
    E. The statement has no relevance to the conclusion.

    17.____

Questions 18-25.

DIRECTIONS: Questions 18 through 25 each provide four factual statements and a conclusion based on these statements. After reading the entire question, you will decide whether:
A. The conclusion is proved by Statements 1-4;
B. The conclusion is disproved by Statements 1-4;
C. The facts are not sufficient to prove or disprove the conclusion.

18. FACTUAL STATEMENTS:
    1) Gear X rotates in a clockwise direction if Switch C is in the OFF position.
    2) Gear X will rotate in a counter-clockwise direction if Switch C is ON.
    3) If Gear X is rotating in a clockwise direction, then Gear Y will not be rotating at all.
    4) Switch C is OFF.

    CONCLUSION: Gear Y is rotating.

    A. The conclusion is proved by Statements 1-4;
    B. The conclusion is disproved by Statements 1-4;
    C. The facts are not sufficient to prove or disprove the conclusion.

    18.____

19. **FACTUAL STATEMENTS:**
    1) Mark is older than Jim but younger than Dan.
    2) Fern is older than Mark but younger than Silas.
    3) Dan is younger than Silas but older than Edward.
    4) Edward is older than Mark but younger than Fern.

    CONCLUSION: Dan is older than Fern.

    A. The conclusion is proved by Statements 1-4;
    B. The conclusion is disproved by Statements 1-4;
    C. The facts are not sufficient to prove or disprove the conclusion.

20. **FACTUAL STATEMENTS:**
    1) Each of Fred's three sofa cushions lies on top of four lost coins.
    2) The cushion on the right covers two pennies and two dimes.
    3) The middle cushion covers two dimes and two quarters.
    4) The cushion on the left covers two nickels and two quarters.

    CONCLUSION: To be guaranteed of retrieving at least one coin of each denomination, and without looking at any of the coins, Frank must take three coins each from under the cushions on the right and the left.

    A. The conclusion is proved by Statements 1-4;
    B. The conclusion is disproved by Statements 1-4;
    C. The facts are not sufficient to prove or disprove the conclusion.

21. **FACTUAL STATEMENTS:**
    1) The door to the hammer mill chamber is locked if light 6 is red.
    2) The door to the hammer mill chamber is locked only when the mill is operating.
    3) If the mill is not operating, light 6 is blue.
    4) The door to the hammer mill chamber is locked.

    CONCLUSION: The mill is in operation.

    A. The conclusion is proved by Statements 1-4;
    B. The conclusion is disproved by Statements 1-4;
    C. The facts are not sufficient to prove or disprove the conclusion.

22. **FACTUAL STATEMENTS:**
    1) In a five-story office building, where each story is occupied by a single professional, Dr. Kane's office is above Dr. Assad's.
    2) Dr. Johnson's office is between Dr. Kane's and Dr. Conlon's.
    3) Dr. Steen's office is between Dr. Conlon's and Dr. Assad's.
    4) Dr. Johnson is on the fourth story.

    CONCLUSION: Dr. Steen occupies the second story.

8 (#1)

    A. The conclusion is proved by Statements 1-4;
    B. The conclusion is disproved by Statements 1-4;
    C. The facts are not sufficient to prove or disprove the conclusion.

23. FACTUAL STATEMENTS:
    1) On Saturday, farmers Hank, Earl, Roy, and Cletus plowed a total of 520 acres.
    2) Hank plowed twice as many acres as Roy.
    3) Roy plowed half as much as the farmer who plowed the most.
    4) Cletus plowed 160 acres.

    CONCLUSION: Hank plowed 200 acres.
        A. The conclusion is proved by Statements 1-4;
        B. The conclusion is disproved by Statements 1-4;
        C. The facts are not sufficient to prove or disprove the conclusion.

24. FACTUAL STATEMENTS:
    1) Four travelers – Tina, Jodie, Alex, and Oscar – each traveled to a different island – Aruba, Jamaica, Nevis, and Barbados – but not necessarily respectively.
    2) Tina did not travel as far to Jamaica as Jodie traveled to her island.
    3) Oscar traveled twice as far as Alex, who traveled the same distance as the traveler who went to Aruba.
    4) Oscar went to Barbados.

    CONCLUSION: Oscar traveled the farthest.

        A. The conclusion is proved by Statements 1-4;
        B. The conclusion is disproved by Statements 1-4;
        C. The facts are not sufficient to prove or disprove the conclusion.

25. FACTUAL STATEMENT:
    1) In the natural history museum, every Native American display that contains pottery also contains beadwork.
    2) Some of the displays containing lodge replicas also contain beadwork.
    3) The display on the Choctaw, a Native American tribe, contains pottery.
    4) The display on the Modoc, a Native American tribe, contains only two of these items.

    CONCLUSION: If the Modoc display contains pottery, it does not contain lodge replicas.

        A. The conclusion is proved by Statements 1-4;
        B. The conclusion is disproved by Statements 1-4;
        C. The facts are not sufficient to prove or disprove the conclusion.

KEY (CORRECT ANSWERS)

1.	A		11.	B
2.	B		12.	C
3.	A		13.	B
4.	A		14.	D
5.	C		15.	E
6.	B		16.	E
7.	B		17.	A
8.	B		18.	B
9.	A		19.	C
10.	B		20.	A

21. A
22. A
23. C
24. A
25. A

TEST 2

DIRECTIONS: Each question or incomplete statement is followed by several suggested answers or completions. Select the one that BEST answers the question or completes the statement. *PRINT THE LETTER OF THE CORRECT ANSWER IN THE SPACE AT THE RIGHT.*

Questions 1-9.

DIRECTIONS: In Questions 1 through 9, you will read a set of facts and a conclusion drawn from them. The conclusion may be valid or invalid, based on the facts. It is your task to determine the validity of the conclusion.
For each question, select the letter before the statement that BEST expresses the relationship between the given facts and the conclusion that has been drawn from them. Your choices are:
  A. The facts prove the conclusion.
  B. The facts disprove the conclusion; or
  C. The facts neither prove nor disprove the conclusion.

1. FACTS: If the maximum allowable income for Medicaid recipients is increased, the number of Medicaid recipients will increase. If the number of Medicaid recipients increases, more funds must be allocated to the Medicaid program, which will require a tax increase. Taxes cannot be approved without the approval of the legislature. The legislature probably will not approve a tax increase.

   CONCLUSION: The maximum allowable income for Medicaid recipients will increase.

   A. The facts prove the conclusion.
   B. The facts disprove the conclusion; or
   C. The facts neither prove nor disprove the conclusion.

1.____

2. FACTS: All the dentists on the baseball team are short. Everyone in the dugout is a dentist, but not everyone in the dugout is short. The baseball team is not made up of people of any particular profession.

   CONCLUSION: Some people who are not dentists are in the dugout.

   A. The facts prove the conclusion.
   B. The facts disprove the conclusion; or
   C. The facts neither prove nor disprove the conclusion.

2.____

3. FACTS: A taxi company's fleet is divided into two fleets. Fleet One contains cabs A, B, C, and D. Fleet Two contains E, F, G, and H. Each cab is either yellow or green. Five of the cabs are yellow. Cabs A and E are not both yellow. Either Cab C or F, or both, are not yellow. Cabs B and H are either both yellow or both green.

   CONCLUSION: Cab H is green.

3.____

138

2 (#2)

   A. The facts prove the conclusion.
   B. The facts disprove the conclusion; or
   C. The facts neither prove nor disprove the conclusion.

4. FACTS: Most people in the skydiving club are not afraid of heights. Everyone in the skydiving club makes three parachute jumps a month.

   CONCLUSION: At least one person who is afraid of heights makes three parachute jumps a month.

   A. The facts prove the conclusion.
   B. The facts disprove the conclusion; or
   C. The facts neither prove nor disprove the conclusion.

4.____

5. FACTS: If the Board approves the new rule, the agency will move to a new location immediately. If the agency moves, five new supervisors will be immediately appointed. The Board has approved the new proposal.

   CONCLUSION: No new supervisors were appointed.

   A. The facts prove the conclusion.
   B. The facts disprove the conclusion; or
   C. The facts neither prove nor disprove the conclusion.

5.____

6. FACTS: All the workers at the supermarket chew gum when they sack groceries. Sometimes Lance, a supermarket worker, doesn't chew gum at all when he works. Another supermarket worker, Jenny, chews gum the whole time she is at work.

   CONCLUSION: Jenny always sacks groceries when she is at work.

6.____

7. FACTS: Lake Lottawatta is bigger than Lake Tacomi. Lake Tacomi and Lake Ottawa are exactly the same size. All lakes in Montana are bigger than Lake Ottawa.

   CONCLUSION: Lake Lottawatta is in Montana.

   A. The facts prove the conclusion.
   B. The facts disprove the conclusion; or
   C. The facts neither prove nor disprove the conclusion.

7.____

8. FACTS: Two men, Cox and Taylor, are playing poker at a table. Taylor has a pair of aces in his hand. One man is smoking a cigar. One of them has no pairs in his hand and is wearing an eye patch. The man wearing the eye patch is smoking a cigar. One man is bald.

   CONCLUSION: Cox is smoking a cigar.

8.____

A. The facts prove the conclusion.
B. The facts disprove the conclusion; or
C. The facts neither prove nor disprove the conclusion.

9. FACTS: All Kwakiutls are Wakashan Indians. All Wakashan Indians originated on Vancouver Island. The Nootka also originated on Vancouver Island.

   CONCLUSION: Kwakiutls originated on Vancouver Island.

   A. The facts prove the conclusion.
   B. The facts disprove the conclusion; or
   C. The facts neither prove nor disprove the conclusion.

9.____

Questions 10-17.

DIRECTIONS: Questions 10 through 17 are based on the following reading passage. It is not your knowledge of the particular topic that is being tested, but your ability to reason based on what you have read. The passage is likely to detail several proposed courses of action and factors affecting these proposals. The reading passage is followed by a conclusion or outcome based on the facts in the passage, or a description of a decision taken regarding the situation. The conclusion is followed by a number of statements that have a possible connection to the conclusion. For each statement, you are to determine whether:
A. The statement proves the conclusion.
B. The statement supports the conclusion but does not prove it.
C. The statement disproves the conclusion.
D. The statement weakens the conclusion but does not disprove it.
E. The statement has no relevance to the conclusion.

Remember that the conclusion after the passage is to be accepted as the outcome of what actually happened, and that you are being asked to evaluate the impact each statement would have had on the conclusion.

PASSAGE

   The World Wide Web portal and search engine, HipBot, is considering becoming a subscription-only service, locking out nonsubscribers from the content on its web site. HipBot currently relies solely on advertising revenues.
   HipBot's content director says that by taking in an annual fee from each customer, the company can both increase profits and provide premium content that no other portal can match.
   The marketing director disagrees, saying that there is no guarantee that anyone who now visits the web site for free will agree to pay for the privilege of visiting it again. Most will probably simply use the other major portals. Also, HipBot's advertising clients will not be happy when they learn that the site will be viewed by a more limited number of people.

4 (#2)

CONCLUSION: In January of 2016, the CEO of HipBot decides to keep the portal open to all web users, with some limited "premium content" available to subscribers who don't mind paying a little extra to access it. The company will aim to maintain, or perhaps increase, its advertising revenue.

10. In an independent marketing survey, 62% of respondents said they "strongly agree" with the following statement: "I almost never pay attention to advertisements that appear on the World Wide Web."
    A. The statement proves the conclusion.
    B. The statement supports the conclusion but does not prove it.
    C. The statement disproves the conclusion.
    D. The statement weakens the conclusion but does not disprove it.
    E. The statement has no relevance to the conclusion.

10.____

11. When it learns about the subscription-only debate going on at HipBot, Wernham Hogg Entertainment, one of HipBot's most reliable clients, says it will withdraw its ads and place them on a free web portal if HipBot decides to limit its content to subscribers. Wernham Hogg pays HipBot about $6 million annually – about 12% of HipBot's gross revenues – to run its ads online.
    A. The statement proves the conclusion.
    B. The statement supports the conclusion but does not prove it.
    C. The statement disproves the conclusion.
    D. The statement weakens the conclusion but does not disprove it.
    E. The statement has no relevance to the conclusion.

11.____

12. At the end of the second quarter of FY 2016, after continued stagnant profits, the CEO of HipBot assembles a blue ribbon commission to gather and analyze data on the costs, benefits, and feasibility of adding a limited amount of "premium" content to the HipBot portal.
    A. The statement proves the conclusion.
    B. The statement supports the conclusion but does not prove it.
    C. The statement disproves the conclusion.
    D. The statement weakens the conclusion but does not disprove it.
    E. The statement has no relevance to the conclusion.

12.____

13. In the following fiscal year, Wernham Hogg Entertainment, satisfied with the "hit counts" on HipBot's free web site, spends another $1 million on advertisements that will appear on web pages that are available to HipBot's "premium subscribers.
    A. The statement proves the conclusion.
    B. The statement supports the conclusion but does not prove it.
    C. The statement disproves the conclusion.
    D. The statement weakens the conclusion but does not disprove it.
    E. The statement has no relevance to the conclusion.

13.____

14. HipBot's information technology director reports that the engineers in his department have come up with a feature that will search not only individual web pages, but tie into other web-based search engines, as well, and then comb through all these results to find those most relevant to the user's search.

14.____

A. The statement proves the conclusion.
B. The statement supports the conclusion but does not prove it.
C. The statement disproves the conclusion.
D. The statement weakens the conclusion but does not disprove it.
E. The statement has no relevance to the conclusion.

15. In an independent marketing survey, 79% of respondents said they "strongly agree" with the following statement: "Many web sites are so dominated by advertisements these days that it is increasingly frustrating to find the content I want to read or see."
    A. The statement proves the conclusion.
    B. The statement supports the conclusion but does not prove it.
    C. The statement disproves the conclusion.
    D. The statement weakens the conclusion but does not disprove it.
    E. The statement has no relevance to the conclusion.

15.____

16. After three years of studies at the federal level, the Department of Commerce releases a report suggesting that, in general, the only private "subscriber-only" web sites that do well financially are those with a very specialized user population.
    A. The statement proves the conclusion.
    B. The statement supports the conclusion but does not prove it.
    C. The statement disproves the conclusion.
    D. The statement weakens the conclusion but does not disprove it.
    E. The statement has no relevance to the conclusion.

16.____

17. HipBot's own marketing research indicates that the introduction of premium content has the potential to attract new users to the HipBot portal.
    A. The statement proves the conclusion.
    B. The statement supports the conclusion but does not prove it.
    C. The statement disproves the conclusion.
    D. The statement weakens the conclusion but does not disprove it.
    E. The statement has no relevance to the conclusion.

17.____

Questions 18-25.

DIRECTIONS: Questions 18 through 25 each provide four factual statements and a conclusion based on these statements. After reading the entire question, you will decide whether:
A. The conclusion is proved by Statements 1-4;
B. The conclusion is disproved by Statements 1-4;
C. The facts are not sufficient to prove or disprove the conclusion.

18. FACTUAL STATEMENTS:
    1) If the alarm goes off, Sam will wake up.
    2) If Tandy wakes up before 4:00, Linda will leave the bedroom and sleep on the couch.
    3) If Linda leaves the bedroom, she'll check the alarm to make sure it is working.
    4) The alarm goes off.

    CONCLUSION: Tandy woke up before 4:00.

    A. The conclusion is proved by Statements 1-4;
    B. The conclusion is disproved by Statements 1-4;
    C. The facts are not sufficient to prove or disprove the conclusion.

18.____

19. FACTUAL STATEMENTS:
    1) Four brothers are named Earl, John, Gary, and Pete.
    2) Earl and Pete are unmarried.
    3) John is shorter than the youngest of the four.
    4) The oldest brother is married, and is also the tallest.

    CONCLUSION: Pete is the youngest brother.

    A. The conclusion is proved by Statements 1-4;
    B. The conclusion is disproved by Statements 1-4;
    C. The facts are not sufficient to prove or disprove the conclusion.

19.____

20. FACTUAL STATEMENTS:
    1) Automobile engines are cooled either by air or by liquid.
    2) If the engine is small and simple enough, air from a belt-driven fan will cool it sufficiently.
    3) Most newer automobile engines are too complicated to be air-cooled.
    4) Air-cooled engines are cheaper and easier to build then liquid-cooled engines.

    CONCLUSION: Most newer automobile engines use liquid coolant.

    A. The conclusion is proved by Statements 1-4;
    B. The conclusion is disproved by Statements 1-4;
    C. The facts are not sufficient to prove or disprove the conclusion.

20.____

21. FACTUAL STATEMENTS:
    1) Erica will only file a lawsuit if she is injured while parasailing.
    2) If Rick orders Trip to run a rope test, Trip will check the rigging.
    3) If the rigging does not malfunction, Erica will not be injured.
    4) Rick orders Trip to run a rope test.

21.____

CONCLUSION: Erica does not file a lawsuit.

   A. The conclusion is proved by Statements 1-4;
   B. The conclusion is disproved by Statements 1-4;
   C. The facts are not sufficient to prove or disprove the conclusion.

22. FACTUAL STATEMENTS:
   1) On Maple Street, which is four blocks long, Bill's shop is two blocks east of Ken's shop.
   2) Ken's shop is one block west of the only shop on Maple Street with an awning.
   3) Erma's shop is one block west of the easternmost block.
   4) Bill's shop is on the easternmost block.

   CONCLUSION: Bill's shop has an awning.

   A. The conclusion is proved by Statements 1-4;
   B. The conclusion is disproved by Statements 1-4;
   C. The facts are not sufficient to prove or disprove the conclusion.

23. FACTUAL STATEMENTS:
   1) Gear X rotates in a clockwise direction if Switch C is in the OFF position.
   2) Gear X will rotate in a counter-clockwise direction if Switch C is ON.
   3) If Gear X is rotating in a clockwise direction, then Gear Y will not be rotating at all.
   4) Gear Y is rotating.

   CONCLUSION: Gear X is rotating in a counter-clockwise direction.

   A. The conclusion is proved by Statements 1-4;
   B. The conclusion is disproved by Statements 1-4;
   C. The facts are not sufficient to prove or disprove the conclusion.

24. FACTUAL STATEMENTS:
   1) The Republic of Garbanzo's currency system has four basic denominations: the pastor, the noble, the donner, and the rojo.
   2) A pastor is worth 2 nobles.
   3) 2 donners can be exchanged for a rojo.
   4) 3 pastors are equal in value to 2 donners.

   CONCLUSION: The rojo is most valuable.

   A. The conclusion is proved by Statements 1-4;
   B. The conclusion is disproved by Statements 1-4;
   C. The facts are not sufficient to prove or disprove the conclusion.

25. FACTUAL STATEMENTS:
   1) At Prickett's Nursery, the only citrus trees left are either Meyer lemons or Valencia oranges, and every citrus tree left is either a dwarf or a semidwarf.
   2) Half of the semidwarf trees are Meyer lemons.
   3) There are more semidwarf trees left than dwarf trees.
   4) A quarter of the dwarf trees are Valencia oranges.

   CONCLUSION: There are more Valencia oranges left at Prickett's Nursery than Meyer lemons.

   A. The conclusion is proved by Statements 1-4;
   B. The conclusion is disproved by Statements 1-4;
   C. The facts are not sufficient to prove or disprove the conclusion.

25.____

KEY (CORRECT ANSWERS)

1.	C		11.	B
2.	B		12.	C
3.	B		13.	A
4.	A		14.	E
5.	B		15.	D
6.	C		16.	B
7.	C		17.	B
8.	A		18.	C
9.	A		19.	C
10.	E		20.	A

21.	C
22.	B
23.	C
24.	A
25.	B

PREPARING WRITTEN MATERIAL

PARAGRAPH REARRANGEMENT
COMMENTARY

The sentences that follow are in scrambled order. You are to rearrange them in proper order and indicate the letter choice containing the correct answer at the space at the right.

Each group of sentences in this section is actually a paragraph presented in scrambled order. Each sentence in the group has a place in that paragraph; no sentence is to be left out. You are to read each group of sentences and decide upon the best order in which to put the sentences so as to form a well-organized paragraph.

The questions in this section measure the ability to solve a problem when all the facts relevant to its solution are not given.

More specifically, certain positions of responsibility and authority require the employee to discover connection between events sometimes, apparently, unrelated. In order to do this, the employee will find it necessary to correctly infer that unspecified events have probably occurred or are likely to occur. This ability becomes especially important when action must be taken on incomplete information.

Accordingly, these questions require competitors to choose among several suggested alternatives, each of which presents a different sequential arrangement of the events. Competitors must choose the MOST logical of the suggested sequences.

In order to do so, they may be required to draw on general knowledge to infer missing concepts or events that are essential to sequencing the given events. Competitors should be careful to infer only what is essential to the sequence. The plausibility of the wrong alternatives will always require the inclusion of unlikely events or of additional chains of events which are NOT essential to sequencing the given events.

It's very important to remember that you are looking for the best of the four possible choices, and that the best choice of all may not even be one of the answers you're given to choose from.

There is no one right way to solve these problems. Many people have found it helpful to first write out the order of the sentences, as they would have arranged them, on their scrap paper before looking at the possible answers. If their optimum answer is there, this can save them some time. If it isn't, this method can still give insight into solving the problem. Others find it most helpful to just go through each of the possible choices, contrasting each as they go along. You should use whatever method feels comfortable and works for you.

While most of these types of questions are not that difficult, we've added a higher percentage of the difficult type, just to give you more practice. Usually there are only one or two questions on this section that contain such subtle distinctions that you're unable to answer confidently. And you then may find yourself stuck deciding between two possible choices, neither of which you're sure about.

EXAMINATION SECTION

TEST 1

DIRECTIONS: The sentences that follow are in scrambled order. You are to rearrange them in proper order and indicate the letter choice containing the correct answer. *PRINT THE LETTER OF THE CORRECT ANSWER IN THE SPACE AT THE RIGHT.*

1. Below are four statements labeled W, X, Y and Z.
   W. He was a strict and fanatic drillmaster.
   X. The word is always used in a derogatory sense and generally shows resentment and anger on the part of the user.
   Y. It is from the name of this Frenchman that we derive our English word, martinet.
   Z. Jean Martinet was the Inspector-General of Infantry during the reign of King Louis XIV.
   The PROPER order in which these sentences should be placed in a paragraph is:
   A. X, Z, W, Y   B. X, Z, Y, W   C. Z, W, Y, X   D. Z, Y, W, X

   1.____

2. In the following paragraph, the sentences, which are numbered, have been jumbled.
   I. Since then it has undergone changes.
   II. It was incorporated in 1955 under the laws of the State of New York.
   III. Its primary purposes, a cleaner city, has, however, remained the same.
   IV. The Citizens Committee works in cooperation with the Mayor's Inter-departmental Committee for a Clean City.
   The order in which these sentences should be arranged to form a well-organized paragraph is:
   A. II, IV, I, III   B. III, IV, I, II   C. IV, II, I, III   D. IV, III, II, I

   2.____

   3.____

Questions 3-5.

DIRECTIONS: The sentences listed below are part of a meaningful paragraph but they are not given in their proper order. You are to decide what would be the BEST order in which to put the sentences so as to form a well-organized paragraph. Each sentence has a place in the paragraph; there are no extra sentences. You are then to answer Questions 3 through 5 inclusive on the basis of your rearrangements of these scrambled sentences into a properly organized paragraph.

In 1887 some insurance companies organized an Inspection Department to advise their clients on all phases of fire prevention and protection. Probably this has been due to the smaller annual fire losses in Great Britain than in the United States. It tests various fire prevention devices and appliances and determines manufacturing hazards and their safeguards. Fire research began earlier in the United States and is more advanced than in Great Britain. Later they established a laboratory specializing in electrical, mechanical, hydraulic, and chemical fields.

149

3. When the five sentences are arranged in proper order, the paragraph starts with the sentence which begins
    A. "In 1887…"   B. "Probably this…"   C. "It tests…"
    D. "Fire research…"   E. "Later they…"

3.____

4. In the last sentence listed above, "they" refers to
    A. the insurance companies   B. the United States and Great Britain
    C. the Inspection Department   D. clients
    E. technicians

4.____

5. When the above paragraph is properly arranged, it ends with the words
    A. "…and protection."   B. "…the United States."
    C. "…their safeguards."   D. "…in Great Britain."
    E. "…chemical fields."

5.____

KEY (CORRECT ANSWERS)

1. C
2. C
3. D
4. A
5. C

TEST 2

DIRECTIONS: In each of the questions numbered I through V, several sentences are given. For each question, choose as your answer the group of number that represents the MOST logical order of these sentences if they were arranged in paragraph form. *PRINT THE LETTER OF THE CORRECT ANSWER IN THE SPACE AT THE RIGHT.*

1. I. It is established when one shows that the landlord has prevented the tenant's enjoyment of his interest in the property leased.
    II. Constructive eviction is the result of a breach of the covenant of quiet enjoyment implied in all leases.
    III. In some parts of the United States, it is not complete until the tenant vacates within a reasonable time.
    IV. Generally, the acts must be of such serious and permanent character as to deny the tenant the enjoyment of his possessing rights.
    V. In this event, upon abandonment of the premises, the tenant's liability for that ceases.
    The CORRECT answer is:
    A. II, I, IV, III, V
    B. V, II, III, I, IV
    C. IV, III, I, II, V
    D. I, III, V, IV, II

2. I. The powerlessness before private and public authorities that is the typical experience of the slum tenant is reminiscent of the situation of blue-collar workers all through the nineteenth century.
    II. Similarly, in recent years, this chapter of history has been reopened by anti-poverty groups which have attempted to organize slum tenants to enable them to bargain collectively with their landlords about the conditions of their tenancies.
    III. It is familiar history that many of the worker remedied their condition by joining together and presenting their demands collectively.
    IV. Like the workers, tenants are forced by the conditions of modern life into substantial dependence on these who possess great political aid and economic power.
    V. What's more, the very fact of dependence coupled with an absence of education and self-confidence makes them hesitant and unable to stand up for what they need from those in power.
    The CORRECT answer is:
    A. V, IV, I, II, III
    B. II, III, I, V, IV
    C. III, I, V, IV, II
    D. I, IV, V, III, II

3. I. A railroad, for example, when not acting as a common carrier may contract away responsibility for its own negligence.
    II. As to a landlord, however, no decision has been found relating to the legal effect of a clause shifting the statutory duty of repair to the tenant.
    III. The courts have not passed on the validity of clauses relieving the landlord of this duty and liability.
    IV. They have, however, upheld the validity of exculpatory clauses in other types of contracts.

V. Housing regulations impose a duty upon the landlord to maintain leased premises in safe condition.
VI. As another example, a bailee may limit his liability except for gross negligence, willful acts, or fraud.

The CORRECT answer is:
A. II, I, VI, IV, III, V
B. I, III, IV, V, VI, II
C. III, V, I, IV, II, VI
D. V, III, IV, I, VI, II

4. I. Since there are only samples in the building, retail or consumer sales are generally eschewed by mart occupants, and in some instances, rigid controls are maintained to limit entrance to the mart only to those persons engaged in retailing.
    II. Since World War I, in many larger cities, there has developed a new type of property, called the mart building.
    III. It can, therefore, be used by wholesalers and jobbers for the display of sample merchandise.
    IV. This type of building is most frequently a multi-storied, finished interior property which is a cross between a retail arcade and a loft building.
    V. This limitation enables the mart occupants to ship the orders from another location after the retailer or dealer makes his selection from the samples.

    The CORRECT answer is:
    A. II, IV, III, I, V
    B. IV, III, V, I, II
    C. I, III, II, IV, V
    D. I, IV, II, III, V

5. I. In general, staff-line friction reduces the distinctive contribution of staff personnel.
    II. The conflicts, however, introduce an uncontrolled element into the managerial system.
    III. On the other hand, the natural resistance of the line to staff innovations probably usefully restrains over-eager efforts to apply untested procedures on a large scale.
    IV. Under such conditions, it is difficult to know when valuable ideas are being sacrificed.
    V. The relatively weak position of staff, requiring accommodation to the line, tends to restrict their ability to engage in free, experimental innovation.

    The CORRECT answer is:
    A. IV, II, III, I, V
    B. I, V, III, II, IV
    C. V, III, I, II, IV
    D. II, I, IV, V, III

KEY (CORRECT ANSWERS)

1. A
2. D
3. D
4. A
5. B

TEST 3

DIRECTIONS: Questions 1 through 4 consist of six sentences which can be arranged in a logical sequence. For each question, select the choice which places the numbered sentences in the MOST logical sequent. *PRINT THE LETTER OF THE CORRECT ANSWER IN THE SPACE AT THE RIGHT.*

1.
   I. The burden of proof as to each issue is determined before trial and remains upon the same party throughout the trial.
   II. The jury is at liberty to believe one witness' testimony as against a number of contradictory witnesses.
   III. In a civil case, the party bearing the burden of proof is required to prove his contention by a fair preponderance of the evidence.
   IV. However, it must be noted that a fair preponderance of evidence does not necessarily mean a greater number of witnesses.
   V. The burden of proof is the burden which rests upon one of the parties to an action to persuade the trier of the facts, generally the jury, that a proposition he asserts is true.
   VI. If the evidence is equally balanced, or if it leaves the jury in such doubt as to be unable to decide the controversy either way, judgment must be given against the party upon whom the burden of proof rests.

   The CORRECT answer is:
   A. III, II, V, IV, I, VI B. I, II, VI, V, III, IV
   C. III, IV, V, I, II, VI D. V, I, III, VI, IV, II

   1._____

2.
   I. If a parent is without assets and is unemployed, he cannot be convicted of the crime of non-support of a child.
   II. The term "sufficient ability" has been held to mean sufficient financial ability.
   III. It does not matter if his unemployment is by choice or unavoidable circumstances.
   IV. If he fails to take any steps at all, he may be liable to prosecution for endangering the welfare of a child.
   V. Under the penal law, a parent is responsible for the support of his minor child only if the parent is "of sufficient ability."
   VI. An indigent parent may meet his obligation by borrowing money or by seeking aid under the provisions of the Social Welfare Law.

   The CORRECT answer is:
   A. VI, I, V, III, II, IV B. I, III, V, II, IV, VI
   C. V, II, I, III, VI, IV D. I, VI, IV, V, II, III

   2._____

3.
   I. Consider, for example, the case of a rabble rouser who urges a group of twenty people to go out and break the windows of a nearby factory.
   II. Therefore, the law fills the indicated gap with the crime of inciting to riot.
   III. A person is considered guilty of inciting to riot when he urges ten or more persons to engage in tumultuous and violent conduct of a kind likely to create public alarm.
   IV. However, if he has not obtained the cooperation of at least four people, he cannot be charged with unlawful assembly.

   3._____

153

V. The charge of inciting to riot was added to the law to cover types of conduct which cannot be classified as either the crime of "riot" or the crime of "unlawful assembly."
VI. If he acquires the acquiescence of at least four of them, he is guilty of unlawful assembly even if the project does not materialize.

The CORRECT answer is:
A. III, V, I, VI, IV, II
B. V, I, IV, VI, II, III
C. III, IV, I, V, II, VI
D. V, I, IV, VI, III, II

4.
I. If, however, the rebuttal evidence presents an issue of credibility, it is for the jury to determine whether the presumption has, in fact, been destroyed.
II. Once sufficient evidence to the contrary is introduced, the presumption disappears from the trial.
III. The effect of a presumption is to place the burden upon the adversary to come forward with evidence to rebut the presumption.
IV. When a presumption is overcome and ceases to exist in the case, the fact or facts which gave rise to the presumption still remain.
V. Whether a presumption has been overcome is ordinarily a question for the court.
VI. Such information may furnish a basis for a logical inference.

The CORRECT answer is:
A. IV, VI, II, V, I, III
B. III, II, V, I, IV, VI
C. V, III, VI, IV, II, I
D. V, IV, I, II, VI, III

4.____

KEY (CORRECT ANSWERS)

1. D
2. C
3. A
4. B

EXAMINATION SECTION
TEST 1

DIRECTIONS: The sentences that follow are in scrambled order You are to rearrange them in proper order and indicate the letter choice containing the correct answer. *PRINT THE LETTER OF THE CORRECT ANSWER IN THE SPACE AT THE RIGHT.*

PARAGRAPH REARRANGEMENT

The following questions deal with paragraph rearrangement. Read the listed sentences and then select the suggested answer which MOST CORRECTLY indicates the proper continuity of sentences.

1.
   1. One of the main benefits of the conference procedure is that those who are performing the actual operation can be given an opportunity to participate in making the decisions which affect them.
   2. They will usually respond more favorably when given this opportunity.
   3. Consultation between management and the members of an organization wherein employees share in the decision-making process will enhance morale and give employees a special feeling of status.
   4. The conference is particularly valuable when used by supervisors as a means of sharing information and experiences with subordinates and learning of their needs and desires.

   A. 2-1-4-3
   B. 1-2-3-4
   C. 2-4-1-3
   D. 4-3-2-1

   1.____

2.
   1. It is highly desirable that he be occupationally competent to perform the task he expects his subordinates to learn about; but having technical proficiency does not insure that he can impart it to others.
   2. Rather, the technically competent supervisor who is also a good teacher will achieve a high degree of success in the training function because one ability will complement the other.
   3. Often a lack of competency or a failure on the part of the supervisor to prepare himself for his training role is the cause of his teaching ineffectiveness.
   4. It would be erroneous to assume that just because an individual is an excellent burglary investigator, he can effectively teach others how to catch burglars.

   A. 4-1-3-2
   B. 2-3-1-4
   C. 3-1-4-2
   D. 2-3-4-1

   2.____

3.
   1. The true importance usually lies somewhere between these two diverse evaluations.
   2. Its determination is an important step in providing well-rounded police service.
   3. Policy decisions must be made about the extent of patrol participation in the performance of all tasks in the fields covered by special units.
   4. When the importance of a special task is evaluated differently by the patrol division and the specialized division, the effort spent by patrol in its performance is likely to be less than the specialists think it should be.
   5. As the range between the evaluations is diminished, the advantages of having the tasks performed by the members of the special divisions are lessened.

   A. 3-4-1-2-5
   B. 1-4-3-5-2
   C. 2-5-4-3-1
   D. 4-2-3-1-5

   3.____

155

4.
1. In some instances such action may be desirable, but the indiscriminate transfer of the most capable personnel from patrol to special units jeopardizes effective patrol service.
2. Not only are men drawn from patrol, but generally the most competent are taken in the creation of specialized units.
3. Police manpower is limited, and increased specialization usually results in a diminished patrol.
4. Although patrol is essential to effective police service, some specialization also is essential, and present evidence indicates a continuance of the marked trend of the past two decades toward specialization.

A. 1-2-3-4 B. 2-1-4-3
C. 3-4-1-2 D. 4-3-2-1

5.
1. He is a roving eity-hall information and complaint counter for the distressed citizen, disgruntled by the inconvenience of trips to the city hall, unsatisfactory telephone calls, and sometimes apparent lack of attention to his complaints.
2. The consonant availability and mobility of the patrolman make his services useful to other city departments, and he improves both public and inter-department relationships by attending more immediately to citizen needs.
3. The patrolman is the ultimate in the decentralization of municipal service.
4. The extent to which patrol officers will provide extra police services is determined by the chief executive of the city and his department heads.

A. 1-3-2-4 B. 4-1-3-2
C. 2-4-1-3 D. 3-1-2-4

6.
1. For one thing, despite the objections of the administration and most business leaders, we must move to a shorter work week or work year, combined, if desired, with multiple shift operations.
2. If the national goal is to minimize technological displacement and unemployment without going back to horse-and-buggy production methods, then a variety of possible policies would achieve optimum employment.
3. For another, young people should be required to stay in school longer.
4. This would keep more people employed and would prevent expensive equipment from standing idle.
5. This requirement, combined with an earlier retirement age, would cut persons off from both ends of the labor force, thereby reducing the number of job seekers.

A. 2-1-4-3-5 B. 2-1-4-5-3
C. 3-1-5-2-4 D. 2-1-5-4-3

7.
1. Overly severe or excessively lenient penalties may cause a reaction from employees just opposite to that intended by the supervisor.
2. In neither case will the punishment accomplish what it should.
3. Such penalties may make the recipient a martyr or indicate that management considers the dereliction inconsequential.
4. Rather, it may set a dangerous precedent which may tend to "bindn management to an indesirable course of action in the future.

A. 1-3-2-4 B. 1-2-3-4
C. 1-4-2-3 D. 2-1-3-4

8. 1. Many of the personal traits supervisors are called upon to evaluate cannot be measured by precise tests.
    2. Extreme difficulties are encountered in trying to compare the performance of the detective with that of the jailor, or the performance of the patrol officer with that of the staff officer.
    3. Rating systems are inherently subjective since they involve a personal audit by one person of another's conduct or performance.
    4. One of the inherently difficult problems in the police service is that of fairly comparing persons assigned to widely different tasks.

    A. 4-2-1-3   B. 4-1-2-3
    C. 3-1-4-2   D. 3-4-2-1

9. 1. Procedures should be standardized so that all raters may perform their tasks uniformly.
    2. Employees may be ranked, they may be rated on the basis of a comparison with selected employees, or in comparison with the ideal employee, or they may be rated on a numerical basis.
    3. He should be made conscious of the difference between ability and performance.
    4. One of the biggest problems in performance evaluations is the selection of a rating method which will yield reliable results.
    5. Whatever standards the supervisor is expected to use as guides in interpreting the performance norms of his subordinates should be clearly defined.

    A. 4-3-2-1-5   B. 1-2-4-3-5
    C. 4-2-5-3-1   D. 5-3-1-2-4

10. 1. It is the type of police behavior that is most objectionable to citizens.
    2. Police decision making is complex enough in cases where discretion is authorized, let alone in situations where discretion is not authorized.
    3. This leads to judgments that are of questionable validity and provides a controversial basis for subsequent actions.
    4. In reacting to perceived dangers and to threats to their authority, policemen often rely on stereotypic symbolic assailants and other perceptual traits of suspiciousness.

    A. 1-3-4-2   B. 2-4-3-1
    C. 3-1-4-2   D. 2-4-3-1

11. 1. All of the councils have been active on an informal basis in promoting interjurisdictional agreements.
    2. A council of governments, with a committee on law enforcement, can be an effective vehicle in metropolitan areas for promoting consolidation or cooperation in law enforcement activities.
    3. It is a simple step to include law enforcement as part of a council's total program.
    4. Four of the councils are now engaged in negotiating cooperative agreements among member units, and three also mediate disputes.

    A. 3-2-1-4   B. 2-4-1-3
    C. 1-2-4-3   D. 4-3-1-2

12. 1. However, in their attempts to uncover basic feelings regarding these factors, the researcher found that direct questions designed to find out how the subjects felt about specific aspects of their jobs resulted in superficial, "lifeless" answers.
    2. These studies were primarily concerned with the determinants of morale and productivity.
    3. Management first became aware of the value of interviewing in industrial relations during the 1930's as a consequence of studies conducted at the Hawthorne plant of the Western Electric Company.
    4. Even worse - or so it seemed at the time - instead of giving "straightforward" responses, some of the people interviewed tended to talk about what interested them most at the moment.

    A. 2-1-4-3   B. 3-2-1-4
    C. 1-2-3-4   D. 3-2-4-1

13. 1. Provision should be made for use of the system by Federal and regional law enforcement agencies, but parallel or duplicatory systems should be avoided unless for specific backup purposes.
    2. It is intended to complement, not to replace, local and State systems.
    3. The National system should be a coordinating mechanism that will further the exchange of information of mutual concern among smaller, independent but coordinated systems.
    4. The concept of the National Crime Information Center (NCIC) is clear.

    A. 4-2-3-1   B. 2-4-1-3
    C. 2-3-1-4   D. 3-2-4-1

14. 1. Traditionally, purchasing was primarily conducted on a departmental basis with little or no centralized purchasing for the jurisdiction.
    2. Purchasing is an activity undertaken by every public jurisdiction, large or small.
    3. The cities of Chicago, Cincinnati, and Milwaukee are in the forefront of this type of buying.
    4. More recently, however, governments, and especially the larger jurisdictions, are abandoning departmental in favor of centralized purchasing.

    A. 2-1-4-3   B. 1-2-3-4
    C. 3-2-1-4   D. 1-4-3-2

15. 1. These "qualities" are really a state of mind.
    2. They exist or are possessed by people who have their heads turned a special way.
    3. We all understand that "ethics and professionalism" do not come in a can or jar.
    4. You cannot order a supply for your department.

    A. 1-3-4-2   B. 3-1-2-4
    C. 3-4-1-2   D. 2-3-1-4

16.
1. This suggests to us that the greater stress lies upon the anvil and not the hammer.
2. It has been written that "Every man who strikes blows for power, for influence, for right, must be just as good an anvil as he is a hammer."
3. Here lies the greater stress.
4. But one does not stand reasonless before an anvil and strike it with a hammer.
5. Between the hammer and the anvil we always find an object which is being beaten, pulled, pursuaded, and shaped—at the mercy of both.

A. 1-3-5-2-4   B. 2-1-4-5-3
C. 2-4-5-3-1   D. 2-5-4-1-3

17.
1. The complaint is not centered in the community, but in the emotional context of the family, thus making an objective analysis of the situation very difficult.
2. Not only are the youth and his parents at the peak of escalated emotions, but the issue of ungovernability, by its very nature, is difficult to define and treat.
3. No more challenging situation exists then investigating a complaint of ungovernability.
4. While truly delinquent acts committed in the community can frequently be determined through the accounts of victims and witnesses, such is not the case with ungovernability.

A. 3-2-4-1   B. 3-4-1-2
C. 4-3-2-1   D. 2-1-4-3

18.
1. The private security sector must be sure thai its personnel are of the highest caliber and that their training is the very best that can be produced with available resources.
2. Certain responsibilities face both law enforcement and the private security sector in providing public safety.
3. Complacency can be more devastating than overzealousness.
4. In addition, the private security sector must be constantly aware that it cannot become lethargic to the point of letting its guard drop.

A. 1-2-3-4   B. 2-1-4-3
C. 2-3-4-1   D. 2-4-1-3

19.
1. This important service makes private security a natural ally of the police and a formidable foe of the criminal.
2. Together they can fashion a program which will foster public understanding and enlist public assistance in combating crime.
3. Both police and private security stand to gain, but more importantly, the public stands to gain the most.
4. The business of the private security sector is not only to sell safety and security but to educate people in the many ways they can protect themselves.

A. 2-1-3-4   B. 4-2-1-3
C. 4-1-2-3   D. 4-3-2-1

20.
1. But these mistakes do not change the economic nature of business.
2. Many private, public or institutional organizations to not plan, design, and manage positions on an economical or efficient basis.
3. However, the fact that some organizations manage more efficiently than others does not conflict with the thesis that positions are creatures of economic need.
4. Poorly made decisions on the number and kinds of positions will surely result in losses and inefficient use of funds that might better be used elsewhere.
5. A business management may make poor investments, it may create too many positions, it may not sell its product, it may tolerate high production costs.

A. 1-4-3-5-2
B. 2-3-5-1-4
C. 3-2-5-1-4
D. 1-2-3-4-5

21.
1. The search for release from stress may result in alcohol or chemical abuse, domestic or financial problems, illness, and sometimes suicide.
2. Long exposure to police work creates physical and mental stress on its practitioners.
3. For others, proper supervision and evaluations will identify potential problem areas in handling stress before adverse conditions take their toll.
4. In a small minority, the inability to cope manifests itself in poor job performance, disability or even death.
5. In the ideal, the strain is routinely handled by the officer who meets the demands of law enforcement and achieves the personal satisfaction associated with public service.

A. 1-5-2-3-4
B. 2-5-3-4-1
C. 1-2-5-3-4
D. 2-5-4-3-1

22.
1. Obviously, it benefits the user to have instructions on how to use an item correctly and how to avoid improper use.
2. Proper labeling serves many purposes, including product identification.
3. Similarly, labels often contain detailed information on how to maintain or care for a product.
4. Another purpose of labeling is to lessen the likelihood of product liability on the part of the manufacturer, and, in the case of police use, on the part of the department that issues an item of equipment to its officers for field use.
5. In some cases, the lable may contain shelf-life data that states a date beyond which the product should not be used, or can be expected to degrade as a consequence of aging.

A. 2-1-3-4-5
B. 2-4-5-1-3
C. 2-1-5-3-4
D. 2-1-3-5-4

23.
1. The same is true for those officers who routinely operate speed-measuring radar devices.
2. Each year, law enforcement equipment becomes more complex as the result of technological developments.
3. Consider the widespread use of mobile communication systems.
4. The very nature of this technology causes potential liability problems.
5. Several police departments have had questions raised by their officers as to whether the transmitted signal is a potentional health hazard.

A. 2-4-3-5-1
B. 5-4-3-2-1
C. 2-3-4-5-1
D. 2-4-5-3-1

24.
1. Terrorists generally do not have criminal records, and their motivation is typically political.
2. Combating terrorism is perhaps the most difficult task facing law enforcement.
3. They are organized in small cells and therefore are not as vulnerable to the use of informants and undercover agents.
4. Generally speaking, there has been a downtrend since the late 1970's.
5. Notwithstanding these problems, we have made progress against terrorists and the number of incidents last year was down from 1982's total.

   A. 2-3-1-5-4 B. 1-2-3-5-4
   C. 2-1-3-5-4 D. 1-3-2-5-4

25.
1. It is not uncommon for officers to gather at the corner bar when their shift is over to unwind, drink a few beers, and review the events of the day.
2. In many departments, these activities are the basis for the strong personal bonds that build trust and reliance among colleagues.
3. Unfortunately, they may also be the basis for the beginning stages of alcoholism for that percentage of officers who are either physiologically or psychologically prone to the disease.
4. Both public and law enforcement professionals tend to share a belief that police officers abuse alcohol to a greater extent than the population as a whole.
5. While surveys indicate that this is not true, it has been suggested that police social customs foster regular alcohol consumption.

   A. 1-4-5-2-3 B. 4-5-1-2-3
   C. 1-3-5-4-2 D. 4-5-2-1-3

26.
1. This approach to mental measurement fell out of favor when it became apparent that there was no correlation between performance on the tests and actual scholastic achievement.
2. The work of Alfred Binet in France suggested that questions tapping reasoning skills and general knowledge provided a more direct means of measuring intelligence.
3. With the development of mental tests, the variability hypothesis began to serve not as an explanation for women's inferior social position but as a justification for it.
4. The strength of a student's grip could not predict the student's grades in mathematics.
5. Tests conducted by Francis Galton had been based on the assumption that measurement of sensory and motor capacities could provide an estimate of intellectual functioning, and supported this assumption of women's inferiority.

   A. 2-3-1-4-5 B. 5-3-1-4-2
   C. 5-1-3-4-2 D. 3-5-1-4-2

27.
1. Only because of the rapidity of the enzyme's action can the carbon dioxide be freed fast enough from its compounds to leave the blood during that moment in the alveolus when it is separated from the air by the thinnest of membranes.
2. The result is that each is broken into one water and one carbon dioxide molecule.
3. Our ability to rid ourselves of CO_2 through the exhaled air is then utterly dependent on the presence of these critically located atoms of zinc.
4. During the one second that the blood is racing through the tiny capillaries of the lung, the single atom of zinc that is set in the center of the enzyme carbonic anhydrase is brought into contact with 600,000 of its target molecule, carbonic acid.
5. Yet the total amount of this mineral in the body is so little that it was, up until a few years ago, considered to be of no significance.

A. 3-4-5-1-2 B. 1-2-3-4-5
C. 4-2-1-3-5 D. 3-4-5-2-1

28.
1. The wise person realizes that everything everyone wants is already contained within himself or herself, and he or she begins to embody these qualities rather than search for them from others.
2. What we usually don't realize is that everyone has this tendency, and unless one knows himself or herself well, he or she is probably wondering the same things.
3. Everyone is wanting it, but few people have the courage to be the one to give it.
4. Usually when we relate to others, our normal tendency is to think, "I wonder if he or she likes me? I wonder if he or she thinks well of me?"
5. So normally we are hoping for approval from those who are hoping for our approval.

A. 1-2-3-4-5 B. 1-4-5-2-3
C. 4-2-5-3-1 D. 4-5-2-1-3

29.
1. At an earlier point in the process, some pure energy slowed down to a speed below that of light, at which point it congealed into mass; and at some point in the future, should the equilibrium of this stable form of energy be disturbed in any way, it can shed its temporary property called mass and become pure energy once more.
2. The moment its mass disappears, an energy pattern no longer projects a material appearance.
3. The manifestation we know as "matter" is simply one of the attendant effects of this energy's transformation into mass; thus, an object is really more of an event than it is a thing of substance.
4. Every material object, be it our own body, a tree, or a mountain, is essentially just a temporary phase in a dynamic process involving a certain amount of energy.
5. The fact that the mass of any material entity is nothing but a specific quantity of energy indicates that we can no longer look at the world around us as a collection of static objects, for matter is not composed of solid substance, it is in fact made up of dancing patterns of energy.

A. 5-1-3-4-2 B. 5-4-1-3-2
C. 4-2-1-5-3 D. 3-4-5-1-2

30.
1. As people get jobs, or move up from poverty-level to better paying employment, they stop receiving benefits and start paying taxes, decreasing the federal deficit.
2. The strategy of putting people to work in civilian rein-dustrialization - in clean energy development, public transportation and urban reconstruction - would not only provide socially useful products, but would lower social service costs and reduce the deficit as well.
3. Thus job creation programs are often a bargain for taxpayers, if the reductions in the costs of other programs and the increase in tax payments are counted.
4. Only poor or unemployed people are eligible for food stamps, welfare, unemployment compensation, housing subsidies and so on.
5. The best way to cut costs of many social programs is to create jobs.

A. 5-3-4-1-2
B. 2-3-4-1-5
C. 4-5-2-3-1
D. 2-1-3-4-5

30.____

KEY (CORRECT ANSWERS)

1.	B	16.	B
2.	C	17.	A
3.	D	18.	B
4.	D	19.	C
5.	D	20.	B
6.	A	21.	B
7.	A	22.	D
8.	C	23.	A
9.	C	24.	C
10.	B	25.	B
11.	B	26.	D
12.	B	27.	C
13.	A	28.	C
14.	A	29.	B
15.	C	30.	C

EXAMINATION SECTION
TEST 1

DIRECTIONS: he sentences that follow are in scrambled order. You are to rearrange them in proper order and indicate the letter choice containing the correct answer. *PRINT THE LETTER OF THE CORRECT ANSWER IN THE SPACE AT THE RIGHT.*

PARAGRAPH REARRANGEMENT

1.
   1. Nevertheless, management has devoted a good deal of attention to providing adequate ventilation, heat, and light; in general management attempts to insure working conditions that make a work-place physically satisfactory--even attractive.
   2. The objects of these needs include such things as food, drink, shelter, rent and exercise.
   3. Our society is sufficiently prosperous, however, so that the minimum physiological requirements are usually met.
   4. All human beings have needs that pertain to survival and physiological maintenance of the body.
   5. Until such needs are reasonably well satisfied, they are strong, driving forces.

   A. 4-2-5-3-1 B. 4-1-3-5-2
   C. 3-4-1-2-5 D. 3-5-2-1-4

2.
   1. As in direct-line relationships, a staff man probably consults with whomever he gives instructions to, and the man receiving the instructions may point out difficulties in execution to the staff man and to the line boss
   2. The most extreme formal technique for extending staff influence is the granting of functional authority.
   3. This means that a staff man can give direct orders to operate personnel in his own name, instead of making recommendations to his boss or to other operating executives.
   4. But until orders are recinded or revised, the company expects the worker to carry them out.
   5. His instructions have the same force as those that come down the chain of command.

   A. 1-3-4-2-5 B. 2-1-4-3-5
   C. 2-3-5-1-4 D. 1-4-5-3-2

3.
   1. Our capacity to rebuild the slums, to eliminate pollution, to give individuals an opportunity for self expression, to raise the standard of living, and to achieve our many other social and personal objectives rests on joint activity.
   2. If individuals or even tribes attempt to be self-sufficient producing their own food, clothing and shelter subsistence is meager at best.
   3. Modern man's aims and aspirations call for unprecedented cooperative effort.
   4. But when men join together in various enterprises, pooling their resources and exchanging their outputs with many other people or enterprises, they grasp the means to flourish.

   A. 4-1-2-3 B. 3-1-2-4
   C. 1-3-4-2 D. 2-4-1-3

4.
1. Rather it is more constructive to list the types of problems in the field and then decide how far we expect a staff man to go in dealing with the problem.
2. We can define the work of a staff man in terms of both the subjects or problems he covers and what he does about them.
3. Unless a staff man, his boss, and everyone he works with understand the scope of his work, his efforts may cause more trouble then help.
4. It is not enough, for example, for us to say that a personnel director should handle staff services in the field of personnel relations.

A. 3-1-4-2 B. 4-3-2-1
C. 1-2-3-4 D. 2-3-4-1

5.
1. These attacks come from a media which has no standards for pre-entry testing, no code of ethics, no educational requirements, and no oath to uphold.
2. Yet we are asked to accept their professionalism.
3. Recently, some members of the national media have taken it upon themselves to recommend changes in the internal management of law enforcement agencies.
4. They have targeted on agencies which require graduate degrees, sworn oaths of office, and adherence to high ethical standards as minimum entry level requirements for the privilege to serve.

A. 3-4-1-2 B. 3-1-4-2
C. 2-3-4-1 D. 3-2-1-4

6.
1. The concept of making optimum use of personnel resources and coordination of the resources is called "team police" approach.
2. Overspecialization, however, is a deterrant to the "team police" approach in larger departments because specialists have a tendency to form elite groups within the organization.
3. All personnel are perceived as having a major contribution to make to the success of the organization.
4. The approach removes all personnel from their nice neat boxes which define specific and limited jobs, tasks, and duties.

A. 1-2-3-4 B. 4-3-2-1
C. 1-4-3-2 D. 1-3-4-2

7.
1. People do not understand how difficult it is to be a police officer.
2. This sentiment is often expressed and deeply felt by many police officers.
3. Yet, for many reasons, such mutual understanding has been hard to achieve.
4. Presumably, better police-public cooperation and accomodation would result if police were better able to communicate with citizens.

A. 1-2-3-4 B. 1-4-3-2
C. 1-2-4-3 D. 4-1-2-3

8. 1. But this is not the case.
    2. People in the work of administering criminal justice tend to see themselves in a profession which is static.
    3. Moreover, we tend to think of the criminal justice system as existing only in our time, and it is only an occasional reflection that makes us realize that we are only living in a small turn of the clock.
    4. We must be made to understand that there has been, is now, and always will be a behavior control system.
    5. Yet, as the present differs from the past, surely we must expect the future to be different also.

    A. 1-3-4-2-5   B. 3-4-1-5-2
    C. 2-3-1-4-5   D. 2-1-3-4-5

8._____

9. 1. A positive public image can help a department recruit and hold good personnel, maintain high morale, and gain public cooperation.
    A. One of the most important positions within a department for achieving these positive results is the uniformed patrol officer.
    B. His contacts with law-abiding citizens within the community may be the only contacts those citizens have with a member of the criminal justice system.
    C. It is necessary, therefore, for him to make a conscious effort to positively influence all those persons with whom he comes in contact during his routine daily activities.

    A. 1-2-3-4   B. 2-3-4-1
    C. 1-4-3-2   D. 4-1-2-3

9._____

10. 1. Such experiments are based on the recognition that typically the only meeting between the private citizen and the police is under circumstances of crises or confrontation where the policeman appears in only one segment of his role, and the citizen himself is likely to be out of character.
    2. Hopefully, the benefits of such exposure will be bilateral.
    3. Frequently, these efforts take the form of observational experiments whereby citizens are invited to observe the officers first hand as they carry out their duties.
    4. Increasing efforts have been made in recent years to overcome the often strained relationship between police officers and citizens.
    5. Whether expressed or not, the intent of experiments involving citizen observation of police work is to display the policeman to the public in a more total perspective.

    A. 1-5-3-4-2   B. 5-3-4-2-1
    C. 4-5-3-1-2   D. 4-3-1-5-2

10._____

11.
1. In recent years, partially as a result of the Women's Movement and law enforcement's shift to a more humanistic attitude and approach, the rape victim is beginning to receive different treatment.
2. These attacks on the criminal justice system have been sufficiently justified to result in the creation of new programs by law enforcement, and the passage of new laws by legislatures.
3. However, victims are starting to make their needs known, and the mistreatment they claim to have sometimes received from law enforcement and the criminal justice system has been chronicled by mass media.
4. At present, rape is the least reported and least punished of all felonies, with an estimated 70% to 90% of all rape cases going unreported.

A. 1-2-3-4
B. 1-4-3-2
C. 4-1-3-2
D. 1-3-4-2

12.
1. No one can be prepared for the psychological upheavals that may result.
2. Rape is a very traumatic experience.
3. However, many rape victims do experience some general reactions.
4. Law enforcement officers who deal with these victims should recognize and be aware of these reactions.

A. 2-4-3-1
B. 2-1-3-4
C. 4-2-1-3
D. 1-2-3-4

13.
1. One of the most common reactions to a forcible rape is an acute phase of disruption.
2. The victim seems completely out of control.
3. After this initial acute phase, there is a long term process wherein she attempts to re-integrate her disrupted life style.
4. During this re-integration period, it often appears that the woman has regained her equilibrium, but she has not.
5. The final phase is another period of adjustment when the woman's final level of equilibrium is reached.

A. 1-2-3-4-5
B. 4-3-2-1-5
C. 1-3-2-4-5
D. 3-2-1-4-5

14.
1. The average police department is too ingrown, too stagnant, to undertake this kind of vigorous, sweeping action.
2. For the development of truly efficient police forces, organized along functional lines requires the creation of new governmental structures; such an endeavor lies outside either the scope or the competence of the police.
3. No matter what new models for the reform and reorganization of the police function are chosen, it is hardly realistic to expect that the initiative for these moves are to come solely, or perhaps even mainly, from within the police forces themselves.
4. Nor, in a sense, is it fair to place the whole burden of reform on the shoulders of the police.

A. 3-1-4-2
B. 4-2-1-3
C. 3-2-4-1
D. 1-2-3-4

15.
1. These new technologies have had both positive and negative consequences, and for many of them, it has not yet even been possible to assess their consequences.
2. The twentieth century has witnessed an explosion of technologies as knowledge which has multiplied itself several times over.
3. This has been an ever quickening cycle which has led man into entirely new dimensions of existence.
4. Added knowledge has enhanced technological capacities, and the advancing technologies have then contributed to the expanded existence of knowledge.

A. 4-1-3-2
B. 3-1-4-2
C. 2-4-3-1
D. 1-3-4-2

16.
1. This information, together with consideration of such factors as street design, degree of congestion, and natural barriers which might interfere with the assistance available from other police units, helps in determining the proper areas and times for one- or two-man patrol units.
2. Two-man cars are assigned to those areas and those periods of time where and when the frequency and nature of police activity justifies their use.
3. Consideration is given to the number of situations in which more than one person is arrested at a time; to the number of arrests involving resistance; and to the number of arrests involving the use of weapons.
4. The number of these incidents usually bears a direct relationship to the number of assaults, disturbances, and other acts of violence in a given area.
5. Also, the frequency of calls for police service will influence the decision to assign a two-man car.

A. 4-2-1-3-5
B. 2-3-4-5-1
C. 5-1-3-2-4
D. 3-4-5-2-1

17.
1. There is a little police officer in most everyone, which should be exploited by the police officer to the benefit of all.
2. The goal is to create the illusion that the witness and police officer are "working this case together as a team," while in reality the officer elicits the information he needs to pursue the investigation.
3. A good interview technique to use with eyewitnesses at a crime scene is to make them feel that they are active participants in the investigation.
4. Extreme formality should be avoided as it usually creates a barrier to effective communication.

A. 4-1-3-2
B. 2-3-4-1
C. 3-4-2-1
D. 3-1-4-2

18.
1. Moreover, a person feels immediately the rewards or punishments of his group, whereas benefits provided by a company for following its plan are usually more remote.
2. If he deviates too far from group standards, other members may no longer want to associate with him and may treat him as though he were at least an oddball, if not a traitor.
3. Such treatment is unpleasant even for those people who can move into other social groups.
4. The pressure of a group on its members can be substantial, for an individual gets many of his satisfactions in his job through group responses.

A. 4-2-3-1
B. 3-1-4-2
C. 2-1-3-4
D. 1-3-4-2

19.
1. So, before we examine various means for engendering cooperation, the characteristics of a wholesome boss-subordinate relationship should be made clear.
2. The need to build voluntary cooperation, instead of relying on power, calls for a fundamental shift in the way we think about leadership.
3. Empathetic understanding, ego support, and provision of opportunities become central concepts.
4. As we move away from power the nature of the interaction between boss and subordinate changes sharply.

   A. 1-4-3-2
   B. 2-4-3-1
   C. 3-1-2-4
   D. 4-1-2-3

20.
1. In simple situations, a supervisor watches work while it is being done.
2. Each time a supervisor delegates work to a subordinate, he creates the problem of knowing whether the work is performed satisfactorily, and so delegating inevitably raises the question of control.
3. For if a manager attempts to control the decisions of his subordinate, does he not repudiate his earlier delegation of planning?
4. Then, when a large part of planning as well as operating is delegated, new complications are added.
5. But when the delegated work increases, control by direct observations no longer remains possible.

   A. 4-3-5-2-1
   B. 2-5-4-3-1
   C. 2-1-5-4-3
   D. 1-3-5-2-4

21.
1. New medical research appears to strongly support this claim.
2. These products include such items as bread that is partly made of sawdust, and breakfast cereals that are 85% sugar.
3. Yet people persist in putting every imaginable type of "food product" into their bodies.
4. Anthropologists have found that the phrase "you are what you eat" has existed for years in many cultures around the globe.

   A. 4-1-3-2
   B. 3-2-1-4
   C. 4-3-2-1
   D. 1-3-2-4

22.
1. Por instance, plane fare is usually higher than bus or train fare, but one would probably incur fewer food and lodging expenses.
2. One should consider not only the actual cost of the different modes of transportation, but also the amount of time required to reach one's destination.
3. Thus, the overall cost of a long trip might be minimized by using the more expensive means of transportation.
4. Business travel should be accomplished in the most economical way.

   A. 1-2-3-4
   B. 4-2-1-3
   C. 4-1-3-2
   D. 2-4-3-1

23.
1. When these factors seem too overwhelming, "burnout" is the result.
2. Several factors might be involved.
3. "Burnout" describes a need to escape from a work situation because the job is consuming too much of one's energy and life.
4. Lack of clarity around organizational and personal goals, uncertainty of rewards, lack of job security, lack of organizational and personal processes for saying "no," and poor work habits all can contribute to an unsatisfying job situation.

A. 3-2-4-1
B. 2-3-4-1
C. 3-4-2-1
D. 1-3-4-2

24.
1. During the strike the workers received assistance from the IWW and financial support from outside sympathizers, such as Helen Keller.
2. In protest, the workers in the town struck the mills.
3. In 1912, textile operators responded to protective labor legislation that reduced the hours women could legally work by cutting wages.
4. The state's subsequent investigation of living and working conditions resulted in a report which touched on considerations central to an understanding of women as workers and strike leaders.

A. 3-4-1-2
B. 3-2-1-4
C. 3-1-4-2
D. 4-2-1-3

25.
1. Exposure to low doses of ionizing radiation can cause cancer twelve to forty years later and genetic disease and abnormalities in future generations.
2. Radiation harms human bodies by ionizing or altering the electrical charge of atoms and molecules that comprise the body's cells.
3. Even the smallest dose can affect us because the effects of radiation are cumulative.
4. Thus, there is no safe level of radiation.

A. 3-4-1-2
B. 2-4-1-3
C. 2-4-3-1
D. 2-3-1-4

KEY (CORRECT ANSWERS)

1. A
2. C
3. B
4. D
5. A

6. D
7. C
8. D
9. A
10. C

11. B
12. B
13. A
14. A
15. C

16. B
17. D
18. A
19. B
20. C

21. A
22. B
23. A
24. B
25. D

EXAMINATION SECTION
TEST 1

DIRECTIONS: The sentences that follow are in scrambled order. You are to rearrange them in proper order and indicate the letter choice containing the correct answer.
PRINT THE LETTER OF THE CORRECT ANSWER IN THE SPACE AT THE RIGHT.

PARAGRAPH REARRANGEMENT

1. 1. The more you know about the man, the better you will understand his ways and the more tolerant you will be of him.
    2. We fear and make up stories about things and people we do not know.
    3. Generally it can be said that prejudices are based on ignorance and superstition.
    4. Ignorance of the next man's ways, his culture, his beliefs, forces us to fill the gaps between our knowledge with absurd ideas.

    A. 1-3-2-4　　　　B. 2-4-3-1
    C. 3-2-4-1　　　　D. 4-2-1-3

2. 1. If he deviates too far from group standards, other members may no longer want to associate with him and may treat him as though he were at least an oddball, if not a traitor.
    2. Moreover, a person feels immediately the rewards or punishments of his group, whereas benefits provided by a company for following its plan are usually more remote.
    3. Such treatment is unpleasant even for those people who can move into other social groups.
    4. The pressure of a group on its members can be substantial, because an individual gets many of his satisfactions in his job through peer group responses.

    A. 2-3-4-1　　　　B. 3-4-1-2
    C. 4-2-1-3　　　　D. 4-1-3-2

3. 1. Procedural modification is needed to protect officers from unnecessary physical danger and charges of impropriety.
    2. Most standard search practices are based on the assumption that both the arresting officer and the prisoner are males.
    3. Slight modification to standard procedures must be made when an officer, either male or female, searches a prisoner of the opposite sex.
    4. With the phenomenal increase in both the number of women entering the law enforcement profession and the number of women turning to crime, there is a need to develop procedures that specifically apply to situations where the arrestees are of the opposite sex of the officers.

    A. 3-1-4-2　　　　B. 4-2-3-1
    C. 1-3-2-4　　　　D. 2-1-4-3

4.
1. But this is not the case.
2. People in the work of administering criminal justice tend to see themselves in a profession which is static.
3. Moreover, we tend to think of the criminal justice system as existing only in our time, and it is only an occasional reflection that makes us realize that we are only living in a small turn of the clock.
4. We must be made to understand that there has been, is now, and always will be a behavior control system.
5. Yet, as the present differs from the past, surely we must expect the future to be different also.

A. 1-3-4-2-5   B. 3-4-1-5-2
C. 2-3-1-4-5   D. 2-1-3-4-5

5.
1. A positive public image can help a department recruit and hold good personnel, maintain high morale, and gain public cooperation.
2. One of the most important positions within a department for achieving these positive results is the uniformed patrol officer.
3. His contacts with law-abiding citizens within the community may be the only contacts those citizens have with a member of the criminal justice system.
4. It is necessary, therefore, for him to make a conscious effort to positively influence all those persons with whom he comes in contact with during his routine daily activities

A. 1-2-3-4   B. 2-3-4-1
C. 1-4-3-2   D. 4-1-2-3

6.
1. Such experiments are based on the recognition that typically the only meeting between the private citizen and the police is under circumstances of crises or confrontation where the policeman appears in only one segment of his role, and the citizen himself is likely to be out of character.
2. Hopefully, the benefits of such exposure will be bi-lateral.
3. Frequently, these efforts take the form of observational experiments, whereby citizens are invited to observe the officers first hand as they carry out their duties.
4. Increasing efforts have been made in recent years to overcome the often strained relationship between police officers and citizens.
5. Whether expressed or not, the intent of experiments involving citizen observation of police work is to display the policeman to the public in a more total perspective.

A. 1-5-3-4-2   B. 5-3-4-2-1
C. 4-5-3-1-2   D. 4-3-1-5-2

7.
1. These attacks come from a media which has no standards for pre-entry testing, no code of ethics, no educational requirements, and no oath to uphold.
2. Yet we are asked to accept their professionalism.
3. Recently, some members of the national media have taken it upon themselves to recommend changes in the internal management of law enforcement agencies.
4. They have targeted on agencies which require graduate degrees, sworn oaths of office, and adherence to high ethical standards as minimum entry level requirements for the privilege to serve.

A. 3-4-1-2   B. 3-1-4-2
C. 2-3-4-1   D. 3-2-1-4

8. 1. How can he expect his subordinates to continue to regard him as a source of help, when discipline is by nature painful?
   2. This rule draws an analogy between touching a hot stove and undergoing discipline.
   3. Inflicting discipline puts the manager in a dilemma.
   4. When you touch a red-hot stove, your discipline is immediate, with warning, consistent, and impersonal.
   5. Can he impose discipline without generating resentment?
   6. We think so - through what Douglas McGregor called the

   A. 1-3-6-4-2-5 B. 3-1-5-6-2-4
   C. 3-2-5-6-4-1 D. 2-4-6-1-3-5

8._____

9. 1. Morale may be low in a concentration camp, yet production very high.
   2. The term "morale" has been used in different ways; but if morale means the employees' attitude toward the organization as a whole, there is little evidence that high morale leads to high productivity.
   3. Similarly, workers may well be satisfied to "goof off" in a department where the work pace is extremely slow.
   4. Indeed, numerous careful psychological studies show that the relationship between productivity and satisfaction is close to zero.
   5. Just the reverse is true.

   A. 1-4-3-2-5 B. 2-3-4-1-5
   C. 2-5-1-3-4 D. 2-1-3-4-5

9._____

10. 1. Indeed, subordinates often subject a new supervisor to a period of testing and initiation to determine whether he measures up to their standards.
    2. To put it another way, managers will find their authority more easily accepted if they are authorities *on* as well as authorities *over*.
    3. It is important for supervisors to be technically skilled in their work, even if they rarely practice their skill on the job.
    4. If subordinates feel their supervisor is master of skills they themselves regard as important, then in a way he has beaten them in a fair race - he has earned his job and is respected for doing so.

    A. 3-1-4-2 B. 1-2-3-4
    C. 4-2-1-3 D. 3-4-1-2

10._____

11. 1. Business cars have been generating a flow of hundreds of millions of dollars in tax deductions.
    2. In addition, special rules affecting depreciation and investment credit are now effective for all cars placed in service after June 18, 2004.
    3. There are millions of businesses in this country and most of them have at least one business ear.
    4. Effective for 2005 and later, that flow will cease unless the business use of the car is substantiated by records made contemporaneously with the use of the car for business.

    A. 1-2-3-4 B. 3-1-4-2
    C. 3-4-1-2 D. 3-1-2-4

11._____

12.
1. Denial on the part of the officer of the individual's problem and withdrawal or lack of attention or human kindness could literally cause this individual to decide to kill himself.
2. It may also confirm the inmate's feelings that his life is not worth living and that death is the only answer to his problems.
3. The inmate could be desperately searching for a reason to live and seeking help.
4. One of the most important reasons for an officer to be attentive to the emotional needs of a prison inmate is that the inmate may not be suicidal yet.

A. 1-3-2-4 B. 4-1-3-2
C. 4-3-1-2 D. 4-2-1-3

13.
1. Do not be judgmental; always assume a suicidal threat or attempt is of a serious nature.
2. An officer will not endanger a prison inmate's life by discussing his suicidal thoughts.
3. On the contrary, the officer should acknowledge the suicidal thoughts and encourage the inmate to talk about them.
4. All cries for help are genuine and cannot be measured by the apparent seriousness of the threat.

A. 2-3-1-4 B. 2-1-4-3
C. 1-4-2-3 D. 1-2-4-3

14.
1. It is important to note that police officers play an important role in ;dealing with intoxicated persons who may be suicidal.
2. As the realization of his immediate circumstances sets in, the possibility of suicide increases.
3. It is common for depression to set in as the individual begins to sober up.
4. These individuals should be watched carefully and all precautions should be taken if the person is remanded to a precinct cell.

A. 1-4-3-2 B. 4-1-3-2
C. 1-4-2-3 D. 1-3-2-4

15.
1. Alcohol or drug abuse are common denominators often found in suicide victims both in the jail setting and in the general population.
2. Regardless of whether alcohol or drug abuse is seen as the symptom or the disease, it often distorts the individual's perception of reality and may lead to the formation of suicidal thoughts.
3. According to an authoritative source, in one year 65% of the people who comitted suicide were charged with being under the influence and were found dead in their cells a few hours after arrest.
4. In a published statistic, 43% of those committing suicide in county facilities or police cells were known to have a history of drug abuse.

A. 1-2-3-4 B. 1-3-4-2
C. 4-3-1-2 D. 2-3-4-1

16.
1. There is also good reason for careful attention to internal communication.
2. Effective communication with those inside the organization makes for fewer misunderstandings, and fewer disgruntled employees.
3. Harmony within the business carries over into public relations with outsiders.
4. In the area of office communication, primary attention is usually centered upon relations with outsiders -customers, suppliers, and others.

A. 2-3-1-4
B. 4-1-2-3
C. 3-2-1-4
D. 1-3-2-4

16._____

17.
1. The underlying theory of dictation is that it enables the executive to pass on to others his mature judgment on important matters in a minimum of time, leaving him free to exercise executive direction in other phases of management.
2. What are the characteristics of an efficient dictator, an inefficient dictator?
3. How does one go about dictating?
4. Research studies and personal experiences tell us that sometimes only time and effort in practicing good dictation procedure can turn a poor dictator into a good one.

A. 2-1-4-3
B. 4-2-1-3
C. 1-3-4-2
D. 3-2-1-4

17._____

18.
1. A systematic plan for handling the mail will speed up performance of office workers.
2. Regardless of the volume of mail, competent supervision and control are necessary.
3. The provision of facilities for handling mail will depend largely upon the volume to be handled.
4. The number of persons forming the mail-room staff, in turn, varies with the volume of correspondence to be handled and the degree to which mechanical equipment is used.

A. 1-3-4-2
B. 2-1-3-4
C. 3-1-4-2
D. 4-3-2-1

18._____

19.
1. A budget is a plan of financial requirements during a given time period.
2. It necessarily is based upon analysis of the situation which faces the enterprise.
3. It develops a course of action to be followed.
4. The general uses of any budget are those of planning financial needs in advance and providing a basis for controlling current expenditures.

A. 3-2-4-1
B. 4-2-3-1
C. 2-4-3-1
D. 1-2-3-4

19._____

20.
1. The employee has little control over any of them.
2. The cost of the training period and its effectiveness will depend upon the degree to which these conditions are properly controlled by the employer.
3. The conditions under which the employee must learn will materially affect the length of the training period.
4. These conditions can be controlled by the employer.

A. 1-2-4-3
B. 4-2-1-3
C. 3-4-2-1
D. 2-4-3-1

20._____

21.
1. Others prefer questions that reflect how accurately they read.
2. Most test takers, however, would prefer to spend their Saturday morning grocery shopping or even watching cartoons with their children.
3. But some people actually enjoy answering the math questions on exams.
4. Taking promotional examinations is usually an anxiety producing past time.

   A. 2-3-1-4 B. 3-4-2-1
   C. 4-3-1-2 D. 4-1-3-2

21.____

22.
1. For example, a conference on childcare in industry that costs $100 to attend may be inaccessible to childcare workers who earn less that that weekly.
2. Accessibility means more than being able to get in the front door.
3. The structure of an event, the language used, the attitudes represented by the service providers, and the cost also may make an event more of less accessible.
4. Further, nonavailability of childcare at an event may prevent mothers of small children from attending.

   A. 3-2-1-4 B. 2-4-1-3
   C. 3-4-1-2 D. 2-3-1-4

22.____

23.
1. When a historian interprets these records, they reveal much more than simply facts and figures.
2. To discover how ordinary people lived in a community, historians must go beyond the obvious sources and sift through a variety of documents and objects.
3. Social historians today are more concerned with the lives of ordinary people than those of the famous, rich, or powerful.
4. Marriage and birth certificates, deeds, contracts, company logs, military enlistment records, and photographs all can tell a historian a great deal about day-to-day life.

   A. 1-4-2-3 B. 2-4-1-3
   C. 3-2-4-1 D. 2-1-4-3

23.____

24.
1. In spite of this overkill capability, world leaders continue to insist that more weapons are needed.
2. According to recent estimates, there are 40,000 to 50,000 nuclear weapons existing in the world today.
3. To put it differently, it is the equivalent of 13 billion tons of TNT, which is more than three tons for every person on the earth.
4. The combined explosive power of these weapons is equivalent to one million bombs like the one dropped on Hiroshima.

   A. 2-1-3-4 B. 4-1-2-3
   C. 2-4-3-1 D. 2-3-4-1

24.____

25.
1. Western culture has not sufficiently distinguished between assertiveness and aggression.
2. Any show of assertive firmness or anger is often equated with aggression.
3. Women, in particular, are told that their natural, assertive behavior is aggressive and masculine.
4. Thus, many mislabel their own naturally assertive impulses as negative, even disturbed, urges that should be controlled.

   A. 2-1-3-4 B. 1-2-3-4
   C. 1-3-4-2 D. 1-3-2-4

25.____

KEY (CORRECT ANSWERS)

1.	C	11.	B
2.	D	12.	C
3.	B	13.	A
4.	D	14.	A
5.	A	15.	B
6.	D	16.	B
7.	A	17.	D
8.	B	18.	A
9.	C	19.	D
10.	A	20.	C

21. C
22. D
23. C
24. C
25. B

READING COMPREHENSION
UNDERSTANDING AND INTERPRETING
WRITTEN MATERIAL

COMMENTARY

The ability to read and understand written materials—texts, publications, newspapers, orders, directions, expositions—is a skill basic to a functioning democracy and to an efficient business or viable government.

That is why almost all examinations—for beginning, middle, and senior levels—test reading comprehension, directly or indirectly.

The reading test measures how well you understand what you read. This is how it is done: You read a short paragraph and five statements. From the five statements, you choose the one statement, or answer, that is BEST supported by, or best matches, what is said in the paragraph.

SAMPLE QUESTIONS

DIRECTIONS: Each question has five suggested answers, lettered A, B, C, D, and E. Decide which one is the BEST answer. *PRINT THE LETTER OF THE CORRECT ANSWER IN THE SPACE AT THE RIGHT.*

1. The prevention of accidents makes it necessary not only that safety devices be used to guard exposed machinery but also that mechanics be instructed in safety rules which they must follow for their own protection and that the light in the plant be adequate.
   The paragraph BEST supports the statement that industrial accidents
   A. are always avoidable
   B. may be due to ignorance
   C. usually result from inadequate machinery
   D. cannot be entirely overcome
   E. result in damage to machinery

1.____

ANALYSIS

Remember what you have to do:
- First - Read the paragraph
- Second - Decide what the paragraph means
- Third - Read the five suggested answers.
- Fourth - Select the one answer which BEST matches what the paragraph says or is BEST supported by something in the paragraph. (Sometimes you may have to read the paragraph again in order to be sure which suggested answer is best.

This paragraph is talking about three steps that should be taken to prevent industrial accidents
1. Use safety devices on machines
2. Instruct mechanics in safety rules
3. provide adequate lighting

SELECTION

With this in mind, let's look at each suggested answer. Each one starts with "Industrial accidents…"

SUGGESTED ANSWER A
   Industrial accidents (A) are always avoidable.
   (The paragraph talks about how to avoid accidents, but does not say that accidents are always avoidable.)

SUGGESTED ANSWER B
   Industrial accidents (B) may be due to ignorance.
   (One of the steps given in the paragraph to prevent accidents is to instruct mechanics on safety rules. This suggests that lack of knowledge or ignorance of safety rules causes accidents. This suggested answer sounds like a good possibility for being the right answer.)

SUGGESTED ANSWER C
   Industrial accidents (C) usually result from inadequate machinery.
   (The paragraph does suggest that exposed machines cause accidents, but it doesn't say that it is the usual cause of accidents. The word usually makes this a wrong answer.)

SUGGESTED ANSWER D
   Industrial accidents (D) cannot be entirely overcome.
   (You may know from your own experience that this is a true statement. But that is not what the paragraph is talking about. Therefore, it is NOT the correct answer.)

SUGGESTED ANSWER E
   Industrial accidents (E) result in damage to machinery.
   (This is a statement that may or may not be true, but in any case it is NOT covered by the paragraph.)

Looking back, you see that the one suggested answer of the five given that BEST matches what the paragraph says is: Industrial accidents (B) may be due to ignorance.

The CORRECT answer then is B.

Be sure to read ALL the possible answers before you make your choice. You may think that none of the five answers is really good, but choose the BEST one of the five.

---

2. Probably few people realize, as they drive on a concrete road, that steel is used to keep the surface flat in spite of the weight of the busses and trucks. Steel bars, deeply embedded in the concrete, provide sinews to take the stresses so that the stresses cannot crack the slab or make it wavy.
The paragraph BEST supports the statement that a concrete road
   A. is expensive to build
   B. usually cracks under heavy weights
   C. looks like any other road
   D. is used only for heavy traffic
   E. is reinforced with other material

2.____

ANALYSIS

This paragraph is commenting on the fact that
1. few people realize, as they drive on a concrete road, that steel is deeply embedded
2. steel keeps the surface flat
3. steel bars enable the road to take the stresses without cracking or becoming wavy

SELECTION

Now read and think about the possible answers:
   A. A concrete road is expensive to build. (Maybe so but that is not what the paragraph is about.)
   B. A concrete road usually cracks under heavy weights. (The paragraph talks about using steel bars to prevent heavy weights from cracking concrete roads. It says nothing about how usual it is for the roads to crack. The word usually makes this suggested answer wrong.)
   C. A concrete road looks like any other road. (This may or may not be true. The important thing to note is that it has nothing to do with what the paragraph is about.)
   D. A concrete road is used only for heavy traffic. (This answer at least has something to do with the paragraph—concrete roads are used with heavy traffic—but it does not say "used only.")
   E. A concrete road is reinforced with other material. (This choice seems to be the correct one on two counts: First, the paragraph does suggest that concrete roads are made

stronger by embedding steel bars in them. This is another way of saying "concrete roads are reinforced with steel bars." Second, by the process of elimination, the other four choices are ruled out as correct answers simply because they do not apply.)

You can be sure that not all the reading questions will be so easy as these.

HINTS FOR ANSWERING READING QUESTIONS

1. Read the paragraph carefully. Then read each suggested answer carefully. Read every word, because often one word can make the difference between a right and a wrong answer.

2. Choose that answer which is supported in the paragraph itself. Do not choose an answer which is a correct statement unless it is based on information in the paragraph.

3. Even though a suggested answer has many of the words used in the paragraph, it may still be wrong.

4. Look out for words—such as *always, never, entirely,* or *only*—which tend to make a suggested answer wrong.

5. Answer first those questions which you can answer most easily. Then work on the other questions.

6. If you can't figure out the answer to the question, guess.

READING COMPREHENSION
UNDERSTANDING AND INTERPRETING WRITTEN MATERIAL
EXAMINATION SECTION
TEST 1

DIRECTIONS: Each question has five suggested answers, lettered A to E. Decide which one is the BEST answer. *PRINT THE LETTER OF THE CORRECT ANSWER IN THE SPACE AT THE RIGHT.*

1. Some specialists are willing to give their services to the Government entirely free of charge; some feel that a nominal salary, such as will cover traveling expenses, is sufficient for a position that is recognized as being somewhat honorary in nature; many other specialists value their time so highly that they will not devote any of it to public service that does not repay them at a rate commensurate with the fees that they can obtain from a good private clientele.
The paragraph BEST supports the statement that the use of specialists by the Government
    A. is rare because of the high cost of securing such persons
    B. may be influenced by the willingness of specialists to serve
    C. enables them to secure higher salaries in private fields
    D. has become increasingly common during the past few years
    E. always conflicts with private demands for their services

1.____

2. The fact must not be overlooked that only about one-half of the international trade of the world crosses the oceans. The other half is merely exchanges of merchandise between countries lying alongside each other or at least within the same continent.
The paragraph BEST supports the statement that
    A. the most important part of any country's trade is transoceanic
    B. domestic trade is insignificant when compared with foreign trade
    C. the exchange of goods between neighboring countries is not considered international trade
    D. foreign commerce is not necessarily carried on by water
    E. about one-half of the trade of the world is international

2.____

3. Individual differences in mental traits assume importance in fitting workers to jobs because such personal characteristics are persistent and are relatively little influenced by training and experience.
The paragraph BEST supports the statement that training and experience
    A. are limited in their effectiveness in fitting workers to jobs
    B. do not increase a worker's fitness for a job
    C. have no effect upon a person's mental traits
    D. have relatively little effect upon the individual's chances for success
    E. should be based on the mental traits of an individual

3.____

4. The competition of buyers tends to keep prices up, the competition of sellers to send them down. Normally, the pressure of competition among sellers is stronger than that among buyers since the seller has his article to sell and must get rid of it, whereas the buyer is not committed to anything.
The paragraph BEST supports the statement that low prices are caused by
   A. buyer competition
   B. competition of buyers with sellers
   C. fluctuations in demand
   D. greater competition among sellers than among buyers
   E. more sellers than buyers

5. In seventeen states, every lawyer is automatically a member of the American Bar Association. In some other states and localities, truly representative organizations of the Bar have not yet come into being, but are greatly needed.
The paragraph IMPLIES that
   A. representative Bar Associations are necessary in states where they do not now exist
   B. every lawyer is required by law to become a member of the Bar
   C. the Bar Association is a democratic organization
   D. some states have more lawyers than others
   E. every member of the American Bar Association is automatically a lawyer in seventeen states

KEY (CORRECT ANSWERS)

1. B
2. D
3. A
4. D
5. A

TEST 2

DIRECTIONS: Each question has five suggested answers, lettered A to E. Decide which one is the BEST answer. *PRINT THE LETTER OF THE CORRECT ANSWER IN THE SPACE AT THE RIGHT.*

1. We hear a great deal about the new education, and see a great deal of it in action. But the school house, though prodigiously magnified in scale, is still very much the same old school house.
   The paragraph IMPLIES
   A. the old education was, after all, better than the new
   B. although the modern school buildings are larger than the old ones, they have not changed very much in other respects
   C. the old school houses do not fit in with modern educational theories
   D. a fine school building does not make up for poor teachers
   E. schools will be schools

   1.____

2. No two human beings are of the same pattern—not even twins and the method of bringing out the best in each one necessarily according to the nature of the child.
   The paragraph IMPLIES that
   A. individual differences should be considered in dealing with children
   B. twins should be treated impartially
   C. it is an easy matter to determine the special abilities of children
   D. a child's nature varies from year to year
   E. we must discover the general technique of dealing with children

   2.____

3. Man inhabits today a world very different from that which encompassed even his parents and grandparents. It is a world geared to modern machinery—automobiles, airplanes, power plants; it is linked together and served by electricity.
   The paragraph IMPLIES that
   A. the world has no changed much during the last few generations
   B. modern inventions and discoveries have brought about many changes in man's way of living
   C. the world is run more efficiently today than it was in our grandparents' time
   D. man is much happier today than he was a hundred years ago
   E. we must learn to see man as he truly is, underneath the veneers of man's contrivances

   3.____

4. Success in any study depends largely upon the interest taken in that particular subject by the student. This being the case, each teacher earnestly hopes that her students will realize at the vey onset that shorthand can be made an intensely fascinating study.
   The paragraph IMPLIES that
   A. Everyone is interested in shorthand
   B. success in a study is entirely impossible unless the student finds the study very interesting

   4.____

187

C. if a student is eager to study shorthand, he is likely to succeed in it
D. shorthand is necessary for success
E. anyone who is not interested in shorthand will not succeed in business

5. The primary purpose of all business English is to move the reader to agreeable and mutually profitable action. This action may be indirect or direct, but in either case a highly competitive appeal for business should be clothed with incisive diction tending to replace vagueness and doubt with clarity, confidence, and appropriate action.
The paragraph IMPLIES that the
   A. ideal business letter uses words to conform to the reader's language level
   B. business correspondent should strive for conciseness in letter writing
   C. keen competition of today has lessened the value of the letter as an appeal for business
   D. writer of a business letter should employ incisive diction to move the reader to compliant and gainful action
   E. the writer of a business letter should be himself clear, confident, and forceful

5.____

KEY (CORRECT ANSWERS)

1. B
2. A
3. B
4. C
5. D

TEST 3

DIRECTIONS: Each question has five suggested answers, lettered A to E. Decide which one is the BEST answer. *PRINT THE LETTER OF THE CORRECT ANSWER IN THE SPACE AT THE RIGHT.*

1. To serve the community best, a comprehensive city plan must coordinate all physical improvements, even at the possible expense of subordinating individual desires, to the end that a city may grow in a more orderly way and provide adequate facilities for its people
   The paragraph IMPLIES that
   A. city planning provides adequate facilities for recreation
   B. a comprehensive city plan provides the means for a city to grow in a more orderly fashion
   C. individual desires must always be subordinated to civic changes
   D. the only way to serve a community is to adopt a comprehensive city plan
   E. city planning is the most important function of city government

   1.____

2. Facility in writing letters, the knack of putting into these quickly written letters the same personal impression that would mark an interview, and the ability to boil down to a one-page letter the gist of what might be called a five- or ten-minute conversation —all these are essential to effective work under conditions of modern business organization.
   The paragraph IMPLIES that
   A. letters are of more importance in modern business activities than ever before
   B. letters should be used in place of interviews
   C. the ability to write good letters is essential to effective work in modern business organization
   D. business letters should never be more than one page in length
   E. the person who can write a letter with great skill will get ahead more readily than others

   2.____

3. The general rule is that it is the city council which determines the amount to be raised by taxation and which therefore determines, within the law, the tax rates. As has been pointed out, however, no city council or city authority has the power to determine what kind of taxes should be levied.
   The paragraph IMPLIES that
   A. the city council has more authority than any other municipal body
   B. while the city council has a great deal of authority in the levying of taxes, its power is not absolute
   C. the kinds of taxes levied in different cities vary greatly
   D. the city council appoints the tax collectors
   E. the mayor determines the kinds of taxes to be levied

   3.____

4. The growth of modern business has made necessary mass production, mass distribution, and mass selling. As a result, the problems of personnel and industrial relations have increased so rapidly that grave injustice in the handling of personal relationships have frequently occurred. Personnel administration is complex because, as in all human problems, many intangible elements are involved. Therefore a thorough, systematic, and continuous study of the psychology of human behavior is essential to the intelligent handling of personnel.
The paragraph IMPLIES that
   A. complex modern industry makes impossible the personal relationships which formerly existed between employer and employee
   B. mass decisions are successfully applied to personnel problems
   C. the human element in personnel administration makes continuous study necessary to is intelligent application
   D. personnel problems are less important than the problems of mass production and mass distribution
   E. since personnel administration is so complex and costly, it should be subordinated to the needs of good industrial relations

5. The Social Security Act is striving toward the attainment of economic security for the individual and for his family. It was stated, in outlining this program, that security for the individual and for the family concerns itself with three factors: (1) decent homes to live in; (2) development of the natural resources of the country so as to afford the fullest opportunity to engage in productive work; and (3) safeguards against the major misfortunes of life. The Social Security Act is concerned with the third of these factors —"safeguards against misfortunes which cannot be wholly eliminated in this man-made world of ours."
The paragraph IMPLIES that the
   A. Social Security Act is concerned primarily with supplying to families decent homes in which to live
   B. development of natural resources is the only means of offering employment to the masses of the unemployed
   C. Social Security Act has attained absolute economic security for the individual and his family
   D. Social Security Act deals with the first (1) factor as stated in the paragraph above
   E. Social Security Act deals with the third (3) factor as stated in the paragraph above

KEY (CORRECT ANSWERS)

1. B
2. C
3. B
4. C
5. E

TEST 4

DIRECTIONS: Each question has five suggested answers, lettered A to E. Decide which one is the BEST answer. *PRINT THE LETTER OF THE CORRECT ANSWER IN THE SPACE AT THE RIGHT.*

PASSAGE 1

Free unrhymed verse has been practiced for some thousands of years and reaches back to the incantation which linked verse with the ritual dance. It provided a communal emotion; the aim of the cadenced phrases was to create a state of mind. The general coloring of free rhythms in the poetry of today is that of speech rhythm, composed in the sequence of the musical phrase, not in the sequence of the metronome, the regular beat. In the twenties, conventional rhyme fell into almost complete disuse. This liberation from rhyme became as well a liberation of rhyme. Freed of its exacting task of supporting lame verse, it would be applied with greater effect where wanted for some special effect. Such break in the tradition of rhymed verse had the healthy effect of giving it a fresh start, released from the hampering convention of too familiar cadences. This refreshing and subtilizing of the use of rhythm can be seen everywhere in the poetry today.

1. The title below that BEST expresses the ideas of this paragraph is:
   A. Primitive Poetry
   B. The Origin of Poetry
   C. Rhyme and Rhythm in Modern Verse
   D. Classification of Poetry
   E. Purposes in All Poetry

2. Free verse had its origin in primitive
   A. fairytales   B. literature   C. warfare
   D. chants   E. courtship

3. The object of early free verse was to
   A. influence the mood of the people   B. convey ideas
   C. produce mental pictures   D. create pleasing sounds
   E. provide enjoyment

PASSAGE 2

Control of the Mississippi had always been goals of nations having ambitions in the New World. LaSalle claimed it for France in 1682. Iberville appropriated it to France when he colonized Louisiana in 1700. Bienville founded New Orleans, its principal port, as a French city in 1718. The fleur-de-lis were the blazon of the delta country until 1762. Then Spain claimed all of Louisiana. The Spanish were easy neighbors. American products from western Pennsylvania and the Northwest Territory were barged down the Ohio and Mississippi to New Orleans; here they were reloaded on ocean-going vessels that cleared for the great seaports of the world.

4. The title below that BEST expresses the ideas of this paragraph is:
   A. Importance of Seaports
   B. France and Spain in the New World
   C. Early Control of the Mississippi
   D. Claims of European Nations
   E. American Trade on the Mississippi

5. Until 1762, the lower Mississippi area was held by
   A. England   B. Spain   C. the United States
   D. France   E. Indians

6. In doing business with Americans, the Spaniards were
   A. easy to outsmart
   B. friendly to trade
   C. inclined to charge high prices for use of their ports
   D. shrewd
   E. suspicious

PASSAGE 3

Our humanity is by no means so materialistic as foolish talk is continually asserting it to be. Judging by what I have learned about men and women, I am convinced that there is far more in them of idealistic willpower than ever comes to the surface of the world. Just as the water of streams is small in amount compared to that which flows underground, so the idealism which becomes visible is small in amount compared with that which men and women bear locked in their hearts, unreleased or scarcely released. To unbind what is bound, to bring the underground waters to the surface—mankind is waiting and longing for men who can do that.

7. The title below that BEST expresses the ideas of the paragraph is:
   A. Releasing Underground Riches
   B. The Good and Bad in Man
   C. Materialism in Humanity
   D. The Surface and the Depths of Idealism
   E. Unreleased Energy

8. Human beings are more idealistic than
   A. the water in underground streams
   B. their waiting and longing proves
   C. outward evidence shows
   D. the world
   E. other living creatures

PASSAGE 4

The total impression made by any work of fiction cannot be rightly understood without a sympathetic perception of the artistic aims of the writer. Consciously or unconsciously, he has accepted certain facts, and rejected or suppressed other facts, in order to give unity to the particular aspect of human life which he is depicting. No novelist possesses the impartiality, the indifference, the infinite tolerance of nature. Nature displays to use, with complete unconcern, the beautiful and the ugly, the precious and the trivial, the pure and the impure. But a writer must select the aspects of nature and human nature which are demanded by the work in hand. He is forced to select, to combine, to create.

9. The title below that BEST expresses the ideas of this paragraph is:
   A. Impressionists in Literature
   B. Nature as an Artist
   C. The Novelist as an Imitator
   D. Creative Technic of the Novelist
   E. Aspects of Nature

10. A novelist rejects some facts because they
    A. are impure and ugly
    B. would show he is not impartial
    C. are unrelated to human nature
    D. would make a bad impression
    E. mar the unity of his story

11. It is important for a reader to know
    A. the purpose of the author
    B. what facts the author omits
    C. both the ugly and the beautiful
    D. something about nature
    E. what the author thinks of human nature

PASSAGE 5

If you watch a lamp which is turned very rapidly on and off, and you keep your eyes open, "persistence of vision" will bridge the gaps of darkness between the flashes of light, and the lamp will seem to be continuously lit. This "topical afterglow" explains the magic produced by the stroboscope, a new instrument which seems to freeze the swiftest motions while they are still going on, and to stop time itself dead in its tracks. The "magic" is all in the eye of the beholder.

12. The "magic" of the stroboscope is due to
    A. continuous lighting
    B. intense cold
    C. slow motion
    D. behavior of the human eye
    E. a lapse of time

13. "Persistence of vision" is explained by
    A. darkness
    B. winking
    C. rapid flashes
    D. gaps
    E. after impression

KEY (CORRECT ANSWERS)

1.	C	6.	B	11.	A
2.	D	7.	D	12.	D
3.	A	8.	C	13.	E
4.	C	9.	D		
5.	D	10.	E		

TEST 5

DIRECTIONS: Each question has five suggested answers, lettered A to E. Decide which one is the BEST answer. *PRINT THE LETTER OF THE CORRECT ANSWER IN THE SPACE AT THE RIGHT.*

PASSAGE 1

During the past fourteen years, thousands of top-lofty United States elms have been marked for death by the activities of the tiny European elm bark beetle. The beetles, however, do not do fatal damage. Death is caused by another importation, Dutch elm disease, a fungus infection which the beetles carry from tree to tree. Up to 1941, quarantine and tree-sanitation measures kept the beetles and the disease pretty well confined within 510 miles around metropolitan New York. War curtailed these measures and made Dutch elm disease a wider menace. Every household and village that prizes an elm-shaded lawn or commons must now watch for it. Since there is as yet no cure for it, the infected trees must be pruned or felled, and the wood must be burned in order to protect other healthy trees.

1. The title below that BEST expresses the ideas of this paragraph is: 1.____
   A. A Menace to Our Elms
   B. Pests and Diseases of the Elm
   C. Our Vanishing Elms
   D. The Need to Protect Dutch Elms
   E. How Elms are Protected

2. The danger of spreading the Dutch elm disease was increased by 2.____
   A. destroying infected trees   B. the war
   C. the lack of a cure   D. a fungus infection
   E. quarantine measures

3. The European elm bark beetle is a serious threat to our elms because it 3.____
   A. chews the bark
   B. kills the trees
   C. is particularly active on the eastern seaboard
   D. carries infection
   E. cannot be controlled

PASSAGE 2

It is elemental that the greater the development of man, the greater the problems he has to concern him. When he lived in a cave with stone implements, his mind no less than his actions was grooved into simple channels. Every new invention, every new way of doing things posed fresh problems for him. And, as he moved along the road, he questioned each step, as indeed he should, for he trod upon the beliefs of his ancestors. It is equally elemental to say that each step upon this later road posed more questions than the earlier ones. It is only the educated man who realizes the results of his actions; it is only the thoughtful one who questions his own decisions.

4. The title below that BEST expresses the ideas of this paragraph is: 4.____
   A. Channels of Civilization
   B. The Mark of a Thoughtful Man
   C. The Cave Man in Contrast with Man Today
   D. The Price of Early Progress
   E. Man's Never-Ending Challenge

PASSAGE 3

Spring is one of those things that man has no hand in, any more than he has a part in sunrise or the phases of the moon. Spring came before man was here to enjoy it, and it will go right on coming even if man isn't here some time in the future. It is a matter of solar mechanics and celestial order. And for all our knowledge of astronomy and terrestrial mechanics, we haven't yet been able to do more than bounce a radar beam off the moon. We couldn't alter the arrival of the spring equinox by as much as one second, if we tried.

Spring is a matter of growth, of chlorophyll, of bud and blossom. We can alter growth and change the time of blossoming in individual plants; but the forests still grow in nature's way, and the grass of the plains hasn't altered its nature in a thousand years. Spring is a magnificent phase of the cycle of nature; but man really hasn't any guiding or controlling hand in it. He is here to enjoy it and benefit by it. And April is a good time to realize it; by May perhaps we will want to take full credit.

5. The title below that BEST expresses the ideas of this passage is: 5.____
   A. The Marvels of the Spring Equinox
   B. Nature's Dependence on Mankind
   C. The Weakness of Man Opposed to Nature
   D. The Glories of the World
   E. Eternal Growth

6. The author of the passage states that 6.____
   A. man has a part in the phases of the moon
   B. April is a time for taking full-credit
   C. April is a good time to enjoy nature
   D. man has a guiding hand in spring
   E. spring will cease to be if civilization ends

PASSAGE 4

The walled medieval town was as characteristic of its period as the cut of a robber baron's beard. It sprang out of the exigencies of war, and it was not without its architectural charm, whatever is hygienic deficiencies may have been. Behind its high, thick walls not only the normal inhabitants but the whole countryside fought and cowered in an hour of need. The capitals of Europe now forsake the city when the sirens scream and death from the sky seems imminent. Will the fear of bombs accelerate the slow decentralization which began with the automobile and the wide distribution of electrical energy and thus reverse the medieval flow to the city?

7. The title below that BEST expresses the ideas in this paragraph is:
   A. A Changing Function of the Town
   B. The Walled Medieval Town
   C. The Automobile's Influence on City Life
   D. Forsaking the City
   E. Bombs Today and Yesterday

   7._____

8. Conditions in the Middle Ages made the walled town
   A. a natural development
   B. the most dangerous of all places
   C. a victim of fires
   D. lacking in architectural charm
   E. healthful

   8._____

9. Modern conditions may
   A. make cities larger
   B. make cities more hygienic
   C. protect against floods
   D. cause people to move from population centers
   E. encourage good architecture

   9._____

PASSAGE 5

The literary history of this nation began when the first settler from abroad of sensitive mind paused in his adventure long enough to feel that he was under a different sky, breathing new air and that a New World was all before him with only his strength and Providence for guides. With him began a new emphasis upon an old theme in literature, the theme of cutting loose and faring forth, renewed, under the powerful influence of a fresh continent for civilized literature, whose other flow has come from a nostalgia for the rich culture of Europe, so much of which was perforce left behind.

10. The title below that BEST expresses the ideas of this paragraph is:
    A. America's Distinctive Literature   B. Pioneer Authors
    C. The Dead Hand of the Past   D. Europe's Literary Grandchild
    E. America Comes of Age

    10._____

11. American writers, according to the author, because of their colonial experiences
    A. were antagonistic to European writers
    B. cut loose from Old World influences
    C. wrote only on New World events and characters
    D. created new literary themes
    E. gave fresh interpretation to an old literary idea

    11._____

KEY (CORRECT ANSWERS)

1.	A	7.	A
2.	B	8.	A
3.	D	9.	D
4.	E	10.	A
5.	C	11.	E
6.	C		

TEST 6

DIRECTIONS: Each question has five suggested answers, lettered A to E. Decide which one is the BEST answer. *PRINT THE LETTER OF THE CORRECT ANSWER IN THE SPACE AT THE RIGHT.*

1. Any business not provided with capable substitutes to fill all important positions is a weak business. Therefore, a foreman should train each man not on to perform his own particular duties but also to do those of two or three positions.
   The paragraph BEST supports the statement that
   A. dependence on substitutes is a sign of weak organization
   B. training will improve the strongest organization
   C. the foreman should be the most expert at any particular job under him
   D. every employee can be trained to perform efficiency work other than his own
   E. vacancies in vital positions should be provided for in advance

   1.____

2. The coloration of textile fabrics composed of cotton and wool generally requires two processes, as the process used in dyeing wool is seldom capable of fixing the color upon cotton. The usual method is to immerse the fabric in the requisite baths to dye the wool and then to treat the partially dyed material in the manner found suitable for cotton.
   The paragraph BEST supports the statement that the dyeing of textile fabrics composed of cotton and wool is
   A. less complicated than the dyeing of wool alone
   B. more successful when the material contains more cotton than wool
   C. not satisfactory when solid colors are desired
   D. restricted to two colors for any one fabric
   E. usually based upon the methods required for dyeing the different materials

   2.____

3. The serious investigator must direct his whole effort toward success in his work. If he wishes to succeed in each investigation, his work will be by no means easy, smooth, or peaceful; on the contrary, he will have to devote himself completely and continuously to a task that requires all his ability.
   The paragraph BEST supports the statement that an investigator's success depends most upon
   A. ambition to advance rapidly in the service
   B. persistence in the face of difficulty
   C. training and experience
   D. willingness to obey orders without delay
   E. the number of investigations which he conducts

   3.____

4. Honest people in one nation find it difficult to understand the viewpoint of honest people in another. State departments and their ministers exist for the purpose of explaining the viewpoints of one nation in terms understood by another. Some of their most important work lies in this direction.

   4.____

The paragraph BEST supports the statement that
- A. people of different nations may not consider matters in the same light
- B. it is unusual for many people to share similar ideas
- C. suspicion prevents understanding between nations
- D. the chief work of state departments is to guide relations between nations united by a common cause
- E. the people of one nation must sympathize with the viewpoints of others

5. Economy once in a while is just not enough. I expect to find it at every level of responsibility, from cabinet member to the newest and youngest recruit. Controlling waste is something like bailing a boat; you have to keep at it. I have no intention of easing up on my insistence on getting a dollar of value for each dollar we spend.
The paragraph BEST supports the statement that
- A. we need not be concerned about items which cost less than a dollar
- B. it is advisable to buy the cheaper of two items
- C. the responsibility of economy is greater at high levels than at low levels
- D. economy becomes easy with practice
- E. economy is a continuing responsibility

KEY (CORRECT ANSWERS)

1. E
2. E
3. B
4. A
5. E

TEST 7

DIRECTIONS: Each question has five suggested answers, lettered A to E. Decide which one is the BEST answer. *PRINT THE LETTER OF THE CORRECT ANSWER IN THE SPACE AT THE RIGHT.*

1. On all permit imprint mail the charge for postage has been printed by the mailer before he presents it for mailing and pays the postage. Such mail of any class is mailable only at the post office that issued a permit covering it. Since the postage receipts for such mail represent only the amount of permit imprint mail detected and verified, employees in receiving, handling, and outgoing sections must be alert constantly to route such mail to the weighing section before it is handled or dispatched.
   The paragraph BEST supports the statement that, at post offices where permit mail is received for dispatch,
   A. dispatching units make a final check on the amount of postage payable on permit imprint mail
   B. employees are to check the postage chargeable on mail received under permit
   C. neither more nor less postage is to be collected than the amount printed on permit imprint mail
   D. the weighing section is primarily responsible for failure to collect postage on such mail
   E. unusual measures are taken to prevent unstamped mail from being accepted

1.____

2. Education should not stop when the individual has been prepared to make a livelihood and to live in modern society. Living would be mere existence were there were no appreciation and enjoyment of the riches of art, literature, and science.
   The paragraph BEST supports the statement that true education
   A. is focused on the routine problems of life
   B. prepares one for full enjoyment of life
   C. deals chiefly with art, literature, and science
   D. is not possible for one who does not enjoy scientific literature
   E. disregards practical ends

2.____

3. Insured and c.o.d. air and surface mail is accepted with the understanding that the sender guarantees any necessary forwarding or return postage. When such mail is forwarded or returned, it shall be rated up for collection of postage; except that insured or c.o.d. air mail weighing 8 ounces or less and subject to the 40 cents an ounce rate shall be forwarded by air if delivery will be advanced, and returned by surface means without additional postage.
   The paragraph BEST supports the statement that the return postage for undeliverable insured mail is
   A. included in the original prepayment on air mail parcels
   B. computed but not collected before dispatching surface patrol post mail to sender

3.____

C. not computed or charged for any air mail that is returned by surface transportation
D. included in the amount collected when the sender mails parcel post
E. collected before dispatching for return if any amount due has been guaranteed

4. All undeliverable first-class mail, except first-class parcels and parcel post paid with first-class postage, which cannot be returned to the sender, is sent to a dead-letter branch. Undeliverable matter of the third- and fourth-classes of obvious value for which the sender does not furnish return postage and undeliverable first-class parcels and parcel-post matter bearing postage of the first-class, which cannot be returned, is sent to a dead parcel-post branch.
The paragraph BEST supports the statement that matter that is sent to a dead parcel-post branch includes all undeliverable
   A. mail, except for first-class letter mail, that appears to be valuable
   B. mail, except that of the first-class, on which the sender failed to prepay the original mailing costs
   C. parcels on which the mailer prepaid the first-class rate of postage
   D. third- and fourth-class matter on which the required return postage has not been paid
   E. parcels on which first-class postage has been prepaid, when the sender's address is not known

5. Civilization started to move rapidly when man freed himself of the shackles that restricted his search for truth.
The passage BEST supports the statement that the progress of civilization
   A. came as a result of man's dislike for obstacles
   B. did not begin until restrictions on learning were removed
   C. has been aided by man's efforts to find the truth
   D. is based on continually increasing efforts
   E. continues at a constantly increasing rate

KEY (CORRECT ANSWERS)

1. B
2. B
3. B
4. E

TEST 8

DIRECTIONS: Each question has five suggested answers, lettered A to E. Decide which one is the BEST answer. *PRINT THE LETTER OF THE CORRECT ANSWER IN THE SPACE AT THE RIGHT.*

1. E-mails should be clear, concise, and brief. Omit all unnecessary words. The parts of speech most often used in e-mails are nouns, verbs, adjectives, and adverbs. If possible, do without pronouns, prepositions, articles, and copulative verbs. Use simple sentences, rather than complex and compound.
   The paragraph BEST supports the statement that in writing e-mails one should always use
   A. common and simple words
   B. only nouns, verbs, adjectives, and adverbs
   C. incomplete sentences
   D. only words essential to the meaning
   E. the present tense of verbs

   1.____

2. The function of business is to increase the wealth of the country and the value and happiness of life. It does this by supplying the material needs of men and women. When the nation's business is successfully carried on, it renders public service of the highest value.
   The paragraph BEST supports the statement that
   A. all businesses which render public service are successful
   B. human happiness is enhanced only by the increase of material wants
   C. the value of life is increased only by the increase of wealth
   D. the material needs of men and women are supplied by well-conducted business
   E. business is the only field of activity which increases happiness

   2.____

3. In almost every community, fortunately, there are certain men and women known to be public-spirited. Others, however, may be selfish and act only as their private interests seem to require.
   The paragraph BEST supports the statement that those citizens who disregard others are
   A. fortunate   B. needed
   C. found only in small communities   D. not known
   E. not public spirited

   3.____

KEY (CORRECT ANSWERS)

1. D
2. D
3. E

READING COMPREHENSION
UNDERSTANDING AND INTERPRETING WRITTEN MATERIAL
EXAMINATION SECTION
TEST 1

DIRECTIONS: Each question or incomplete statement is followed by several suggested answers or completions. Select the one that BEST answers the question or completes the statement. *PRINT THE LETTER OF THE CORRECT ANSWER IN THE SPACE AT THE RIGHT.*

Questions 1-3.

DIRECTIONS: Questions 1 through 3 are to be answered SOLELY on the basis of the following statement.

The equipment in a mailroom may include a mail metering machine. This machine simultaneously stamps, postmarks, seals, and counts letters as fast as the operator can feed them. It can also print the proper postage directly on a gummed strip to be affixed to bulky items. It is equipped with a meter which is removed from the machine and sent to the postmaster to be set for a given number of stampings of any denomination. The setting of the meter must be paid for in advance. One of the advantages of metered mail is that it bypasses the cancellation operation and thereby facilitates handling by the post office. Mail metering also makes the pilfering of stamps impossible, but does not prevent the passage of personal mail in company envelopes through the meters unless there is established a rigid control or censorship over outgoing mail.

1. According to this statement, the postmaster

    A. is responsible for training new clerks in the use of mail metering machines
    B. usually recommends that both large and small firms adopt the use of mail metering machines
    C. is responsible for setting the meter to print a fixed number of stampings
    D. examines the mail metering machine to see that they are properly installed in the mailroom

1.____

2. According to this statement, the use of mail metering machines

    A. requires the employment of more clerks in a mailroom than does the use of postage stamps
    B. interferes with the handling of large quantities of outgoing mail
    C. does not prevent employees from sending their personal letters at company expense
    D. usually involves smaller expenditures for mailroom equipment than does the use of postage stamps

2.____

3. On the basis of this statement, it is MOST accurate to state that

    A. mail metering machines are often used for opening envelopes
    B. postage stamps are generally used when bulky packages are to be mailed
    C. the use of metered mail tends to interfere with rapid mail handling by the post office
    D. mail metering machines can seal and count letters at the same time

3.____

Questions 4-5.

DIRECTIONS: Questions 4 and 5 are to be answered SOLELY on the basis of the following statement.

Forms are printed sheets of paper on which information is to be entered. While what is printed on the form is most important, the kind of paper used in making the form is also important. The kind of paper should be selected with regard to the use to which the form will be subjected. Printing a form on an unnecessarily expensive grade of papers is wasteful. On the other hand, using too cheap or flimsy a form can materially interfere with satisfactory performance of the work the form is being planned to do. Thus, a form printed on both sides normally requires a heavier paper than a form printed only on one side. Forms to be used as permanent records, or which are expected to have a very long life in files, requires a quality of paper which will not disintegrate or discolor with age. A form which will go through a great deal of handling requires a strong, tough paper, while thinness is a necessary qualification where the making of several copies of a form will be required.

4. According to this statement, the type of paper used for making forms 4.___

    A. should be chosen in accordance with the use to which the form will be put
    B. should be chosen before the type of printing to be used has been decided upon
    C. is as important as the information which is printed on it
    D. should be strong enough to be used for any purpose

5. According to this statement, forms that are 5.___

    A. printed on both sides are usually economical and desirable
    B. to be filed permanently should not deteriorate as time goes on
    C. expected to last for a long time should be handled carefully
    D. to be filed should not be printed on inexpensive paper

Questions 6-8.

DIRECTIONS: Questions 6 through 8 are to be answered SOLELY on the basis of the following paragraph.

The increase in the number of public documents in the last two centuries closely matches the increase in population in the United States. The great number of public documents has become a serious threat to their usefulness. It is necessary to have programs which will reduce the number of public documents that are kept and which will, at the same time, assure keeping those that have value. Such programs need a great deal of thought to have any success.

6. According to the above paragraph, public documents may be LESS useful if 6.___

    A. the files are open to the public
    B. the record room is too small
    C. the copying machine is operated only during normal working hours
    D. too many records are being kept

7. According to the above paragraph, the growth of the population in the United States has matched the growth in the quantity of public documents for a period of MOST NEARLY _____ years.

   A. 50   B. 100   C. 200   D. 300

8. According to the above paragraph, the increased number of public documents has made it necessary to

   A. find out which public documents are worth keeping
   B. reduce the great number of public documents by decreasing government services
   C. eliminate the copying of all original public documents
   D. avoid all new copying devices

Questions 9-10.

DIRECTIONS: Questions 9 and 10 are to be answered SOLELY on the basis of the following paragraph.

The work goals of an agency can best be reached if the employees understand and agree with these goals. One way to gain such understanding and agreement is for management to encourage and seriously consider suggestions from employees in the setting of agency goals.

9. On the basis of the above paragraph, the BEST way to achieve the work goals of an agency is to

   A. make certain that employees work as hard as possible
   B. study the organizational structure of the agency
   C. encourage employees to think seriously about the agency's problems
   D. stimulate employee understanding of the work goals

10. On the basis of the above paragraph, understanding and agreement with agency goals can be gained by

    A. allowing the employees to set agency goals
    B. reaching agency goals quickly
    C. legislative review of agency operations
    D. employee participation in setting agency goals

Questions 11-13.

DIRECTIONS: Questions 11 through 13 are to be answered SOLELY on the basis of the following paragraph.

In order to organize records properly, it is necessary to start from their very beginning and trace each copy of the record to find out how it is used, how long it is used, and what may finally be done with it. Although several copies of the record are made, one copy should be marked as the copy of record. This is the formal legal copy, held to meet the requirements of the law. The other copies may be retained for brief periods for reference purposes, but these copies should not be kept after their usefulness as reference ends. There is another reason for tracing records through the office and that is to determine how long it takes the copy of record to reach the central file. The copy of record must not be kept longer than necessary by the section of the office which has prepared it, but should be sent to the central file as soon as possible so that it can be available to the various sections of the office. The central file can make the copy of record available to the various sections of the office at an early date only if it arrives at the central file as quickly as possible. Just as soon as its immediate or active service period is ended, the copy of record should be removed from the central file and put into the inactive file in the office to be stored for whatever length of time may be necessary to meet legal requirements, and then destroyed.

11. According to the above paragraph, a reason for tracing records through an office is to

    A. determine how long the central file must keep the records
    B. organize records properly
    C. find out how many copies of each record are required
    D. identify the copy of record

12. According to the above paragraph, in order for the central file to have the copy of record available as soon as possible for the various sections of the office, it is MOST important that the

    A. copy of record to be sent to the central file meets the requirements of the law
    B. copy of record is not kept in the inactive file too long
    C. section preparing the copy of record does not unduly delay in sending it to the central file
    D. central file does not keep the copy of record beyond its active service period

13. According to the above paragraph, the length of time a copy of a record is kept in the inactive file of an office depends CHIEFLY on the

    A. requirements of the law
    B. length of time that is required to trace the copy of record through the office
    C. use that is made of the copy of record
    D. length of the period that the copy of record is used for reference purposes

Questions 14-16.

DIRECTIONS: Questions 14 through 16 are to be answered SOLELY on the basis of the following paragraph.

The office was once considered as nothing more than a focal point of internal and external correspondence. It was capable only of dispatching a few letters upon occasion and of preparing records of little practical value. Under such a concept, the vitality of the office force was impaired. Initiative became stagnant, and the lot of the office worker was not likely to be a happy one. However, under the new concept of office management, the possibilities of waste and mismanagement in office operation are now fully recognized, as are the possibilities for the modern office to assist in the direction and control of business operations. Fortunately, the modern concept of the office as a centralized service-rendering unit is gaining ever greater acceptance in today's complex business world, for without the modern office, the production wheels do not turn and the distribution of goods and services is not possible.

14. According to the above paragraph, the fundamental difference between the old and the new concept of the office is the change in the

   A. accepted functions of the office
   B. content and the value of the records kept
   C. office methods and systems
   D. vitality and morale of the office force

14.____

15. According to the above paragraph, an office operated today under the old concept of the office MOST likely would

   A. make older workers happy in their jobs
   B. be part of an old thriving business concern
   C. have a passive role in the conduct of a business enterprise
   D. attract workers who do not believe in modern methods

15.____

16. Of the following, the MOST important implication of the above paragraph is that a present-day business organization cannot function effectively without the

   A. use of modern office equipment
   B. participation and cooperation of the office
   C. continued modernization of office procedures
   D. employment of office workers with skill and initiative

16.____

Questions 17-20.

DIRECTIONS: Questions 17 through 20 are to be answered SOLELY on the basis of the following paragraph.

A report is frequently ineffective because the person writing it is not fully acquainted with all the necessary details before he actually starts to construct the report. All details pertaining to the subject should be known before the report is started. If the essential facts are not known, they should be investigated. It is wise to have essential facts written down rather than to depend too much on memory, especially if the facts pertain to such matters as amounts, dates, names of persons, or other specific data. When the necessary information has been gathered, the general plan and content of the report should be thought out before the writing is actually begun. A person with little or no experience in writing reports may find that it is wise to make a brief outline. Persons with more experience should not need a written outline, but they should make mental notes of the steps they are to follow. If writing reports without dictation is a regular part of an office worker's duties, he should set aside a certain time during the day when he is least likely to be interrupted. That may be difficult, but in most offices there are certain times in the day when the callers, telephone calls, and other interruptions are not numerous. During those times, it is best to write reports that need undivided concentration. Reports that are written amid a series of interruptions may be poorly done.

17. Before starting to write an effective report, it is necessary to

   A. memorize all specific information
   B. disregard ambiguous data
   C. know all pertinent information
   D. develop a general plan

17.____

18. Reports dealing with complex and difficult material should be   18.____

    A. prepared and written by the supervisor of the unit
    B. written when there is the least chance of interruption
    C. prepared and written as part of regular office routine
    D. outlined and then dictated

19. According to the paragraph, employees with no prior familiarity in writing reports may find   19.____
    it helpful to

    A. prepare a brief outline
    B. mentally prepare a synopsis of the report's content
    C. have a fellow employee help in writing the report
    D. consult previous reports

20. In writing a report, needed information which is unclear should be   20.____

    A. disregarded   B. memorized
    C. investigated   D. gathered

Questions 21-25.

DIRECTIONS: Questions 21 through 25 are to be answered SOLELY on the basis of the following passage.

Positive discipline minimizes the amount of personal supervision required and aids in the maintenance of standards. When a new employee has been properly introduced and carefully instructed, when he has come to know the supervisor and has confidence in the supervisor's ability to take care of him, when he willingly cooperates with the supervisor, that employee has been under positive discipline and can be put on his own to produce the quantity and quality of work desired. Negative discipline, the fear of transfer to a less desirable location, for example, to a limited extent may restrain certain individuals from overt violation of rules and regulations governing attendance and conduct which in governmental agencies are usually on at least an agency-wide basis. Negative discipline may prompt employees to perform according to certain rules to avoid a penalty such as, for example, docking for tardiness.

21. According to the above passage, it is reasonable to assume that in the area of discipline,   21.____
    the first-line supervisor in a governmental agency has GREATER scope for action in

    A. *positive* discipline, because negative discipline is largely taken care of by agency rules and regulations
    B. *negative* discipline, because rules and procedures are already fixed and the supervisor can rely on them
    C. *positive* discipline, because the supervisor is in a position to recommend transfers
    D. *negative* discipline, because positive discipline is reserved for people on a higher supervisory level

22. In order to maintain positive discipline of employees under his supervision, it is MOST   22.____
    important for a supervisor to

    A. assure each employee that he has nothing to worry about
    B. insist at the outset on complete cooperation from employees

C. be sure that each employee is well trained in his job
D. inform new employees of the penalties for not meeting standards

23. According to the above passage, a feature of negative discipline is that it   23._____

    A. may lower employee morale
    B. may restrain employees from disobeying the rules
    C. censures equal treatment of employees
    D. tends to create standards for quality of work

24. A REASONABLE conclusion based on the above passage is that positive discipline benefits a supervisor because   24._____

    A. he can turn over orientation and supervision of a new employee to one of his subordinates
    B. subordinates learn to cooperate with one another when working on an assignment
    C. it is easier to administer
    D. it cuts down, in the long run, on the amount of time the supervisor needs to spend on direct supervision

25. Based on the above passage, it is REASONABLE to assume, that an important difference between positive discipline and negative discipline is that positive discipline   25._____

    A. is concerned with the quality of work and negative discipline with the quantity of work
    B. leads to a more desirable basis for motivation of the employee
    C. is more likely to be concerned with agency rules and regulations
    D. uses fear while negative discipline uses penalties to prod employees to adequate performance

KEY (CORRECT ANSWERS)

1.	C	11.	B
2.	C	12.	C
3.	D	13.	A
4.	A	14.	A
5.	B	15.	C
6.	D	16.	B
7.	C	17.	C
8.	A	18.	B
9.	D	19.	A
10.	D	20.	B

21. A
22. C
23. B
24. D
25. B

TEST 2

Questions 1-6.

DIRECTIONS: Questions 1 through 6 are to be answered SOLELY on the basis of the following passage.

Inherent in all organized endeavors is the need to resolve the individual differences involved in conflict. Conflict may be either a positive or negative factor since it may lead to creativity, innovation and progress on the one hand, or it may result, on the other hand, in a deterioration or even destruction of the organization. Thus, some forms of conflict are desirable, whereas others are undesirable and ethically wrong.

There are three management strategies which deal with interpersonal conflict. In the *divide-and-rule strategy*, management attempts to maintain control by limiting the conflict to those directly involved and preventing their disagreement from spreading to the larger group. The *suppression-of-differences strategy* entails ignoring conflicts or pretending they are irrelevant. In the *working-through-differences strategy*, management actively attempts to solve or resolve intergroup or interpersonal conflicts. Of the three strategies, only the last directly attacks and has the potential for eliminating the causes of conflict. An essential part of this strategy, however, is its employment by a committed and relatively mature management team.

1. According to the above passage, the *divide-and-rule strategy tor* dealing with conflict is the attempt to

   A. involve other people in the conflict
   B. restrict the conflict to those participating in it
   C. divide the conflict into positive and negative factors
   D. divide the conflict into a number of smaller ones

2. The word *conflict* is used in relation to both positive and negative factors in this passage. Which one of the following words is MOST likely to describe the activity which the word *conflict*, in the sense of the passage, implies?

   A. Competition   B. Confusion
   C. Cooperation   D. Aggression

3. According to the above passage, which one of the following characteristics is shared by both the *suppression-of-differences strategy* and the *divide-and-rule strategy*?

   A. Pretending that conflicts are irrelevant
   B. Preventing conflicts from spreading to the group situation
   C. Failure to directly attack the causes of conflict
   D. Actively attempting to resolve interpersonal conflict

4. According to the above passage, the successful resolution of interpersonal conflict requires

   A. allowing the group to mediate conflicts between two individuals
   B. division of the conflict into positive and negative factors
   C. involvement of a committed, mature management team
   D. ignoring minor conflicts until they threaten the organization

5. Which can be MOST reasonably inferred from the above passage? Conflict between two individuals is LEAST likely to continue when management uses

   A. the *working-through differences strategy*
   B. the *suppression-of differences strategy*
   C. the *divide-and-rule strategy*
   D. a combination of all three strategies

6. According to the above passage, a DESIRABLE result of conflict in an organization is when conflict

   A. exposes production problems in the organization
   B. can be easily ignored by management
   C. results in advancement of more efficient managers
   D. leads to development of new methods

Questions 7-13.

DIRECTIONS: Questions 7 through 13 are to be answered SOLELY on the basis of the passage below.

Modern management places great emphasis on the concept of communication. The communication process consists of the steps through which an idea or concept passes from its inception by one person, the sender, until it is acted upon by another person, the receiver. Through an understanding of these steps and some of the possible barriers that may occur, more effective communication may be achieved. The first step in the communication process is ideation by the sender. This is the formation of the intended content of the message he wants to transmit. In the next step, encoding, the sender organizes his ideas into a series of symbols designed to communicate his message to his intended receiver. He selects suitable words or phrases that can be understood by the receiver, and he also selects the appropriate media to be used—for example, memorandum, conference, etc. The third step is transmission of the encoded message through selected channels in the organizational structure. In the fourth step, the receiver enters the process by tuning in to receive the message. If the receiver does not function, however, the message is lost. For example, if the message is oral, the receiver must be a good listener. The fifth step is decoding of the message by the receiver, as for example, by changing words into ideas. At this step, the decoded message may not be the same idea that the sender originally encoded because the sender and receiver have different perceptions regarding the meaning of certain words. Finally, the receiver acts or responds. He may file the information, ask for more information, or take other action. There can be no assurance, however, that communication has taken place unless there is some type of feedback to the sender in the form of an acknowledgement that the message was received.

7. According to the above passage, *ideation* is the process by which the

   A. sender develops the intended content of the message
   B. sender organizes his ideas into a series of symbols
   C. receiver tunes in to receive the message
   D. receiver decodes the message

8. In the last sentence of the passage, the word *feedback* refers to the process by which the sender is assured that the

   A. receiver filed the information
   B. receiver's perception is the same as his own
   C. message was received
   D. message was properly interpreted

9. Which one of the following BEST shows the order of the steps in the communication process as described in the passage?

   A. 1 - ideation   2 - encoding
      3 - decoding   4 - transmission
      5 - receiving   6 - action
      7 - feedback to the sender

   B. 1 - ideation   2 - encoding
      3 - transmission   4 - decoding
      5 - receiving   6 - action
      7 - feedback to the sender

   C. 1 - ideation   2 - decoding
      3 - transmission   4 - receiving
      5 - encoding   6 - action
      7 - feedback to the sender

   D. 1 - ideation   2 - encoding
      3 - transmission   4 - receiving
      5 - decoding   6 - action
      7 - feedback to the sender

10. Which one of the following BEST expresses the main theme of the passage?

    A. Different individuals have the same perceptions regarding the meaning of words.
    B. An understanding of the steps in the communication process may achieve better communication.
    C. Receivers play a passive role in the communication process.
    D. Senders should not communicate with receivers who transmit feedback.

11. The above passage implies that a receiver does NOT function properly when he

    A. transmits feedback   B. files the information
    C. is a poor listener   D. asks for more information

12. Which one of the following, according to the above passage, is included in the SECOND step of the communication process?

    A. Selecting the appropriate media to be used in transmission
    B. Formulation of the intended content of the message
    C. Using appropriate media to respond to the receiver's feedback
    D. Transmitting the message through selected channels in the organization

13. The above passage implies that the *decoding process* is MOST NEARLY the reverse of the _____ process.

    A. transmission   B. receiving
    C. feedback   D. encoding

Questions 14-19.

DIRECTIONS: Questions 14 through 19 are to be answered SOLELY on the basis of the following passage.

It is often said that no system will work if the people who carry it out do not want it to work. In too many cases, a departmental reorganization that seemed technically sound and economically practical has proved to be a failure because the planners neglected to take the human factor into account. The truth is that employees are likely to feel threatened when they learn that a major change is in the wind. It does not matter whether or not the change actually poses a threat to an employee; the fact that he believes it does or fears it might is enough to make him feel insecure. Among the dangers he fears, the foremost is the possibility that his job may cease to exist and that he may be laid off or shunted into a less skilled position at lower pay. Even if he knows that his own job category is secure, however, he is likely to fear losing some of the important intangible advantages of his present position—for instance, he may fear that he will be separated from his present companions and thrust in with a group of strangers, or that he will find himself in a lower position on the organizational ladder if a new position is created above his.

It is important that management recognize these natural fears and take them into account in planning any kind of major change. While there is no cut-and-dried formula for preventing employee resistance, there are several steps that can be taken to reduce employees' fears and gain their cooperation. First, unwarranted fears can be dispelled if employees are kept informed of the planning from the start and if they know exactly what to expect. Next, assurance on matters such as retraining, transfers, and placement help should be given as soon as it is clear what direction the reorganization will take. Finally, employees' participation in the planning should be actively sought. There is a great psychological difference between feeling that a change is being forced upon one from the outside, and feeling that one is an insider who is helping to bring about a change.

14. According to the above passage, employees who are not in real danger of losing their jobs because of a proposed reorganization   14.____

    A. will be eager to assist in the reorganization
    B. will pay little attention to the reorganization
    C. should not be taken into account in planning the reorganization
    D. are nonetheless likely to feel threatened by the reorganization

15. The passage mentions the *intangible advantages* of a position.   15.____
    Which of the following BEST describes the kind of advantages alluded to in the passage?

    A. Benefits such as paid holidays and vacations
    B. Satisfaction of human needs for things like friendship and status
    C. Qualities such as leadership and responsibility
    D. A work environment that meets satisfactory standards of health and safety

16. According to the passage, an employee's fear that a reorganization may separate him from his present companions is a (n)   16.____

    A. childish and immature reaction to change
    B. unrealistic feeling since this is not going to happen

C. possible reaction that the planners should be aware of
D. incentive to employees to participate in the planning

17. On the basis of the above passage, it would be DESIRABLE, when planning a departmental reorganization, to

   A. be governed by employee feelings and attitudes
   B. give some employees lower positions
   C. keep employees informed
   D. lay off those who are less skilled

18. What does the passage say can be done to help gain employees' cooperation in a reorganization?

   A. Making sure that the change is technically sound, that it is economically practical, and that the human factor is taken into account
   B. Keeping employees fully informed, offering help in fitting them into new positions, and seeking their participation in the planning
   C. Assuring employees that they will not be laid off, that they will not be reassigned to a group of strangers, and that no new positions will be created on the organization ladder
   D. Reducing employees' fears, arranging a retraining program, and providing for transfers

19. Which of the following suggested titles would be MOST appropriate for this passage?

   A. PLANNING A DEPARTMENTAL REORGANIZATION
   B. WHY EMPLOYEES ARE AFRAID
   C. LOOKING AHEAD TO THE FUTURE
   D. PLANNING FOR CHANGE: THE HUMAN FACTOR

Questions 20-22.

DIRECTIONS: Questions 20 through 22 are to be answered SOLELY on the basis of the following passage.

The achievement of good human relations is essential if a business office is to produce at top efficiency and is to be a pleasant place in which to work. All office workers plan an important role in handling problems in human relations. They should, therefore, strive to acquire the understanding, tactfulness, and awareness necessary to deal effectively with actual office situations involving co-workers on all levels. Only in this way can they truly become responsible, interested, cooperative, and helpful members of the staff.

20. The selection implies that the MOST important value of good human relations in an office is to develop

   A. efficiency   B. cooperativeness
   C. tact   D. pleasantness and efficiency

21. Office workers should acquire understanding in dealing with

   A. co-workers   B. subordinates
   C. superiors   D. all members of the staff

22. The selection indicates that a highly competent secretary who is also very argumentative is meeting office requirements   22.____

    A. wholly
    B. partly
    C. slightly
    D. not at all

Questions 23-25.

DIRECTIONS: Questions 23 through 25 are to be answered SOLELY on the basis of the following passage.

It is common knowledge that ability to do a particular job and performance on the job do not always go hand in hand. Persons with great potential abilities sometimes fall down on the job because of laziness or lack of interest in the job, while persons with mediocre talents have often achieved excellent results through their industry and their loyalty to the interests of their employers. It is clear; therefore, that in a balanced personnel program, measures of employee ability need to be supplemented by measures of employee performance, for the final test of any employee is his performance on the job.

23. The MOST accurate of the following statements, on the basis of the above paragraph, is that   23.____

    A. employees who lack ability are usually not industrious
    B. an employee's attitudes are more important than his abilities
    C. mediocre employees who are interested in their work are preferable to employees who possess great ability
    D. superior capacity for performance should be supplemented with proper attitudes

24. On the basis of the above paragraph, the employee of most value to his employer is NOT necessarily the one who   24.____

    A. best understands the significance of his duties
    B. achieves excellent results
    C. possesses the greatest talents
    D. produces the greatest amount of work

25. According to the above paragraph, an employee's efficiency is BEST determined by an   25.____

    A. appraisal of his interest in his work
    B. evaluation of the work performed by him
    C. appraisal of his loyalty to his employer
    D. evaluation of his potential ability to perform his work

KEY (CORRECT ANSWERS)

1. B
2. A
3. C
4. C
5. A

6. D
7. A
8. C
9. D
10. B

11. C
12. A
13. D
14. D
15. B

16. C
17. C
18. B
19. D
20. D

21. D
22. B
23. D
24. C
25. B

TEST 3

Questions 1-8.

DIRECTIONS: Questions 1 through 8 are to be answered SOLELY on the basis of the following information and directions.

Assume that you are a clerk in a city agency. Your supervisor has asked you to classify each of the accidents that happened to employees in the agency into the following five categories:

A. An accident that occurred in the period from January through June, between 9 A.M. and 12 Noon, that was the result of carelessness on the part of the injured employee, that caused the employee to lose less than seven working hours, that happened to an employee who was 40 years of age or over, and who was employed in the agency for less than three years;

B. An accident that occurred in the period from July through December, after 1 P.M., that was the result of unsafe conditions, that caused the injured employee to lose less than seven working hours, that happened to an employee who was 40 years of age or over, and who was employed in the agency for three years or more;

C. An accident that occurred in the period from January through June, after 1 P.M., that was the result of carelessness on the part of the injured employee, that caused the injured employee to lose seven or more working hours, that happened to an employee who was less than 40 years old, and who was employed in the agency for three years or more;

D. An accident that occurred in the period from July through December, between 9 A.M. and 12 Noon, that was the result of unsafe conditions, that caused the injured employee to lose seven or more working hours, that happened to an employee who was less than 40 years old, and who was employed in the agency for less than three years;

E. Accidents that cannot be classified in any of the foregoing groups. NOTE: In classifying these accidents, an employee's age and length of service are computed as of the date of accident. In all cases, it is to be assumed that each employee has been employed continuously in city service, and that each employee works seven hours a day, from 9 A.M. to 5 P.M., with lunch from 12 Noon to 1 P.M. In each question, consider only the information which will assist you in classifying the accident. Any information which is of no assistance in classifying an accident should not be considered.

1. The unsafe condition of the stairs in the building caused Miss Perkins to have an accident on October 14, 2003 at 4 P.M. When she returned to work the following day at 1 P.M., Miss Perkins said that the accident was the first one that had occurred to her in her ten years of employment with the agency. She was born on April 27, 1962.

2. On the day after she completed her six-month probationary period of employment with the agency, Miss Green, who had been considered a careful worker by her supervisor, injured her left foot in an accident caused by her own carelessness. She went home immediately after the accident, which occurred at 10 A.M., March 19, 2004, but returned to work at the regular time on the following morning. Miss Green was born July 12, 1963 in New York City.

3. The unsafe condition of a duplicating machine caused Mr. Martin to injure himself in an accident on September 8, 2006 at 2 P.M. As a result of the accident, he was unable to work the remainder of the day, but returned to his office ready for work on the following morning. Mr. Martin, who has been working for the agency since April 1, 2003, was born in St. Louis on February 1, 1968.

3.____

4. Mr. Smith was hospitalized for two weeks because of a back injury resulted from an accident on the morning of November 16, 2006. Investigation of the accident revealed that it was caused by the unsafe condition of the floor on which Mr. Smith had been walking. Mr. Smith, who is an accountant, has been anemployee of the agency since March 1, 2004, and was born in Ohio on June 10, 1968.

4.____

5. Mr. Allen cut his right hand because he was careless in operating a multilith machine. Mr. Allen, who was 33 years old when the accident took place, has been employed by the agency since August 17, 1992. The accident, which occurred on January 26, 2006, at 2 P.M., caused Mr. Allen to be absent from work for the rest of the day. He was able to return to work the next morning.

5.____

6. Mr. Rand, who is a college graduate, was born on December, 28, 1967, and has been working for the agency since January 7, 2002. On Monday, April 25, 2005, at 2 P.M., his carelessness in operating a duplicating machine caused him to have an accident and to be sent home from work immediately. Fortunately, he was able to return to work at his regular time on the following Wednesday.

6.____

7. Because he was careless in running down a flight of stairs, Mr. Brown fell, bruising his right hand. Although the accident occurred shortly after he arrived for work on the morning of May 22, 2006, he was unable to resume work until 3 P.M. that day. Mr. Brown was born on August 15, 1955, and began working for the agency on September 12, 2003, as a clerk, at a salary of $22,750 per annum.

7.____

8. On December 5, 2005, four weeks after he had begun working for the agency, the unsafe condition of an automatic stapling machine caused Mr. Thomas to injure himself in an accident. Mr. Thomas, who was born on May 19,1975, lost three working days because of the accident, which occurred at 11:45 A.M.

8.____

Questions 9-10.

DIRECTIONS: Questions 9 and 10 are to be answered SOLELY on the basis of the following paragraph.

An impending reorganization within an agency will mean loss by transfer of several professional staff members from the personnel division. The division chief is asked to designate the persons to be transferred. After reviewing the implications of this reduction of staff with his assistant, the division chief discusses the matter at a staff meeting. He adopts the recommendations of several staff members to have volunteers make up the required reduction.

9. The decision to permit personnel to volunteer for transfer is 9._____

   A. *poor;* it is not likely that the members of a division are of equal value to the division chief
   B. *good;* dissatisfied members will probably be more productive elsewhere
   C. *poor;* the division chief has abdicated his responsibility to carry out the order given to him
   D. *good;* morale among remaining staff is likely to improve in a more cohesive framework

10. Suppose that one of the volunteers is a recently appointed employee who has completed 10._____
    his probationary period acceptably, but whose attitude toward division operations and
    agency administration tends to be rather negative and sometimes even abrasive.
    Because of his lack of commitment to the division, his transfer is recommended. If the
    transfer is approved, the division chief should, prior to the transfer,

    A. discuss with the staff the importance of commitment to the work of the agency and its relationship with job satisfaction
    B. refrain from any discussion of attitude with the employee
    C. discuss with the employee his concern about the employee's attitude
    D. avoid mention of attitude in the evaluation appraisal prepared for the receiving division chief

Questions 11-16.

DIRECTIONS: Questions 11 through 16 are to be answered SOLELY on the basis of the following paragraph.

Methods of administration of office activities, much of which consists of providing information and *know-how* needed to coordinate both activities within that particular office and other offices, have been among the last to come under the spotlight of management analysis. Progress has been rapid during the past decade, however, and is now accelerating at such a pace that an *information revolution* in office management appears to be in the making. Although triggered by technological breakthroughs in electronic computers and other giant steps in mechanization, this information revolution must be attributed to underlying forces, such as the increased complexity of both governmental and private enterprise, and ever-keener competition. Size, diversification, specialization of function, and decentralization are among the forces which make coordination of activities both more imperative and more difficult. Increased competition, both domestic and international, leaves little margin for error in managerial decisions. Several developments during recent years indicate an evolving pattern. In 1960, the American Management Association expanded the scope of its activities and changed the name of its Office Management Division to Administrative Services Division. Also in 1960, the magazine *Office Management* merged with the magazine *American Business*, and this new publication was named *Administrative Management*.

11. A REASONABLE inference that can be made from the information in the above paragraph is that an important role of the office manager today is to

    A. work toward specialization of functions performed by his subordinates
    B. inform and train subordinates regarding any new developments in computer technology and mechanization
    C. assist the professional management analysts with the management analysis work in the organization
    D. supply information that can be used to help coordinate and manage the other activities of the organization

11._____

12. An IMPORTANT reason for the *information revolution* that has been taking place in office management is the

    A. advance made in management analysis in the past decade
    B. technological breakthrough in electronic computers and mechanization
    C. more competitive and complicated nature of private business and government
    D. increased efficiency of office management techniques in the past ten years

12._____

13. According to the above paragraph, specialization of function in an organization is MOST likely to result in

    A. the elimination of errors in managerial decisions
    B. greater need to coordinate activities
    C. more competition with other organizations, both domestic and international
    D. a need for office managers with greater flexibility

13._____

14. The word *evolving*, as used in the third from last sentence in the above paragraph, means MOST NEARLY

    A. developing by gradual changes
    B. passing on to others
    C. occurring periodically
    D. breaking up into separate, constituent parts

14._____

15. Of the following, the MOST reasonable implication of the changes in names mentioned in the last part of the above paragraph is that these groups are attempting to

    A. professionalize the field of office management and the title of Office Manager
    B. combine two publications into one because of the increased costs of labor and materials
    C. adjust to the fact that the field of office management is broadening
    D. appeal to the top managerial people rather than the office management people in business and government

15._____

16. According to the above paragraph, intense competition among domestic and international enterprises makes it MOST important for an organization's managerial staff to

    A. coordinate and administer office activities with other activities in the organization
    B. make as few errors in decision-making as possible
    C. concentrate on decentralization and reduction of size of the individual divisions of the organization
    D. restrict decision-making only to top management officials

16._____

Questions 17-21.

DIRECTIONS: Questions 17 through 21 are to be answered SOLELY on the basis of the following passage.

For some office workers, it is useful to be familiar with the four main classes of domestic mail; for others, it is essential. Each class has a different rate of postage, and some have requirements concerning wrapping, sealing, or special information to be placed on the package. First class mail, the class which may not be opened for postal inspection, includes letters, postcards, business reply cards, and other kinds of written matter. There are different rates for some of the kinds of cards which can be sent by first class mail. The maximum weight for an item sent by first class mail is 70 pounds. An item which is not letter size should be marked *First Class* on all sides. Although office workers most often come into contact with first class mail, they may find it helpful to know something about the other classes. Second class mail is generally used for mailing newspapers and magazines. Publishers of these articles must meet certain U.S. Postal Service requirements in order to obtain a permit to use second class mailing rates. Third class mail, which must weigh less than 1 pound, includes printed materials and merchandise parcels. There are two rate structures for this class - a single piece rate and a bulk rate. Fourth class mail, also known as parcel post, includes packages weighing from one to 40 pounds. For more information about these classes of mail and the actual mailing rates, contact your local post office.

17. According to this passage, first class mail is the *only* class which

    A. has a limit on the maximum weight of an item
    B. has different rates for items within the class
    C. may not be opened for postal inspection
    D. should be used by office workers

18. According to this passage, the one of the following items which may CORRECTLY be sent by fourth class mail is a

    A. magazine weighing one-half pound
    B. package weighing one-half pound
    C. package weighing two pounds
    D. postcard

19. According to this passage, there are different postage rates for

    A. a newspaper sent by second class mail and a magazine sent by second class mail
    B. each of the classes of mail
    C. each pound of fourth class mail
    D. printed material sent by third class mail and merchandise parcels sent by third class mail

20. In order to send a newspaper by second class mail, a publisher MUST

    A. have met certain postal requirements and obtained a permit
    B. indicate whether he wants to use the single piece or the bulk rate
    C. make certain that the newspaper weighs less than one pound
    D. mark the newspaper *Second Class* on the top and bottom of the wrapper

21. Of the following types of information, the one which is NOT mentioned in the passage is   21.____
    the
    A. class of mail to which parcel post belongs
    B. kinds of items which can be sent by each class of mail
    C. maximum weight for an item sent by fourth class mail
    D. postage rate for each of the four classes of mail

Questions 22-25.

DIRECTIONS: Questions 22 through 25 are to be answered SOLELY on the basis of the following paragraph.

A standard comprises characteristics attached to an aspect of a process or product by which it can be evaluated. Standardization is the development and adoption of standards. When they are formulated, standards are not usually the product of a single person, but represent the thoughts and ideas of a group, leavened with the knowledge and information which are currently available. Standards which do not meet certain basic requirements become a hindrance rather than an aid to progress. Standards must not only be correct, accurate, and precise in requiring no more and no less than what is needed for satisfactory results, but they must also be workable in the sense that their usefulness is not nullified by external conditions. Standards should also be acceptable to the people who use them. If they are not acceptable, they cannot be considered to be satisfactory, although they may possess all the other essential characteristics.

22. According to the above paragraph, a processing standard that requires the use of materials that cannot be procured is MOST likely to be   22.____
    A. incomplete   B. unworkable
    C. inaccurate   D. unacceptable

23. According to the above paragraph, the construction of standards to which the performance of job duties should conform is MOST often   23.____
    A. the work of the people responsible for seeing that the duties are properly performed
    B. accomplished by the person who is best informed about the functions involved
    C. the responsibility of the people who are to apply them
    D. attributable to the efforts of various informed persons

24. According to the above paragraph, when standards call for finer tolerances than those essential to the conduct of successful production operations, the effect of the standards on the improvement of production operations is   24.____
    A. negative   B. negligible
    C. nullified   D. beneficial

25. The one of the following which is the MOST suitable title for the above paragraph is   25.____
    A. THE EVALUATION OF FORMULATED STANDARDS
    B. THE ATTRIBUTES OF SATISFACTORY STANDARDS
    C. THE ADOPTION OF ACCEPTABLE STANDARDS
    D. THE USE OF PROCESS OR PRODUCT STANDARDS

KEY (CORRECT ANSWERS)

1. B
2. A
3. E
4. D
5. E

6. C
7. A
8. D
9. A
10. C

11. D
12. C
13. B
14. A
15. C

16. B
17. C
18. C
19. B
20. A

21. D
22. C
23. D
24. A
25. B

ARITHMETICAL REASONING
EXAMINATION SECTION
TEST 1

DIRECTIONS: Each question or incomplete statement is followed by several suggested answers or completions. Select the one that BEST answers the question or completes the statement. *PRINT THE LETTER OF THE CORRECT ANSWER IN THE SPACE AT THE RIGHT.*

1. The ABC Corporation had a gross income of $125,500.00 in 2019. Of this, it paid 60% for overhead.
   If the gross income for 2020 increased by $6,500 and the cost of overhead increased to 61% of gross income, how much MORE did it pay for overhead in 2020 than in 2019?
   A. $1,320   B. $5,220   C. $7,530   D. $8,052

2. After one year, Mr. Richards paid back a total of $16,950 as payment for a $15,000 loan. All the money paid over $15,000 was simple interest.
   The interest charge was MOST NEARLY
   A. 13%   B. 11%   C. 9%   D. 7%

3. A checking account has a balance of $253.36.
   If deposits of $36.95, $210.23, and $7.34 and withdrawals of $117.35, $23.37, and $15.98 are made, what is the NEW balance of the account?
   A. $155.54   B. $351.18   C. $364.58   D. $664.58

4. In 2020, the W Realty Company spent 27% of its income on rent.
   If it earned $97,254 in 2020, the amount it paid for rent was
   A. $26,258.58   B. 26,348.58   C. $27,248.58   D. $27,358.58

5. Six percent simple annual interest on $2,436.18 is MOST NEARLY
   A. $145.08   B. $145.17   C. $146.08   D. $146.17

6. H. Partridge receives a weekly gross salary (before deductions) of $397.50. Through weekly payroll deductions of $13.18, he is paying back a loan he took from his pension fund.
   If other fixed weekly deductions amount to $122.76, how much pay would Mr. Partridge take home over a period of 33 weeks?
   A. $7,631.28   B. $8,250.46   C. $8,631.48   D. $13,117.50

7. Mr. Robertson is a city employee enrolled in a city retirement system. He has taken out a loan from the retirement fund and is paying it back at the rate of $14.90 every two weeks.
   In eighteen weeks, how much money will he have paid back on the loan?
   A. $268.20   B. $152.80   C. $134.10   D. $67.05

8. In 2019, The Iridor Book Company had the following expenses: rent, $6,500; overhead, $52,585; inventory, $35,700; and miscellaneous, $1,275.
If all of these expenses went up 18% in 2020, what would they TOTAL in 2020?
A. $17,290.80   B. $78,769.20   C. $96,060.00   D. $113,350.80

8.____

9. Ms. Ranier had a gross salary of $710.72 paid once every two weeks.
If the deductions from each paycheck are $125.44, $50.26, $12.58, and $2.54, how much money would Ms. Ranier take home in eight weeks?
A. $2,079.60   B. $2,842.88   C. $4,159.20   D. $5,685.76

9.____

10. Mr. Martin had a net income of $95,500 in 2019.
If he spent 34% on rent and household expenses, 3% on house furnishings, 25% on clothes, and 36% on food, how much was left for savings and other expenses?
A. $980   B. $1,910   C. $3,247   D. $9,800

10.____

11. Mr. Elsberg can pay back a loan of $1,800 from the city employees' retirement system if he pays back $36.69 every two weeks for two full years.
At the end of the two years, how much more than the original $1,800 he borrowed will Mr. Elsberg have paid back?
A. $53.94   B. $107.88   C. $190.79   D. $214.76

11.____

12. Mr. Nusbaum is a city employee receiving a gross salary (salary before deductions) of $20,800. Every two weeks, the following deductions are taken out of his salary: Federal Income Tax, $162.84; FICA, $44.26; State Tax, $29.2; City Tax, $13.94; Health Insurance, $3.14.
If Mr. Nusbaum's salary and deductions remained the same for a full calendar year, what would his net salary (gross salary less deductions) be in that year?
A. $6,596.20   B. $14,198.60   C. $18,745.50   D. $20,546.30

12.____

13. Add: 8936, 7821, 8953, 4297, 9785, 6579.
A. 45,371   B. 45,381   C. 46,371   D. 46,381

13.____

14. Multiply: 987
            867
A. 854,609   B. 854,729   C. 855,709   D. 855,729

14.____

15. Divide: 59)321439.0
A. 5438.1   B. 5447.1   C. 5448.1   D. 5457.1

15.____

16. Divide: .052)721
A. 12,648.0   B. 12,648.1   C. 12,649.0   D. 12,649.1

16.____

17. If the total number of employees in one city agency increased from 1,927 to 2,006 during a certain year, the percentage increase in the number of employees for that year is MOST NEARLY
A. 4%   B. 5%   C. 6%   D. 7%

17.____

3 (#1)

18. During a single fiscal year, which totaled 248 workdays, one account clerk verified 1,488 purchase vouchers.
Assuming a normal work week of five days, what is the AVERAGE number of vouchers verified by the account clerk in a one-week period during this fiscal year?
A. 25	B. 30	C. 35	D. 40

18._____

19. Multiplying a number by .75 is the same as
A. multiplying it by ²/₃
B. dividing it by ²/₃
C. multiplying it by ¾
D. dividing it by ¾

19._____

20. In City Agency A, ²/₃ of the employees are enrolled in a retirement system. City Agency B has the same number of employees as Agency A and 60% of these are enrolled in a retirement system.
If Agency A has a total of 660 employees, how many MORE employees does it have enrolled in a retirement system than does Agency B?
A. 36	B. 44	C. 56	D. 66

20._____

21. Net worth is equal to assets minus liabilities.
If, at the end of 2019, a textile company had assets of $98,695.83 and liabilities of $59,238.29, what was its net worth?
A. $38,478.54	B. $38,488.64	C. $39,457.54	D. $48,557.54

21._____

22. Mr. Martin's assets consist of the following: Cash on hand, $5,233.74, Automobile, $3,206.09; Furniture, $4,925.00; Government Bonds, $5,500.00; and House, $36,69.85.
What are his TOTAL assets?
A. $54,545.68	B. $54,455.68	C. $55,455.68	D. $55,555.68

22._____

23. If Mr. Mitchell has $627.04 in his checking account and then writes three checks for $241.75, $13.24, and $102.97, what will be his new balance?
A. $257.88	B. $269.08	C. $357.96	D. $369.96

23._____

24. An employee's net pay is equal to his total earnings less all deductions.
If an employee's total earnings in a pay period are $497.05, what is his net pay if he has the following deductions: Federal Income Tax, $18.79; City Tax, $7.25; Pension, $1.88?
A. $351.17	B. $351.07	C. $350.17	D. $350.07

24._____

25. A petty cash fund had an opening balance of $85.75 on December 1. Expenditures of $23.00, $15.65, $5.23, $14.75, and $26.38 were made out of this fund during the first 14 days of the month. Then, on December 17, another $38.50 was added to the fund.
If additional expenditures of $17.18, $3.29, and $11.64 were made during the remainder of the month, what was the FINAL balance of the petty cash fund at the end of December?
A. $6.93	B. $7.13	C. $46.51	D. $91.40

25._____

KEY (CORRECT ANSWERS)

1.	B	11.	B
2.	A	12.	B
3.	B	13.	C
4.	A	14.	D
5.	D	15.	C
6.	C	16.	D
7.	C	17.	A
8.	D	18.	B
9.	A	19.	C
10.	B	20.	B

21. C
22. D
23. B
24. D
25. B

5 (#1)

SOLUTIONS TO PROBLEMS

1. ($132,000)(.61) − ($125,500)(.60) = $5,220

2. Interest = $1,950. As a percent, $1950 ÷ 15,000 = 13%

3. New balance = $253.36 + $36.95 + $210.23 + $7.34 - $117.35 - $23.37 - $15.98 = $351.18

4. Rent = ($97,254)(.27) = $26,258.58

5. ($2,436.18)(.06) ≈ $146.17

6. ($397.50 - $13.18 - $122.76) = $8,631.48

7. ($14.90)($\frac{18}{2}$) = $134.10

8. ($6,500 + $52,585 + $35,700 + $1,275)(1.18) = $113,350.80

9. ($710.72 - $125.44 - $50.26 - $12.58 - $2.54)($\frac{8}{2}$) = $2,079.60

10. (1 - .34 - .03 - .25 - .36) - $1,800 = $107.88

11. (36.69)(52) - $1,800 = $107.88

12. $20,800 − (26)($162.84+$44.26+$29.72+$13.94+$3.14) = $14,198.60

13. 8,936 + 7,821 + 8,953 + 4,297 + 9,785 + 6,579 = 46,371

14. (987)(867) − 855,729

15. 321,439 ÷ 59 ≈ 5,448.1

16. 721 ÷ .057 ≈ 12,649.1

17. (2,006-1,927) ÷ 1,927 ≈ 4%

18. Let x = number of vouchers. Then, $\frac{x}{5} = \frac{1488}{248}$. Solving, x = 30

19. Multiplying by .75 is equivalent to multiplying by $\frac{3}{4}$

20. (660)($\frac{2}{3}$) − (660)(.60) = 44

21. Net worth = $98,695.83 - $59,238.29 = $39,457.54

22. Total Assets = $5,233.74 + $3,206.09 + $4,925.00 + $5,500.00) + $36,690.85 = $55,555.68.

23. New balance = $627.04 - $241.75 - $13.24 - $102.97 = $269.08

24. Net pay = $497.05 - $90.32 - $28.74 - $18.79 - $7.25 - $1.88 = $350.07

25. Final balance = $85.75 - $23.00 - $15.65 - $5.23 - $14.75 - $26.38 + $38.50 - $17.18 - $3.29 - $11.64 = $7.13

TEST 2

DIRECTIONS: Each question or incomplete statement is followed by several suggested answers or completions. Select the one that BEST answers the question or completes the statement. *PRINT THE LETTER OF THE CORRECT ANSWER IN THE SPACE AT THE RIGHT.*

1. The formula for computing base salary is: Earnings equals base gross plus additional gross.
   If an employee's earnings during a particular period are in the amounts of $597.45, $535.92, $639.91, and $552.83, and his base gross salary is $525.50 per paycheck, what is the TOTAL of the additional gross earned by the employee during that period?
   A. $224.11   B. $224.21   C. $224.51   D. $244.11

   1.____

2. If a lump sum death benefit is paid by the retirement system in an amount equal to 3/7 of an employee's last yearly salary of $13,486.50, the amount of the death benefit paid is MOST NEARLY
   A. $5,749.29   B. $5,759.92   C. $5,779.92   D. $5,977.29

   2.____

3. Suppose that a member has paid 15 installments on a 28-installment loan. The percentage of the number of installments paid to the retirement system is
   A. 53.57%   B. 53.97%   C. 54.57%   D. 55.37%

   3.____

4. If an employee takes a 1-month vacation during a calendar year, the percentage of the year during which he works is MOST NEARLY
   A. 90.9%   B. 91.3%   C. 91.6%   D. 92.1%

   4.____

5. Suppose that an employee took a leave of absence totaling 7 months during a calendar year.
   Assuming the employee did not take any vacation time during the remainder of that year, the percentage of the year in which he worked is MOST NEARLY
   A. 41.7%   B. 43.3%   C. 46.5%   D. 47.1%

   5.____

6. A member has borrowed $4,725 from her funds in the retirement system. If $3,213 has been repaid, the percentage of the loan which is still outstanding is MOST NEARLY
   A. 16%   B. 32%   C. 48%   D. 68%

   6.____

7. If an employee worked only 24 weeks during the year because of illness, the portion of the year he was out of work was MOST NEARLY
   A. 46%   B. 48%   C. 51%   D. 54%

   7.____

8. If an employee purchased credit for a 16-week period of service which he had prior to rejoining the retirement system, the percentage of a year he purchased credit for was MOST NEARLY
   A. 27.9%   B. 28.8%   C. 30.7%   D. 33.3%

   8.____

2 (#2)

9. If an employee contributes 2/11 of his yearly salary to his pension fund account, the percentage of his yearly salary which he contributes is MOST NEARLY
    A. 17.9%   B. 18.2%   C. 18.4%   D. 19.0%

10. In 2018, the maximum amount of income from which social security tax could be withheld (base salary) was $70,500. In 2020, the base salary was $82,500. The 2020 base salary represents a percentage increase over the 2018 base salary of APPROXIMATELY
    A. 15%   B. 16%   C. 17%   D. 18%

11. If 17.5% of an employee's salary is withheld for taxes, the one of the following which is the fraction of the salary withheld is
    A. 3/20   B. 8/35   C. 7/40   D. 4/25

12. If a person withdraws 42% of the funds from his account with the retirement system, the remaining balance represents a fraction of MOST NEARLY
    A. 7/13   B. 5/9   C. 7/12   D. 4/7

13. A property decreases in value from $45,000 to $35,000.
    The percent of decrease is MOST NEARLY
    A. 20.5%   B. 22.2%   C. 25.0%   D. 28.6%

14. The fraction $\frac{487}{101326}$ expressed as a decimal is MOST NEARLY
    A. .0482   B. .00481   C. .0049   D. .00392

15. The reciprocal of the sum of 2/3 and 1/6 can be expressed as
    A. 0.83   B. 1.20   C. 1.25   D. 1.50

16. Total land and building costs for a new commercial property equal $50 per square foot.
    If the investors expect a 10 percent return on their costs, and if total operating expenses average 5 percent of total costs, annual gross rentals per square foot must be AT LEAST
    A. $7.50   B. $8.50   C. $10.00   D. $12.00

17. The formula for computing the amount of annual deposit in a compound interest bearing account to provide a lump sum at the end of a period of years is
    $X = \frac{r \cdot L}{(1+r)^{n-1}}$ (X is the amount of annual deposit, r is the rate of interest, and n is the number of years and L = lump sum).
    Using the formula, the annual amount of the deposit at the end of each year to accumulate $20,000 at the end of 3 years with interest at 2 percent on annual balances is
    A. $6,120.00   B. $6,203.33   C. $6,535.09   D. $6,666.66

18. An investor sold two properties at $150,000 each. On one he made a 2.5 percent profit. On the other, he suffered a 25 percent loss.
    The NET result of his sales was
    A. neither a gain nor a loss
    B. a $20,000 loss
    C. a $75,000 gain
    D. a $75,000 loss

    18._____

19. A contractor decides to install a chain fence covering the perimeter of a parcel 75 feet wide and 112 feet in depth.
    Which one of the following represents the number of feet to be covered?
    A. 187   B. 364   C. 374   D. 8,400

    19._____

20. A builder estimates he can build an average of 4½ one-family homes to an acre. There are 640 acres to one square mile.
    Which one of the following CORRECTLY represents the number of one-family homes the builder would estimate he can build on one square mile?
    A. 1,280   B. 1,920   C. 2,560   D. 2,880

    20._____

21. $.01059 deposit at 7 percent interest will yield $1.00 in 30 years.
    If a person deposited $1,059 at 7 percent interest on April 4, 1991, which one of the following amounts would represent the worth of this deposit on March 31, 2021?
    A. $100   B. $1,000   C. $10,000   D. $100,000

    21._____

22. A building has an economic life of forty years.
    Assuming the building depreciates at a constant annual rate, which one of the following CORRECTLY represents the yearly percentage of depreciation?
    A. 2.0%   B. 2.5%   C. 5.0%   D. 7.0%

    22._____

23. A building produces a gross income of $200,000 with a net income of $20,000, before mortgage charges and capital recapture. The owner is able to increase the gross income 5 percent without a corresponding increase in operating costs.
    The effect upon the net income will be an INCREASE of
    A. 5%   B. 10%   C. 12.5%   D. 50%

    23._____

24. The present value of $1.00 not payable for 8 years, and at 10 percent interest, is $.4665.
    Which of the following amounts represents the PRESENT value of $1,000 payable 8 years hence at 10 percent interest?
    A. $46.65   B. $466.50   C. $4,665.00   D. $46,650.00

    24._____

25. The amount of real property taxes to be levied by a city is $100 million. The assessment roll subject to taxation shows an assessed valuation of $2 billion. Which one of the following tax rates CORRECTLY represents the tax rate to be levied per $100 of assessed valuation?
    A. $.50   B. $5.00   C. $50.00   D. $500.00

    25._____

KEY (CORRECT ANSWERS)

1.	A	11.	C
2.	C	12.	C
3.	A	13.	B
4.	C	14.	B
5.	A	15.	B
6.	B	16.	A
7.	D	17.	C
8.	C	18.	B
9.	B	19.	C
10.	C	20.	D

21.	D
22.	B
23.	D
24.	B
25.	B

5 (#2)

SOLUTIONS TO PROBLEMS

1. $597.45 + $535.91 + $639.91 + $552.83 = $2,326.11. Then, $2,326.11 − (4)($525.50) = $224.11

2. Death benefit = ($13,486.50)($\frac{3}{7}$) ≈ $5,779.92

3. $\frac{15}{28}$ ≈ 53.57%

4. $\frac{11}{12}$ ≈ 91.6% (closer to 91.7%)

5. $\frac{5}{12}$ ≈ 41.7%

6. ($4,725-$3,213) ÷ $4,725 = 32%

7. $\frac{28}{52}$ ≈ 54%

8. $\frac{16}{52}$ ≈ 30.7% (closer to 30.8%)

9. $\frac{2}{11}$ ≈ 18.2%

10. ($82,500 - $70,500) ÷ $70,500 = 17%

11. 17.5% = $\frac{175}{1000}$ = $\frac{7}{40}$

12. 100% - 42% = 58% = $\frac{58}{100}$ = $\frac{29}{50}$, closest to $\frac{7}{12}$ in selections

13. $\frac{\$10,000}{\$45,000}$ ≈ 22.2%

14. 487/101,216 ≈ .00481

15. $\frac{2}{3} + \frac{1}{6} = \frac{5}{6}$ Then, $1 ÷ \frac{5}{6} = \frac{6}{5}$ = 1.20

16. (.15)($50) = $7.50

17. x = (.02)($20,000)/[(1+.02)^3 − 1] = 400 ÷ .061208 ≈ $6,535.09

18. Sold 150,000, 25% loss = paid 200,000, loss of $50,000 Sold 150,000, 25% profit = paid 120,000, profit of 30,000 − 50,000 + 30,000 = 20,000 (loss)

19. Perimeter = (2)(75) + (2)(112) = 374 ft.

20. (640)(4½) = 2,880 homes

21. (1÷.01059)(1059) = $100,000

22. 1÷4 = .025 = 2.5%

23. New gross income = ($200,000)(X1.05) = $210,000
    Then, ($210,000-$200,000) ÷ $20,000 = 50%

24. Let x = present value of $1,000. Then, $\frac{\$1.00}{\$.4665} = \frac{\$1000}{x}$
    Solving, x = $466.50

25. Let x = tax rate. Then, $\frac{\$100,000,000}{\$2,000,000,000} = \frac{x}{\$100}$
    Solving, x = $5.00

TEST 3

DIRECTIONS: Each question or incomplete statement is followed by several suggested answers or completions. Select the one that BEST answers the question or completes the statement. *PRINT THE LETTER OF THE CORRECT ANSWER IN THE SPACE AT THE RIGHT.*

1. It is found that for the past three years the average weekly number of inspections per inspector ranged from 20 inspections to 40 inspections.
On the basis of this information, it is MOST reasonable to conclude that
   A. on the average, 30 inspections per week were made
   B. the average weekly number of inspections never fell below 20
   C. the performance of inspectors deteriorated over the three-year period
   D. the range in average weekly inspections was 60

1.____

Questions 2-4.

DIRECTIONS: Questions 2 through 4 are to be answered on the basis of the following information.

The number of students admitted to University X in 2019 from High School Y was 268 students. This represented 13.7 percent of University X's entering freshman classes. In 2020, it is expected that University X will admit 591 students from High School Y, which is expected to represent 19.4 percent of the 2020 entering freshman classes of University X.

2. Which of the following is CLOSEST estimate of the size of University's expected 2020 entering freshman classes?
   _____ students
   A. 2,000   B. 2,500   C. 3,000   D. 3,500

2.____

3. Of the following, the expected percentage of increase from 2019 to 2020 in the number of students graduating from High School Y and entering University X as freshmen is MOST NEARLY
   A. 5.7%   B. 20%   C. 45%   D. 120%

3.____

4. Assume that the cost of processing admission to University X from High School Y in 2019 was an average of $28. Also, that this was 1/3 more than the average cost of processing each of the other 2019 freshmen admissions to University X.
Then, the one of the following that MOST closely shows the total processing cost of all 2019 freshman admissions to University X is
   A. $6,500   B. $20,000   C. $30,000   D. $40,000

4.____

5. Assume that during the fiscal year 2019-2020, a bureau produced 20% more work units than it produced in the fiscal year 2018-2019. Also assume that during the fiscal year 2019-2020 that bureau's staff was 20% smaller than it was in the fiscal year 2018-2019.

5.____

239

On the basis of this information, it would be MOST proper to conclude that the number of work units produced per staff member in that bureau in the fiscal year 2019-2020 exceeded the number of work units produced per staff member in that bureau in the fiscal year 2018-2019 by which one of the following percentages?
A. 20%   B. 25%   C. 40%   D. 50%

6. Assume that during the following fiscal years (FY), a bureau has received the following appropriations:
   FY 2015-2016 - $200,000
   FY 2016-2017 - $240,000
   FY 2017-2018 - $280,000
   FY 2018-2019 - $390,000
   FY 2019-2020 - $505,000
   The bureau's appropriation for which one of the following fiscal years showed the LARGEST percentage of increase over the bureau's appropriation for the immediately previous fiscal year?
   A. FY 2016-2017   B. FY 2017-2018
   C. FY 2018-2019   D. FY 2010-2020

7. Assume that the number of buses (U_t) required for a given line-haul system serving the Central Business District depends upon roundtrip time (t), capacity of bus (c), and the total number of people to be moved in a peak hour (P) in the major direction, i.e., in the morning and out in the evening.
   The formula for the number of buses required is U_t =
   A. Ptc   B. $\frac{tP}{c}$ C. $\frac{cP}{t}$ D. $\frac{ct}{P}$

8. The area, in blocks, that can be served by a single stop for any maximum walking distance is given by the following formula: $a = 2w^2$. In this formula, a = the area served by a stop and w = maximum walking distance.
   If people will tolerate a walk of up to three blocks, how many stops would be needed to service an area of 288 square blocks?
   A. 9   B. 16   C. 18   D. 27

Questions 9-11.

DIRECTIONS: Questions 9 through 11 are to be answered on the basis of the following information.

In 2019, a police precinct records 456 cases of car thefts, which is 22.6 percent of all grand larcenies. In 2020, there were 560 such cases, which constituted 35% of the broader category.

9. The number of crimes in the broader category in 2020 was MOST NEARLY
   A. 1,600   B. 1,700   C. 1,960   D. 2,800

10. The change from 2019 to 2020 in the number of crimes in the broader category represented MOST NEARLY a
    A. 2.5% decrease
    B. 10.1% increase
    C. 12.5% increase
    D. 20% decrease

    10.____

11. In 2020, one out of every 6 of these crimes was solved.
    This represents MOST NEARLY what percentage of the total number of crimes in the broader category that year?
    A. 5.8
    B. 6
    C. 9.3
    D. 12

    11.____

12. Assume that a maintenance shop does 5 brake jobs to every 3 front-end jobs. It does 8,000 jobs altogether in a 240-day year. In one day, one worker can do 3 front-end jobs or 4 brake jobs.
    About how many workers will be needed in the shop?
    A. 3
    B. 5
    C. 10
    D. 18

    12.____

13. Assume that the price of a certain item declines by 6% one year, and then increases by 5 and 10 percent, respectively, during the next two years.
    What is the OVERALL increase in price over the three-year period?
    A. 4.2
    B. 6
    C. 8.6
    D. 10.1

    13.____

14. After finding the total percent change in a price (TO) over a three-year period, as in the preceding question, one could compute the average annual percent change in the price by using the formula
    A. $(1+TC)^{1/3}$
    B. $\frac{(1+TC)}{3}$
    C. $(1+TC)^{1/3-1}$
    D. $\frac{1}{(1+TC)^{1/3}-1}$

    14.____

15. 357 is 6% of
    A. 2,142
    B. 5,950
    C. 4,140
    D. 5,900

    15.____

16. In 2019, a department bought n pieces of a certain supply item for a total of $x. In 2020, the department bought k percent fewer of the item but had to pay a total of g percent more for it.
    Which of the following formulas is CORRECT for determining the average price per item in 2020?
    A. $100\frac{xg}{nk}$
    B. $\frac{x(100+g)}{n(100-k)}$
    C. $\frac{x(100-g)}{n(100+k)}$
    D. $\frac{x}{n} - 100\frac{g}{k}$

    16.____

17. A sample of 18 income tax returns, each with 4 personal exemptions, is taken for 2019 and 2020. The breakdown is as follows in terms of income:

Average Gross Income (in thousands)	Number of Returns	
	2019	2020
40	6	2
80	10	11
120	2	5

    There is a personal deduction per exemption of $500.
    There are no other expense deductions. In addition, there is an exclusion of $3,000 for incomes less than $50,000 and $2,000 for incomes from $50,000 to $99,999.99. From $100,000 upward there is no exclusion.

    17.____

The average net taxable income for the samples in thousands for 2019 is MOST NEARLY
A. $67 B. $85 C. $10 D. $128

18. In the preceding question, the increase in average net taxable income for the sample (in thousands) between 2019 and 2020 is
A. 16 B. 20 C. 24 D. 34

19. Assume that supervisor S has four subordinates—A, B, C, and D. The MAXIMUM number of relationships, assuming that all combinations are included, that can exist between S and his subordinates is
A. 28 B. 15 C. 7 D. 4

20. If the workmen's compensation insurance rate for clerical workers is 93 cents per $100 of wages, the total premium paid by a city whose clerical staff earns $8,765,000 is MOST NEARLY
A. $8,150 B. $81,515 C. $87,650 D. $93,765

21. Assume that a budget of $3,240,000,000 for the fiscal year beginning July 1, 2020 has been approved. A city sales tax is expected to provide $1,100,000,000; licenses, fees and sundry revenues ae expected to yield $121,600,000; the balance is to be raised from property taxes. A tax equalization board has appraised all property in the city at a fair value of $42,500,000,000. The council wishes to assess property at 60% of its fair value.
The tax rate would need to be MOST NEARLY _____ per $100 of assessed value.
A. $12.70 B. $10.65 C. $7.90 D. $4.00

22. Men's white linen handkerchiefs cost $12.90 for 3.
The cost per dozen handkerchiefs is
A. $77.40 B. $38.70 C. $144.80 D. $51.60

23. Assume that it is necessary to partition a room measuring 40 feet by 20 feet into eight smaller rooms of equal size.
Allowing no room for aisles, the MINIMUM amount of partitioning that would be needed is _____ feet.
A. 90 B. 100 C. 110 D. 140

24. Assume that two types of files have been ordered: 200 of type A and 100 of type B. When the files are delivered, the buyer discovers that 25% of each type is damaged. Of the remaining files, 20% of type A and 40% of type B are the wrong color.
The total number of files that are the WRONG COLOR is
A. 30 B. 40 C. 50 D. 60

25. In a unit of five inspectors, one inspector makes an average of 12 inspections a day, two inspectors make an average of 10 inspections a day, and two inspectors make an average of 9 inspections a day.
If in a certain week one of the inspectors who makes an average of nine inspections a day is out of work on Monday and Tuesday because of illness and all the inspectors do no inspections for half a day on Wednesday because of a special meeting, the number of inspections this unit can be expected to make in that week is MOST NEARLY

25.____

   A. 215   B. 225   C. 230   D. 250

KEY (CORRECT ANSWERS)

1.	B	11.	A
2.	C	12.	C
3.	D	13.	C
4.	D	14.	C
5.	D	15.	B
6.	C	16.	B
7.	B	17.	A
8.	B	18.	A
9.	A	19.	B
10.	D	20.	B

21. C
22. D
23. B
24. D
25. A

SOLUTIONS TO PROBLEMS

1. Since the number of weekly inspections ranged from 20 to 40, this implies that the average weekly number of inspections never fell below 20.

2. 591 ÷ 194 ≈ 3046, closest to 3,000 students

3. (591-268) ÷ 268 = 120%

4. Total processing cost = (268)(28) + (1,688)($21) = $42,952, closest to $40,000. [Note: Since 268 represents 13.7%, total freshman population = 268 ÷ .137 ≈ 1,956. Then, 1,956 − 268 = 1,688]

5. Let x = staff size in 2018-2019. Then, .80x = staff size in 2019-2020. Since the 2019-2020 staff produced 20% more work, this is represented by 1.20. However, to measure the productivity per staff member, the factor 1/.80 = 1.25 must also be used to equate the 2 staffs. Then, (1.20)(1.25) = 1.50. Thus, the 2019-2020 staff produced 50% more than the 2018-2019 staff.

6. The respective percent increases are ≈ 20%, 17%, 39%, 29%. The largest would be, over the previous fiscal year, for the current fiscal year 2018-2019

7. $\frac{P}{c}$ = number of buses needed per hour. If t = time (in hrs.), then U_t = tP.c

8. a = (2)(9) = 18 for 1 stop. Then, 288 ÷ 18 = 15 stops.

9. 560 ÷ .35 = 1600 grand larcenies.

10. 456 ÷ .226 = 2018; 560 ÷ .35 = 1600. Then, (1,600-2,018) ÷ 2,018 = -20% or a 20% decrease.

11. $(\frac{1}{6})(560) = 93\frac{1}{3}$. Then, $93\frac{1}{3}$ ÷ 1,600 = 5.8%

12. There are 5,000 brake jobs and 3,000 front-end jobs in one year.
    5,000 ÷ 4 = 1,250 days, and 1,250 ÷ 240 ≈ 5.2. Also, 3,000 ÷ 3 = 1,000 days, and 1,000 ÷ 240 ≈ 4.2. Total number of workers needed ≈ 5.2 + 4.2 ≈ 10.

13. (.94)(1.05)(1.10) = 1.0857, which represents an overall increase by about 8.6%.

14. Average annual % change = $(1+TC)^{1/3} - 1 = (1.0857)^{1/3} - 1 ≈ 2.8\%$.

15. 357 ÷ .06 = 5,950

16. In 2020, $(h)(1-\frac{k}{100})$ pieces cost $(x)(1 + \frac{g}{100})$ dollars. To calculate the cost for 1 piece (average cost), find the value of $[(x)(1 + \frac{G}{100})] ÷ [(n)(1 - \frac{K}{100})]$ = [(x)(100+g)/100]. [100/{n(100-k)}] = [x(100+g)]/[n(100-k)

17.
	#	Deductions Up to 50,000	
40,000	6	2000 3000	40,000-3,000-2,000 = 35,000 x 6
80,000	10	2000 2000	80,000-2,000-2,000 = 76,000 x 10
20,000	2	2000	= 118000 x 2

35,000 x 6 = 210,000 = 210
76,000 x 10 = 760,000 = 760
118,800 x 2 = 236,000 = 236
                                    1206

1206 ÷ 18 = 67

18.
2020		Deductions	
40,000	2	2000 3000	35,000 x 2 = 70,000
80,000	11	2000 2000	76,000 x 11 = 836,000
120,000	5	2000	118,000 x 5 = 590,000
			1,496,000

1,496,000/18 = 83,111
83,111 − 67,000 = 16,111 = most nearly 16 (in thousands)

19. We are actually looking for the number of different groups of different sizes involving S. This reduces to $_4C_1 + {_4C_2} + {_4C_2} + {_4C_4} = 4 + 6 + 4 + 1 = 15$. The notation $_nC_r$ means combinations of n things taken R at a time = $[(n)(n-1)(n-2)(...)(n-R+1)]/[(R)(R-1)(...)(1)]$. The 15 groups are: SA, SB, SC, SD, SAB, SAC, SAD, SBC, SBD, SCD, SABC, SABD, SACD, SBCD, SABCD.

20. Let x = total premiums. Then, $\frac{.93}{100} = \frac{X}{8,765,000}$ Solving, x = $81,515

21. The balance, raised from property taxes, = $3,240,000,000 - $1,100,000,000 − $121,600,000 = $2,018,400,000. Now, (.60)($42,500,000,000) = $25,500,000. The tax rate per $100 of assessed value = ($2,018,400,000)($100)(/$25,500,000,00 = $7.90.

22. A dozen costs ($12.90)($\frac{12}{3}$) = $51.60.

23. (40(20) ÷ 8 = 100 ft.

24. Total number of wrong-color files = (200)(.75)(.20)+(100)(.75)(.40) = 60

25. Weekly number of inspections = (12×5) + (10×5) + (10×5) + (9×5) + 9×5) = 250
Subtract: 9 Monday, 9 Tuesday, 25 Wednesday
Total: 250 − 9 − 9 − 25 = 207
Closest entry is choice A.

EXAMINATION SECTION
TEST 1

DIRECTIONS: Each question or incomplete statement is followed by several suggested answers or completions. Select the one that BEST answers the question or completes the statement. *PRINT THE LETTER OF THE CORRECT ANSWER IN THE SPACE AT THE RIGHT.*

Note: Some items will require the use of compound interest or amortization tables.

1. The procedure for determining the net price of something using the complement method involves

    A. multiplying the list price by the discount and subtracting the result from the list price
    B. multiplying the net price by the complement rate
    C. multiplying the list price by the complement rate
    D. multiplying the list price by the discount

    1.____

2. Employees at Rosenberg's Department Store are paid the hourly wages listed below:
$7.50, $9.25, $8.75, $9.50, $7.25, $8.50
What is the range of these hourly wages?

    A. $1.75
    B. $2.25
    C. $3.00
    D. $8.46

    2.____

3. An electrician charges a flat fee of $35 per job and $99 per hour for labor, which includes the $32 per hour she pays her assistant. The electrician also charges for the cost of materials. The total cost (C) of the electrician's work, for a 2-hour job that involves $40 worth of materials would be represented by the equation

    A. $C = 35 + 2(99) + 40$
    B. $C = 2(35 + 99 - 32)$
    C. $C = 2(35 + 99 + 32 + 40)$
    D. $C = 35 + 2(99 + 40)$

    3.____

4. $2000 remains in an account that pays 6% interest. After 5 years, if interest is compounded quarterly, the account will contain

    A. $2693.71
    B. $2600
    C. $2480
    D. $2291.72

    4.____

5. To determine how much one would have needed to deposit three years ago at 10% annually in order to have $50,000 today, which table should be used?

    A. Future value of an annuity due of 1
    B. Future value of 1 or present value of 1
    C. Future value of an ordinary annuity of 1
    D. Present value of an ordinary annuity of 1

    5.____

247

6. A 5-year loan, compounded semiannually, has _____ compounding periods.

    A. 2.5
    B. 5
    C. 10
    D. 20

7. The men's department at Woolridge's Department Store had sales of $96,890. If sales for the entire store were $396,800 and the total overhead for the store is $28,500, how much overhead is allotted to the men's department?

    A. $6959.09
    B. $17,888.34
    C. $21,540.91
    D. $33,450.33

8. The percent decrease from $6.49 to $4.49 is

    A. 3.08 %
    B. 24.75%
    C. 30.82%
    D. 42.23%

9. A 120-day promissory note with a $14,500 face value and an interest rate of 12% exact simple interest per year would have a maturity value of

    A. $14,500
    B. $15,072.05
    C. $15,080
    D. $15,827.08

10. To retire its bonds, Ankh Reliquaries, needs $100,000. What amount does the company need to deposit on January 1, 2008 at 10% interest compounded semiannually in order to accumulate the desired sum by January 1 of 2015?

    A. $25,253
    B. $33,333
    C. $50,507
    D. $75,761

11. $\dfrac{N(3 \times 4)}{(4+2)} = 5(N - 9)$

    $N =$

    A. -12
    B. 12
    C. -15
    D. 15

12. Diamante Motors has a current ratio of 2.1 and an acid test ratio of 1.82. Diamante's current liabilities are $40,000. Assuming no prepaid expenses, the dollar amount of merchandise inventory is

A. $7,280
B. $8,400
C. $11,200
D. $12,400

13. A debtor makes partial payments, at three-month intervals, of $500, $300, and $400 on a one-year loan of $2000 at a 10% simple interest rate.
What is the amount that is due at the end of the year?   13.____

  A. $800
  B. $920.97
  C. $943.99
  D. $967.67

14. Harlan Carnes uses the retail inventory Its annual sales were $70,000, net purchases at cost were $39,500, net purchases at retail were $65,500. Beginning inventory at cost was $20,500 and beginning inventory at retail was $34,500. Harlan Carnes' ending inventory at cost is   14.____

  A. $18,000
  B. $30,000
  C. $60,000
  D. $77,000

15. Which of the following functions would find the lowest degree polynomial that passes through the points (-4, 0), (-2, 0), (1, 0), and (3, 0)?   15.____

  A. $f(x) = (x + 4)(x + 2)(x-1)(x-3)$
  B. $f(x) = (x-4)(x-2)(x+1)(x+3)$
  C. $f(x) = (x + 4)(x + 2) + (x -1)(x -3)$
  D. $f(x) = (x-4)(x-2) + (x+1)(x + 3)$

16. Which of the following would require the use of the present value of an annuity due concept in order to calculate the present value of the asset or liability at the date of incurrence?   16.____

  A. A 10-year, 6% bond is issued on January 1 with interest payable semi-annually on July 1 and January 1 yielding 7%.
  B. A 10-year, 6% bond is issued on January 1 with interest payable semi-annually on July 1 and January 1 yielding 5%.
  C. A company enters a capital lease agreement with the initial payment due within 30 days of the signing of the agreement.
  D. A company enters a capital lease agreement with the initial payment due upon the signing of the agreement.

17. From different parts of the country, three friends met at Mt. Katahdin for a camping trip. Celeste drove 80 1/8 miles and Jennifer drove 76 5/6 miles. All together, the three friends drove 351 miles. How many miles were driven by the third friend, Stella?   17.____

  A. 194 23/72
  B. 193 23/72
  C. 15649/72
  D. 1487/12

18. 19, 5, 16, 12, *m*, 11, 3, 20

    If the mean of the list of numbers above is 12, the median is

    A. 11.5
    B. 11
    C. 10.5
    D. 10

    18.____

19. The present value of an ordinary annuity of $10,000 for 18 months at 6% annual interest, compounded semiannually, is

    A. $3,34.82
    B. $18,000
    C. $28,290
    D. $96,090

    19.____

20. Investors Trust purchased 100 servers and 200 scanner/printers from Globe Technology. The trade discount on the servers was 20%. The series of discounts on the scanner/printers was 20%, 10%. The list price of a server is $800 per unit, and scanner/printers are $700 a unit. The total invoice price was subject to terms of 2/10, n/30. If Investors Trust paid the invoice within the discount period, what was the price per unit of a scanner/printer?

    A. $493.92
    B. $627.20
    C. $686
    D. $784

    20.____

21. Payments of $5000 were made at the end of each quarter into an ordinary annuity that pays 11% compounded quarterly. After six years, the accounts contained

    A. $166,841
    B. $178,954
    C. $187,900
    D. $222,567

    21.____

22. What is the rate of yield to maturity for five 10-year, $1000, 8% bonds for 90?

    A. 9.5%
    B. 9.8%
    C. 10%
    D. 10.9%

    22.____

23. $R(x) = \dfrac{x^2 - 9}{2x^2 - 5x - 3}$

    A graph of the function above will have

    A. one vertical asymptote, one horizontal asymptote, and two equal zeroes
    B. one vertical asymptote, one horizontal asymptote, one distinct zero, and a removable discontinuity at $x = 3$
    C. two vertical asymptotes, two horizontal asymptotes, one distinct zero, and a removable discontinuity at $x = 3$
    D. two vertical asymptotes, one horizontal asymptote, and two distinct zeroes

    23.____

24. In simple interest, the dollar amount of difference between a $12,000 note at 12% for 9 months and the same amount for 15 months would be   24.____

    A. $1900
    B. $1080
    C. $720
    D. $129.60

25. Butcher Pete, a boutique gourmet catalog retailer, imports seasoned Kobe beef Chateaubriand for $55 a The company's past history has demonstrated that about 5% of the meat will pass its expiration date before it can be Butcher Pete needs a 62% markup based on cost. If Butcher Pete receives a shipment of 1300 pounds of Chateaubriand, what should the selling price per pound of this shipment?   25.____

    A. $89
    B. $94
    C. $107
    D. $111

KEY (CORRECT ANSWERS)

1. C		11. D	
2. B		12. C	
3. A		13. C	
4. A		14. A	
5. B		15. A	
6. C		16. D	
7. A		17. A	
8. C		18. A	
9. B		19. C	
10. C		20. A	

21. A
22. A
23. B
24. C
25. B

TEST 2

DIRECTIONS: Each question or incomplete statement is followed by several suggested answers or completions. Select the one that BEST answers the question or completes the statement. *PRINT THE LETTER OF THE CORRECT ANSWER IN THE SPACE AT THE RIGHT.*

Note: Some items will require the use of compound interest or amortization tables.

1. An annuity due of $100 for six months at 8% annual interest, compounded quarterly, will earn _____ in total interest.   1._____

   A. $3.33
   B. $6.04
   C. $16
   D. $36

2. $2.5(b + 7) = 15$ 2._____
   $b =$

   A. -2
   B. -2.5
   C. -1.25
   D. 1.25

3. An in voice for $500 contains terms 3/15, n/45. In order to take advantage of the cash discount, a customer would need to borrow at an ordinary interest rate of   3._____

   A. 15%
   B. 33.34%
   C. 37.11%
   D. 43.45%

4. The equation $(3 + 5) + 8 = 3 + (5 + 8)$ demonstrates the _____ property of numbers.   4._____

   A. commutative
   B. associative
   C. distributive
   D. transitive

5. For an interest rate of 5% for six years, which of the following tables would show the largest value?   5._____

   A. Future value of an ordinary annuity of 1
   B. Present value of an ordinary annuity of 1
   C. Future value of 1
   D. Present value of 1

6. Which of the following statements is TRUE?   6._____

   A. The set of real numbers form a group under addition but the set of $n \times n$ matrices do not.
   B. All real numbers have an additive inverse but some $n \times n$ matrices do not.

C. The multiplication of real numbers is commutative but the multiplication of n x n matrices is not.
D. The product of two real numbers is a real number, but the product of two n x n matrices is a scalar.

7. If the selling price is an item is $45.60 and the cost is $32.57, the markup based on cost is

   A. 20%
   B. 40%
   C. 60%
   D. 80%

8. The percent increase from $16.50 to $20.00 is

   A. 3.08%
   B. 18.96%
   C. 21.21%
   D. 308%

9. In Earl's Sporting Warehouse, the Camping & Gear Department occupies 6000 square feet; the Biking and Boarding Department 3000 square feet; and the Clothing Department occupies 1000 square feet. What percentage of overhead expense would be applied to the clothing department?

   A. 5
   B. 10
   C. 20
   D. 40

10. A 3-year loan of $7000 required interest of $1250 to be If the loan was repaid in monthly installments, the annual percentage rate was

    A. 5.6%
    B. 5.85%
    C. 11%
    D. 11.7%

11. To find the cost of ending inventory using the weighted average method, the units in ending inventory should be multiplied by the

    A. assigned cost per unit
    B. cost per unit
    C. cost of ending inventory
    D. average unit cost

12. A company begins a sinking fund, hoping to make monthly payments that will accumulate $100,000 at the end of 20 years, at an interest rate of 6% compounded annually. The monthly payment will be

    A. $151.04
    B. $200.54
    C. $214.89
    D. $216.43

13. Johnson Little Company has issued 10,000 shares of $100 par value 8% noncumunative preferred stock and $ 100,000 of no-par value common In its first year of operations, Johnson Little declared and paid a $50,000 In its second year, Johnson Little declared and paid a $280,000 The dividend per common share in the second year was

    A. $1.20
    B. $1.70
    C. $1.80
    D. $2.00

14. An investment of $2800, earning 9% compounded monthly, would be worth $3251.31 at the end of _____ months.

    A. 20
    B. 24
    C. 32
    D. 40

15. Gene signs a 120-day promissory note on September 4. The due date of the note is

    A. January 3
    B. January 2
    C. January 1
    D. December 31

16. For illustrating how data are divided into categories, a _____ graph is usually the best

    A. circle/pie
    B. bar
    C. pictorial
    D. line

17. An ice cream factory's energy costs in August are $20,000. The owner estimates that the cost of energy will decrease by 1.7% per month over the next six months. Based on this estimate, the factory's energy costs be in October of the same year should be calculated as

    A. ($20,000 - ($20,000 x 0.83)) x 0.83
    B. $20,000 x 0.983 x 0.983
    C. ($20,000 x 0.983) + ($20,000 x 0.966)
    D. $20,000 - ($20,000 x 0.017 x 0.017)

18. If a savings account pays 4% compounded quarterly, then the amount of $ 1 left on deposit for 7 years would be found in a table using

    A. 28 periods at 1%
    B. 28 periods at 4%
    C. 7 periods at 1%
    D. 7 periods at 4%

19. A ranch is for sale consisting of 112 3/8 acres. After negotiating with a buyer, the seller agreed to sell a 29 5/6-acre parcel of the ranch. After the sale, how many acres of land remain?

    A. 81 3/8
    B. 82 11/24
    C. 82 13/34
    D. 83 11/24

19.____

20. If the current value of a bond with a $5000 face value is 1.01%, its dollar value is

    A. $4950
    B. $5000
    C. $5050
    D. $5500

20.____

21. The federal Social Security tax rate is 6.2% of the first $87,500 in gross earnings. Don, who earns $100,000 in a year, would pay a Social Security tax of

    A. $5449,30
    B. $6200
    C. $6899.80
    D. $9,899.60

21.____

22. The Carlings own a home with a tax assessment of 1.25% of 80% of its market value of $230,000. The Carlings are going to sell the home to a Navy veteran who will receive an 8% exemption from property taxes. The veteran's annual property tax will be

    A. $1840
    B. $2116
    C. $2645
    D. $2932

22.____

23. Hornacek Plumbing Supply sells copper elbows for $2.50 each and gate-valve faucets for $8.00. In the last month the company has sold a total of 300 units for a total of $1,465. What was the total amount of sales for copper elbows?

    A. $324.50
    B. $425
    C. $1040
    D. $1140

23.____

24. Numbers that are both a factor of 2400 and a multiple of 12 include
    I. 8
    II. 36
    III. 48
    IV. 96

    A. I and II
    B. II only
    C. III and IV
    D. I, II, III and IV

24.____

25. Each of the following is used to calculate net sales, EXCEPT
    A. sales discounts
    B. purchases
    C. gross sales
    D. returns and allowances

KEY (CORRECT ANSWERS)

1. B
2. A
3. C
4. B
5. A

6. C
7. B
8. C
9. B
10. C

11. D
12. D
13. D
14. A
15. B

16. A
17. B
18. A
19. C
20. C

21. A
22. B
23. B
24. C
25. B

TEST 3

DIRECTIONS: Each question or incomplete statement is followed by several suggested answers or completions. Select the one that BEST answers the question or completes the statement. *PRINT THE LETTER OF THE CORRECT ANSWER IN THE SPACE AT THE RIGHT.*

Note: Some items will require the use of compound interest or amortization tables.

1. The future value formula for compound interest is

    A. $A = P(1+R)^N$
    B. $A = P + I$
    C. $I = PR$
    D. $I = PRT$

    1.____

2. Wilma purchased 300 shares of Spacely Sprockets for $6000. When she sold her stock a year later, the proceeds were $8015. Her dividends during the year were $678. Her return on investment (excluding possible broker fees or commissions) was

    A. 7.2%
    B. 25.1%
    C. 44.9%
    D. 79.4%

    2.____

3. 25 is 20% of

    A. 85
    B. 110
    C. 110
    D. 125

    3.____

4. The total amount paid for a toaster was $49.78. If the sales tax was 5.6%, what was the sale price of the toaster?

    A. $47.14
    B. $47.99
    C. $48.84
    D. $52.50

    4.____

5. Chockaloff Manufacturing had a beginning inventory that was $8000 at cost and ending inventory of $7800 at cost. Its net sales for the year were $42,000 and the cost of goods sold was $28,000. The inventory turnover at cost was

    A. 1.33
    B. 1.52
    C. 1.77
    D. 2.65

    5.____

6. A car stereo is marked up 37%, based on the selling price. The equivalent markup, based on cost, is

    A. 38.7%
    B. 58.7%

    6.____

C. 59%
D. 63%

7. During the Memorial Day sale, all merchandise is priced at 23% off. If an item from this store originally cost x dollars, its sale price is   7.____

   A. 0.23x
   B. 0.77x
   C. 1.23x
   D. 1.77x

8. If the nominal rate of an investment is 7% and interest is compounded semiannually, the effective rate is   8.____

   A. 6.94%
   B. 7.04%
   C. 7.12%
   D. 7.5%

9. Mr. Halz recently started a new He worked 20% more hours in his third week on the job than he did in the second He worked 30% more hours in the second week than he did in the first week, and he worked 10% fewer hours in the first week than his regularly scheduled weekly hours. If Mr. Halz worked 46 hours in his third week on the job, approximately what are his regularly scheduled weekly work hours?   9.____

   A. 45
   B. 38
   C. 33
   D. 27

10. The Stokelys bought a home for $190,000 with a down payment of $65,000. The rate of interest was 7% for 35 years. The Stokelys' monthly payment is   10.____

    A. $798.75
    B. $834.57
    C. $843.75
    D. $978.57

11. The Hardware Hut had a weekend sale on tools, charging $3.95 for a Phillips screwdriver and $3.49 for a flat screwdriver. During the sale, the Hardware Hut sold three times as many flathead screwdrivers as Phillips screwdrivers. The total revenue for the two sales was $1095.92. How many flathead screwdrivers did the Hardware Hut sell?   11.____

    A. 76
    B. 152
    C. 228
    D. 684

12. The Cloud family purchases a minivan for $24,000 by making a $2000 down payment and amortize the balance over 4 years at 12% annually. The amount of each monthly payment is   12.____

    A. $267.98
    B. $441.45

C. $579.34
D. $610.17

13. The maturity value of a proposed 22-month investment is $6350. At a simple annual interest rate of 9%, the present value of the investment is

    A. $5450
    B. $5500
    C. $5550
    D. $7600

14. On March 1, Universal Faucet purchased $23,000 of fittings for its The purchase was subject to terms of 1/10, n/30. Universal Faucet paid half the invoice purchase price on March 9, and promised the vendor the remainder by the end of the For this partial payment, the vendor should credit Universal payment with a payment of

    A. $11,500
    B. $11,743.69
    C. $11,985.75
    D. $12,000

15. The island of Gaura experienced ten earthquakes last year. Their magnitudes, measured on the Richter scale, are as follows:
    7.0, 6.2, 7.7, 8.0, 6.4, 7.2, 5.4, 6.6, 7.5, 5.9
    The mode of this data set is

    A. There is no
    B. 5.4
    C. 6.4
    D. 7.3

16. On January 1, Greatline Enterprises issued $100,000, 8% bonds with interest payable semiannually, due in three years. The market rate at the time of issue was 10%. In order to have an effective yield of 10% over the three-year period, the bonds would have to sell for

    A. $20,302.76
    B. $74,622.00
    C. $94,924.76
    D. $98,345.31

17. 108/30 as a whole number reduced to the lowest terms is

    A. 3.35
    B. 3 3/5
    C. 3 2/3
    D. 3 18/30

18. If the cost of goods sold is $132,500 and the average inventory at cost is $53,000, the inventory turnover rate at cost is

    A. 1.2
    B. 1.8

C. 2.5
D. 4.0

19. Property in Yolo County is assessed at 82% of its fair market If the tax rate is $13.66 per thousand, what is the property tax on property with a fair market value of $544,000? 19._____

   A. $4852.37
   B. $4940.76
   C. $5450.97
   D. $6093.45

20. A machine that cost $50,000 has an estimated useful life of 5 years and an estimated salvage value of $2000. It is placed in service on January 1. Using the double-declining balance method, what with the book value of the machine be at the end of the third year? 20._____

   A. $7,200
   B. $8,700
   C. $10,800
   D. $18,000

21. The modified accelerated cost recovery system (MACRS) of depreciation allows for _____ of a property's total cost to be 21._____

   A. 20%
   B. 50%
   C. 80%
   D. 100%

22. Which of the following tables has a factor of 1.00000 for 1 period at every interest rate? 22._____

   A. Future value of 1
   B. Present value of 1
   C. Future value of an ordinary annuity of 1
   D. Present value of an ordinary annuity of 1

23. Binford Tools purchased materials under terms of 2/10, 1/15, n/30 on August 1, and paid the $4,500 invoice on August 27. How much was the cash discount? 23._____

   A. $0
   B. $45
   C. $90
   D. $135

24. A quality control engineer takes a random sample of flour from 25,000 bags. The engineer reports that the mean weight of the flour in the bags in the population is 4.87 pounds ± 0.8 ounces, with a confidence level of 95%. If the size of the sample is increased and the engineer retains the 95% confidence level, 24._____

   A. the size of the confidence interval will decrease
   B. the size of the confidence interval will increase
   C. the mean value will decrease
   D. the mean value will increase

25. On September 15, the unpaid balance on Leeds Consulting's expense charge account was $4000. Between September 15 and October 15, Leeds consultants charged $4786 worth of goods and services, and the company paid $6000 on its charge account. On October 15, including a 2.3% monthly finance charge on the previous month's unpaid balance, the account balance is

25.____

A. $2398.37
B. $2589
C. $2650.15
D. $2878

KEY (CORRECT ANSWERS)

1. A
2. C
3. D
4. A
5. C

6. B
7. B
8. C
9. C
10. A

11. C
12. C
13. A
14. B
15. A

16. C
17. B
18. C
19. D
20. C

21. D
22. C
23. A
24. A
25. D

INTERPRETING STATISTICAL DATA GRAPHS, CHARTS, AND TABLES

EXAMINATION SECTION

TEST 1

DIRECTIONS: Each question or incomplete statement is followed by several suggested answers or completions. Select the one that BEST answers the question or completes the statement. *PRINT THE LETTER OF THE CORRECT ANSWER IN THE SPACE AT THE RIGHT.*

Questions 1-5.

DIRECTIONS: Questions 1 through 5 are to be answered SOLELY on the basis of the following chart.

DUPLICATION JOBS							
	DATES					NO. OF COPIES	
JOB NO.	SUBMITTED	REQUIRED	COMPLETED	PROCESS	NO. OF ORIGINALS	OF EACH ORIGINAL	REQUESTING UNIT
324	6/22	6/25	6/25	Xerox	14	25	Research
325	6/25	6/27	6/28	Kodak	10	125	Training
326	6/25	6/25	6/25	Xerox	12	11	Budget
327	6/25	6/27	6/26	Press	17	775	Admin. Div. H
328	6/28	ASAP*	6/25	Press	5	535	Personnel
329	6/26	6/26	6/27	Xerox	15	8	Admin. Div. G
*ASAP – As soon as possible							

1. The unit whose job was to be Xeroxed but was NOT completed by the date required is
   A. Administrative Division H
   B. Administrative Division G
   C. Research
   D. Training

   1.____

2. The job with the LARGEST number of original pages to be Xeroxed is job number
   A. 324   B. 326   C. 327   D. 329

   2.____

3. Jobs were completed AFTER June 26 for
   A. Training and Administrative Division G
   B. Training and Administrative Division H
   C. Research and Budget
   D. Administrative Division G only

   3.____

4. Which one of the following units submitted a job which was completed SOONER than required?
   A. Training
   B. Administrative Division H
   C. Personnel
   D. Administrative Division G

   4.____

263

5. The jobs which were submitted on different days but were completed on the SAME day and used the SAME process had job numbers
   A. 324 and 326
   B. 327 and 328
   C. 324, 326, and 328
   D. 324, 326, and 329

5._____

KEY (CORRECT ANSWERS)

1. B
2. D
3. A
4. B
5. A

TEST 2

DIRECTIONS: Each question or incomplete statement is followed by several suggested answers or completions. Select the one that BEST answers the question or completes the statement. *PRINT THE LETTER OF THE CORRECT ANSWER IN THE SPACE AT THE RIGHT.*

Questions 1-10.

DIRECTIONS: Questions 1 through 10 are to be answered SOLELY on the basis of the Production Record table shown below for the Information Unit in Agency X for the work week ended Friday, December 6. The table shows, for each employee, the quantity of each type of work performed and the percentage of the work week spent in performing each type of work.

NOTE: Assume that each employee works 7 hours a day and 5 days a week, making a total of 35 hours for the work week.

PRODUCTION RECORD – INFORMATION UNIT IN AGENCY X (For the Work Week ended Friday, December 6)				
	NUMBER OF			
	Papers Filed	Sheets Proofread	Visitors Received	Envelopes Addressed
Miss Agar	3120	33	178	752
Mr. Brun	1565	59	252	724
Miss Case	2142	62	214	426
Mr. Dale	4259	29	144	1132
Miss Earl	2054	58	212	878
Mr. Farr	1610	69	245	621
Miss Glen	2390	57	230	790
Mr. Hope	3425	32	176	805
Miss Iver	3726	56	148	650
Mr. Joad	3212	55	181	495

	PERCENTAGE OF WORK WEEK SPENT ON				
	Filing Papers	Proofreading	Receiving Visitors	Addressing Envelopes	Performing Miscellaneous Work
Miss Agar	30%	9%	34%	11%	16%
Mr. Brun	13%	15%	52%	10%	10%
Miss Case	23%	18%	38%	6%	15%
Mr. Dale	50%	7%	17%	16%	10%
Miss Earl	24%	14%	37%	14%	11%
Mr. Farr	16%	19%	48%	8%	9%
Miss Glen	27%	12%	42%	12%	7%
Mr. Hope	38%	8%	32%	13%	9%
Miss Iver	43%	13%	24%	9%	11%
Mr. Joad	33%	11%	36%	7%	13%

1. For the week, the average amount of time which the employees spent in proofreading was MOST NEARLY _____ hours.
   A. 3.1   B. 3.6   C. 4.4   D. 5.1

2. The average number of visitors received daily by an employee was MOST NEARLY
   A. 40   B. 57   C. 198   D. 395

3. Of the following employees, the one who addressed envelopes at the FASTEST rate was
   A. Miss Agar   B. Mr. Brun   C. Miss Case   D. Mr. Dale

4. Mr. Farr's rate of filing papers was MOST NEARLY _____ pages per minute.
   A. 2   B. 1.7   C. 5   D. 12

5. The average number of hours that Mr. Brun spent daily on receiving visitors exceeded the average number of hours that Miss Iver spent daily on the same type of work by MOST NEARLY _____ hours.
   A. 2   B. 3   C. 4   D. 5

6. Miss Earl worked at a FASTER rate than Miss Glen in
   A. filing papers
   B. proofreading sheets
   C. receiving visitors
   D. addressing envelopes

7. Mr. Joad's rate of filing papers _____ Miss Iver's rate of filing papers by APPROXIMATELY _____.
   A. was less than; 10%
   B. exceeded; 33%
   C. was less than; 16%
   D. exceeded; 12%

8. Assume that in the following week Miss Case is instructed to increase the percentage of her time spent on filing papers to 35%.
   If she continued to file papers at the same rate as she did for the week ended December 6, the number of additional papers that she filed the following week was MOST NEARLY
   A. 3260   B. 5400   C. 250   D. 1120

9. Assume that in the following week Mr. Hope increased his weekly total of envelopes addressed to 1092.
   If he continued to spend the same amount of time on this assignment as he did for the week ended December 6, the increase in his rate of addressing envelopes the following week was MOST NEARLY _____ envelopes her hour.
   A. 15   B. 65   C. 155   D. 240

10. Assume that in the following week Miss Agar and Mr. Dale spent 3 and 9 hours less, respectively, on filing papers than they had spent for the week ended December 6, without changing their rates of work.
The total number of papers filed during the following week by both Miss Agar and Mr. Dale was MOST NEARLY
A. 4235 B. 4295 C. 4315 D. 4370

10.____

KEY (CORRECT ANSWERS)

1. C
2. A
3. B
4. C
5. A
6. C
7. D
8. D
9. B
10. B

TEST 3

DIRECTIONS: Each question or incomplete statement is followed by several suggested answers or completions. Select the one that BEST answers the question or completes the statement. *PRINT THE LETTER OF THE CORRECT ANSWER IN THE SPACE AT THE RIGHT.*

Questions 1-6.

DIRECTIONS: Questions 1 through 6 are to be answered SOLELY on the basis of the following chart.

EMPLOYMENT RECORDS				
	Allan	Barry	Cary	David
July	5	4	1	7
August	8	3	9	8
September	7	8	7	5
October	3	6	5	3
November	2	4	4	6
December	5	2	8	4

1. The clerk with the HIGHEST number of errors for the 6-month period was 1.____
   A. Allan   B. Barry   C. Cary   D. David

2. If the number of errors made by Allan in the six months shown represented one-eighth of the total errors made by the unit during the entire ear, what was the TOTAL number of errors made by the unit for the year? 2.____
   A. 124   B. 180   C. 240   D. 360

3. The number of errors made by David in November was what fraction of the total errors made in November? 3.____
   A. 1/3   B. 1/6   C. 378   D. 3/15

4. The average number of errors made per month per clerk was MOST NEARLY 4.____
   A. 4   B. 5   C. 6   D. 7

5. Of the total number of errors made during the six-month period, the percentage made in August was MOST NEARLY 5.____
   A. 2%   B. 4%   C. 23%   D. 44%

6. If the number of errors in the unit were to decrease in the next six months by 30%, what would be MOST NEARLY the total number of errors for the unit for the next six months? 6.____
   A. 87   B. 94   C. 120   D. 137

KEY (CORRECT ANSWERS)

1. C
2. C
3. C
4. B
5. C
6. A

TEST 4

DIRECTIONS: Each question or incomplete statement is followed by several suggested answers or completions. Select the one that BEST answers the question or completes the statement. *PRINT THE LETTER OF THE CORRECT ANSWER IN THE SPACE AT THE RIGHT.*

Questions 1-5.

DIRECTIONS: Questions 1 through 5 are to be answered SOLELY on the basis of the following data. These data show the performance rates of the employees in a particular division for a period of six months.

Employee	Jan.	Feb.	March	April	May	June
A	96	53	64	48	76	72
B	84	58	69	56	67	79
C	73	68	71	54	59	62
D	98	74	79	66	86	74
E	89	78	67	74	75	77

1. According to the above data, the average monthly performance for a worker is MOST NEARLY
   A. 66   B. 69   C. 72   D. 75

2. According to the above data, the mean monthly performance for the division is MOST NEARLY
   A. 350   B. 358   C. 387   D. 429

3. According to the above data, the employee who shows the LEAST month-to-month variation in performance is
   A. A   B. B   C. C   D. D

4. According to the above data, the employee who shows the GREATEST range in performance is
   A. A   B. B   C. C   D. D

5. According to the above data, the median employee with respect to performance for the six-month period is
   A. A   B. B   C. C   D. D

KEY (CORRECT ANSWERS)

1. C
2. B
3. C
4. A
5. B

TEST 5

DIRECTIONS: Each question or incomplete statement is followed by several suggested answers or completions. Select the one that BEST answers the question or completes the statement. *PRINT THE LETTER OF THE CORRECT ANSWER IN THE SPACE AT THE RIGHT.*

Questions 1-5.

DIRECTIONS: Questions 1 through 5 are to be answered SOLELY on the basis of the following chart, which shows the absences in Unit A for the period November 1 through November 15.

ABSENCE RECORD – UNIT A November 1-15															
Date:	1	2	3	4	5	6	7	8	9	10	11	12	13	14	15
Employee															
Ames	X	s	H					X			H			X	X
Bloom	X		H				X	X	S	s	H	S	S		X
Deegan	X	J	H	J	J	J	X	X			H				X
Howard	X		H					X			H			X	X
Jergens	X	M	H	M	M	M		X			X			X	X
Lange	X		H			S	X	X							X
Morton	X						X	X	V	V	H				X
O'Shea	X		H			O		X			H			X	X

CODE FOR TYPES OF ABSENCE
X - Saturday or Sunday
H - Legal Holiday
P - Leave Without Pay
M - Military Leave
J - Jury Duty
V - Vacation
S - Sick Leave
O - Other Leave of Absence

NOTE: If there is no entry against an employee's name under a date, the employee worked on that date.

1. According to the above chart, NO employee in Unit A was absent on
   A. leave without pay
   B. military leave
   C. other leave of absence
   D. vacation

   1._____

2. According to the above chart, all but one of the employees in Unit A were present on the
   A. 3rd   B. 5th   C. 9th   D. 13th

   2._____

3. According to the above chart, the ONLY employee who worked on a legal holiday when the other employees were absent are
   A. Deegan and Morton
   B. Howard and O'Shea
   C. Lange and Morton
   D. Morton and O'Shea

   3._____

2 (#5)

4. According to the above chart, the employee who was absent ONLY on a day that was a Saturday, Sunday, or legal holiday was 4.____
   A. Bloom   B. Howard   C. Morton   D. O'Shea

5. The employees who had more absences than anyone else are 5.____
   A. Bloom and Deegan
   B. Bloom, Deegan, and Jergens
   C. Deegan and Jergens
   D. Deegan, Jergens, and O'Shea

KEY (CORRECT ANSWERS)

1. A
2. D
3. C
4. B
5. B

TEST 6

DIRECTIONS: Each question or incomplete statement is followed by several suggested answers or completions. Select the one that BEST answers the question or completes the statement. *PRINT THE LETTER OF THE CORRECT ANSWER IN THE SPACE AT THE RIGHT.*

Questions 1-7.

DIRECTIONS: Questions 1 through 7 are to be answered SOLELY on the basis of the time sheet and instructions given below.

	MON.		TUES.		WED.		THURS.		FRI.	
	IN	OUT	IN	OUT	IN	OUT	IN	OUT	IN	OUT
Walker	8:45	5:02	9:20	5:00	9:00	5:02	Annual Lv.		9:04	5:05
Jones	9:01	5:00	9:03	5:02	9:08	5:01	8:55	5:04	9:00	5:00
Rubins	8:49	5:04	Sick Lv.		9:05	5:04	9:03	5:03	9:04	3:30 (PB)
Brown	9:00	5:01	8:55	5:03	9:00	5:05	9:04	5:07	9:05	5:03
Roberts	9:30	5:08	8:43	5:07	9:05	5:05	9:09	12:30	8:58	5:04
	PA						PB			

The above time sheet indicates the arrival and leaving times of five telephone operators who punched a time clock in a city agency for the week of April 14. The times they arrived at work in the mornings are indicated in the columns labeled *IN* and the times they left work are indicated in the columns labeled *OUT*. The letters (PA) mean prearranged lateness, and the letters (PB) mean personal business. Time lost for these purposes is charged to annual leave.

The operators are scheduled to arrive at 9:00. However, they are not considered late unless they arrive after 9:05. If they prearrange a lateness, they are not considered late. Time lost through lateness is charged to annual leave. A full day's work is eight hours, from 9:00 to 5:00.

1. Which operator worked the entire week WITHOUT using any annual leave or sick leave time?
   A. Jones
   B. Brown
   C. Roberts
   D. None of the above

   1._____

2. On which days was NONE of the operators considered late?
   A. Monday and Wednesday
   B. Monday and Friday
   C. Wednesday and Thursday
   D. Wednesday and Friday

   2._____

3. Which operator clocked out at a different time each day of the week?
   A. Roberts   B. Jones   C. Rubins   D. Brown

   3._____

4. How many of the operators were considered late on Wednesday?
   A. 0   B. 1   C. 2   D. 3

   4._____

273

5. What was the TOTAL number of charged latenesses for the week of April 14?
   A. 1   B. 3   C. 5   D. 7

   5._____

6. Which day shows the MOST time charged to all types of leave by all the operators?
   A. Monday   B. Tuesday   C. Wednesday   D. Thursday

   6._____

7. What operators were considered ON TIME all week?
   A. Jones and Rubins
   B. Rubins and Brown
   C. Brown and Roberts
   D. Walker and Brown

   7._____

KEY (CORRECT ANSWERS)

1. B
2. B
3. A
4. B
5. B
6. D
7. B

TEST 7

DIRECTIONS: Each question or incomplete statement is followed by several suggested answers or completions. Select the one that BEST answers the question or completes the statement. *PRINT THE LETTER OF THE CORRECT ANSWER IN THE SPACE AT THE RIGHT.*

Questions 1-10.

DIRECTIONS: Questions 1 through 10 are to be answered SOLELY on the basis of the information and code tables given below.

In accordance with these code tables, each employee in the department is assigned a code number consisting of ten digits arranged from left to right in the following order:
  I. Division in Which Employed
  II. Title of Position
  III. Annual Salary
  IV. Age
  V. Number of Years Employed in Department

EXAMPLE: A clerk is 21 years old, has been employed in the department for three years, and is working in the Supply Division at a yearly salary of $25,000. His code number is 90-115-13-02-2.

\multicolumn{10}{c}{DEPARTMENTAL CODE}

TABLE I		TABLE II		TABLE III		TABLE IV		TABLE V	
Code No.	Division in Which Employed	Code No.	Title of Position	Code No.	Annual Salary	Code No.	Age	Code No.	No. of Years Employed in Department
10	Accounting	115	Clerk	11	$18,000 or less	01	Under 20 yrs.	1	Less than 1 year
20	Construction	155	Typist						
30	Engineering	175	Stenographer	12	$18,001 to $24,000	02	20 to 29 yrs.	2	1 to 5 yrs.
40	Information	237	Bookkeeper					3	6 to 10 yrs.
50	Maintenance	345	Statistician			03	30 to 39 yrs.	4	11 to 15 yrs.
60	Personnel	545	Storekeeper	13	$24,001 to $30,000			5	16 to 25 yrs.
70	Record	633	Draftsman			04	40 to 49 yrs.	6	26 to 35 yrs.
80	Research	665	Civil Engineer					7	36 yrs. or over
90	Supply	865	Machinist	14	$30,001 to $36,000	05	50 to 59 yrs.		
		915	Porter			06	60 to 69 yrs.		
				15	$36,001 to $45,000	07	70 yrs. or over		
				16	$45,001 to $60,000				
				17	$60,001 to $70,000				
				18	$70,001 or over				

275

1. A draftsman employed in the Engineering Division at a yearly salary of $34,800 is 36 years old and has been employed in the department for 9 years.
   He should be coded
   A. 20-633-13-04-3
   B. 30-865-13-03-4
   C. 20-665-14-04-4
   D. 30-633-14-03-3

2. A porter employed in the Maintenance Division at a yearly salary of $28,800 is 52 years old and has been employed in the department for 6 years.
   He should be coded
   A. 50-915-12-03-3
   B. 90-545-12-05-3
   C. 50-915-13-05-3
   D. 90-545-13-03-3

3. Richard White, who has been employed in the department for 12 years, receives $50,000 a year as a civil engineer in the Construction Division. He is 38 years old.
   He should be coded
   A. 20-665-16-03-4
   B. 20-665-15-02-1
   C. 20-633-14-04-2
   D. 20-865-15-02-5

4. An 18-year-old clerk appointed to the department six months ago is assigned to the Record Division. His annual salary is $21,600.
   He should be coded
   A. 70-115-11-01-1
   B. 70-115-12-01-1
   C. 70-115-12-02-1
   D. 70-155-12-01-1

5. An employee has been coded 40-155-12-03-3.
   Of the following statements regarding this employee, the MOST accurate one is that he is
   A. a clerk who has been employed in the department for at least 6 years
   B. a typist who receives an annual salary which does not exceed $24,000
   C. under 30 years of age and has been employed in the department for at least 11 years
   D. employed in the Supply Division at a salary which exceeds $18,000 per annum

6. Of the following statements regarding an employee who is coded 60-175-13-01-2, the LEAST accurate statement is that this employee
   A. is a stenographer in the Personnel Division
   B. has been employed in the department for at least one year
   C. receives an annual salary which exceeds $24,000
   D. is more than 20 years of age

7. The following are the names of four employees of the department with their code numbers:
   James Black, 80-345-15-03-4
   William White, 30-633-14-03-4
   Sam Green, 80-115-12-02-3
   John Jones, 10-237-13-04-5

If a salary increase is to be given to the employees who have been employed in the department for 11 years or more and who earn less than $36,001 a year, the two of the above employees who will receive a salary increase are
A. John Jones and William White B. James Black and Sam Green
C. James Black and William White D. John Jones and Sam Green

8. Code number 50-865-14-02-6, which has been assigned to a machinist, contains an obvious inconsistency.
This inconsistency involves the figures
   A. 50-865 B. 865-14 C. 14-02 D. 02-6

9. Ten employees were awarded merit prizes for outstanding service during the year. Their code numbers were:
   80-345-14-04-4   40-155-12-02-2
   40-155-12-04-4   10-115-12-02-2
   10-115-13-03-2   80-115-13-02-2
   80-174-13-05-5   10-115-13-02-3
   10-115-12-04-3   30-633-14-04-4
   Of these outstanding employees, the number who were clerks employed in the Accounting Division at a salary ranging from $24,001 to $30,000 per annum is
   A. 1 B. 2 C. 3 D. 4

10. The MOST accurate of the following statements regarding the ten outstanding employees listed in the previous question is that
    A. fewer than half of the employees were under 40 years of age
    B. there were fewer typists than stenographers
    C. four of the employees were employed in the department 11 years or more
    D. two of the employees in the Research Division receive annual salaries ranging from $30,001 to $36,000

KEY (CORRECT ANSWERS)

1. D   6. D
2. C   7. A
3. A   8. D
4. B   9. B
5. B   10. C

SAMPLE QUESTIONS
BIOGRAPHICAL INVENTORY

The questions included in the Biographical Inventory ask for information about you and your background. These kinds of questions are often asked during an oral interview. For years, employers have been using interviews to relate personal history, preferences, and attitudes to job success. This Biographical Inventory attempts to do the same and includes questions which have been shown to be related to job success. It has been found that successful employees tend to select some answers more often than other answers, while less successful employees tend to select different answers. The questions in the Biographical Inventory do not have a single correct answer. Every choice is given some credit. More credit is given for answers selected more often by successful employees.

These Biographical Inventory questions are presented for illustrative purposes only. The answers have not been linked to the answers of successful employees; therefore, we cannot designate any "correct" answer(s).

DIRECTIONS: You may only mark ONE response to each question. It is possible that none of the answers applies well to you. However, one of the answers will surely be true (or less inaccurate) for you than others. In such a case, mark that answer. <u>Answer each question honestly.</u> The credit that is assigned to each response on the actual test is based upon how successful employees described themselves when honestly responding to the questions. *PRINT THE LETTER OF THE CORRECT ANSWER IN THE SPACE AT THE RIGHT.*

1. Generally, in your work assignments, would you prefer
   A. to work on one thing at a time
   B. to work on a couple of things at a time
   C. to work on many things at the same time

2. In the course of a week, which of the following gives you the GREATEST satisfaction?
   A. Being told you have done a good job.
   B. Helping other people to solve their problems.
   C. Coming up with a new or unique way to handle a situation.
   D. Having free time to devote to personal interests.

EXAMINATION SECTION
TEST 1

For each of the following items, circle the answer that best reflects the accuracy of the given statement, according to your own values, opinions, and experience.

1. In most situations, I value cooperation over competition.

    A. Very Accurate
    C. Neither Accurate nor Inaccurate
    E. Very Inaccurate
    B. Moderately Accurate
    D. Moderately Inaccurate

2. In work or in school, I've tried to do more than what's expected of me.

    A. Very Accurate
    C. Neither Accurate nor Inaccurate
    E. Very Inaccurate
    B. Moderately Accurate
    D. Moderately Inaccurate

3. Most of my problems are caused by other people.

    A. Very Accurate
    C. Neither Accurate nor Inaccurate
    E. Very Inaccurate
    B. Moderately Accurate
    D. Moderately Inaccurate

4. It's reasonable to say that a person's race is in some way related to the likelihood that he or she will commit a crime.

    A. Very Accurate
    C. Neither Accurate nor Inaccurate
    E. Very Inaccurate
    B. Moderately Accurate
    D. Moderately Inaccurate

5. My respect for a person's authority relies entirely on my respect for them as an individual, and has nothing to do with his or her official position.

    A. Very Accurate
    C. Neither Accurate nor Inaccurate
    E. Very Inaccurate
    B. Moderately Accurate
    D. Moderately Inaccurate

6. When I was in school, I never cheated on a test or assignment.

    A. Very Accurate
    C. Neither Accurate nor Inaccurate
    E. Very Inaccurate
    B. Moderately Accurate
    D. Moderately Inaccurate

7. I feel comfortable around most people, even if they're strangers.

    A. Very Accurate
    C. Neither Accurate nor Inaccurate
    E. Very Inaccurate
    B. Moderately Accurate
    D. Moderately Inaccurate

8. It's acceptable for an employee to borrow property from the workplace if the person who takes it intends to return it when he or she is finished with it.

    A. Very Accurate
    C. Neither Accurate nor Inaccurate
    E. Very Inaccurate
    B. Moderately Accurate
    D. Moderately Inaccurate

9. If it's clear that a person is not likely to receive adequate punishment for a crime or infraction, it's only fair to inflict some form of discipline on that person to make up for any likely lapses injustice.

    A. Very Accurate
    B. Moderately Accurate
    C. Neither Accurate nor Inaccurate
    D. Moderately Inaccurate
    E. Very Inaccurate

10. In previous work experience, I have been reluctant or unable to take on extra work or overtime on short notice.

    A. Very Accurate
    B. Moderately Accurate
    C. Neither Accurate nor Inaccurate
    D. Moderately Inaccurate
    E. Very Inaccurate

11. The casual use of illegal substances, if it's done only recreationally and on weekends, has no effect on a person's performance on the job during the work week.

    A. Very Accurate
    B. Moderately Accurate
    C. Neither Accurate nor Inaccurate
    D. Moderately Inaccurate
    E. Very Inaccurate

12. I am sometimes overwhelmed by events.

    A. Very Accurate
    B. Moderately Accurate
    C. Neither Accurate nor Inaccurate
    D. Moderately Inaccurate
    E. Very Inaccurate

13. If I don't agree with a certain rule, I see nothing wrong with breaking it, as long as it doesn't hurt anyone else.

    A. Very Accurate
    B. Moderately Accurate
    C. Neither Accurate nor Inaccurate
    D. Moderately Inaccurate
    E. Very Inaccurate

14. I get angry easily.

    A. Very Accurate
    B. Moderately Accurate
    C. Neither Accurate nor Inaccurate
    D. Moderately Inaccurate
    E. Very Inaccurate

15. As long as an employee finishes all his work on time at the end of the day, there's nothing wrong with coming back from lunch late.

    A. Very Accurate
    B. Moderately Accurate
    C. Neither Accurate nor Inaccurate
    D. Moderately Inaccurate
    E. Very Inaccurate

16. I enjoy beginning new things.

    A. Very Accurate
    B. Moderately Accurate
    C. Neither Accurate nor Inaccurate
    D. Moderately Inaccurate
    E. Very Inaccurate

17. When I have a number of tasks to be done, I prioritize them and tackle them immediately in order of importance.

    A. Very Accurate
    B. Moderately Accurate
    C. Neither Accurate nor Inaccurate
    D. Moderately Inaccurate
    E. Very Inaccurate

18. I would have no reservations about working for a supervisor who is of a different race or gender than I am.

    A. Very Accurate
    B. Moderately Accurate
    C. Neither Accurate nor Inaccurate
    D. Moderately Inaccurate
    E. Very Inaccurate

19. I'd rather help other people to do better than punish them for doing wrong.

    A. Very Accurate
    B. Moderately Accurate
    C. Neither Accurate nor Inaccurate
    D. Moderately Inaccurate
    E. Very Inaccurate

20. In the past, I've had personality clashes with fellow students or co-workers whom I disliked or with whom I disagreed.

    A. Very Accurate
    B. Moderately Accurate
    C. Neither Accurate nor Inaccurate
    D. Moderately Inaccurate
    E. Very Inaccurate

21. Confrontations are usually unpleasant, but sometimes necessary.

    A. Very Accurate
    B. Moderately Accurate
    C. Neither Accurate nor Inaccurate
    D. Moderately Inaccurate
    E. Very Inaccurate

22. I generally believe that other people have good intentions.

    A. Very Accurate
    B. Moderately Accurate
    C. Neither Accurate nor Inaccurate
    D. Moderately Inaccurate
    E. Very Inaccurate

23. When I have a lot of information to sort through, I have difficulty making up my mind.

    A. Very Accurate
    B. Moderately Accurate
    C. Neither Accurate nor Inaccurate
    D. Moderately Inaccurate
    E. Very Inaccurate

24. In tense situations, I choose my words with care.

    A. Very Accurate
    B. Moderately Accurate
    C. Neither Accurate nor Inaccurate
    D. Moderately Inaccurate
    E. Very Inaccurate

25. A person who works through his or her lunch break should automatically be able to go home early.

    A. Very Accurate   B. Moderately Accurate
    C. Neither Accurate nor Inaccurate   D. Moderately Inaccurate
    E. Very Inaccurate

Experiences and Traits

For each of the 25 items, score your response according to the list below. Then add the scores of all 25 items to arrive at a single number.

1. A=4;B=3;C=2;D=1;E=0
2. A=4;B=3;C=2;D=1;E=0
3. A=0;B=1;C=2;D=3;E=4
4. A=0;B=1;C=2;D=3;E=4
5. A=0;B=1;C=2;D=3;E=4

6. A=4;B=3;C=2;D=1;E=0
7. A=4;B=3;C=2;D=1;E=0
8. A=0;B=1;C=2;D=3;E=4
9. A=0;B=1;C=2;D=3;E=4
10. A=0;B=1;C=2;D=3;E=4

11. A=0;B=1;C=2;D=3;E=4
12. A=0;B=1;C=2;D=3;E=4
13. A=0;B=1;C=2;D=3;E=4
14. A=0;B=1;C=2;D=3;E=4
15. A=0;B=1;C=2;D=3;E=4

16. A=4;B=3;C=2;D=1;E=0
17. A=4;B=3;C=2;D=1;E=0
18. A=4;B=3;C=2;D=1;E=0
19. A=4;B=3;C=2;D=1;E=0
20. A=0;B=1;C=2;D=3;E=4

21. A=4;B=3;C=2;D=1;E=0
22. A=4;B=3;C=2;D=1;E=0
23. A=0;B=1;C=2;D=3;E=4
24. A=4;B=3;C=2;D=1;E=0
25. A=0;B=1;C=2;D=3;E=4

The following scores serve as an approximate guide to your compatibility with a career in law enforcement but should not be taken as the final word.

    85-100 points   Most compatible
    70-84 points   Compatible
    50-69 points   Somewhat compatible
    0-49 points   Incompatible

TEST 2

For each of the following items, circle the answer that best reflects the accuracy of the given statement, according to your own values, opinions, and experience.

1. I find it difficult to approach people I don't know well.

    A. Very Accurate
    B. Moderately Accurate
    C. Neither Accurate nor Inaccurate
    D. Moderately Inaccurate
    E. Very Inaccurate

2. I'm not really interested in hearing about other people's problems.

    A. Very Accurate
    B. Moderately Accurate
    C. Neither Accurate nor Inaccurate
    D. Moderately Inaccurate
    E. Very Inaccurate

3. Sometimes I don't know why I do the things I do.

    A. Very Accurate
    B. Moderately Accurate
    C. Neither Accurate nor Inaccurate
    D. Moderately Inaccurate
    E. Very Inaccurate

4. I am hesitant to take charge of a group that has no clear leadership.

    A. Very Accurate
    B. Moderately Accurate
    C. Neither Accurate nor Inaccurate
    D. Moderately Inaccurate
    E. Very Inaccurate

5. I enjoy examining myself and the direction my life is taking.

    A. Very Accurate
    B. Moderately Accurate
    C. Neither Accurate nor Inaccurate
    D. Moderately Inaccurate
    E. Very Inaccurate

6. I believe there is no absolute right or wrong.

    A. Very Accurate
    B. Moderately Accurate
    C. Neither Accurate nor Inaccurate
    D. Moderately Inaccurate
    E. Very Inaccurate

7. I always pay my bills on time.

    A. Very Accurate
    B. Moderately Accurate
    C. Neither Accurate nor Inaccurate
    D. Moderately Inaccurate
    E. Very Inaccurate

8. In this world it's difficult to be both honest and successful.

    A. Very Accurate
    B. Moderately Accurate
    C. Neither Accurate nor Inaccurate
    D. Moderately Inaccurate
    E. Very Inaccurate

9. I am intimidated by strong personalities.

   A. Very Accurate
   B. Moderately Accurate
   C. Neither Accurate nor Inaccurate
   D. Moderately Inaccurate
   E. Very Inaccurate

10. In past work experience, I was unable to find value in work that wasn't personally rewarding to me.

    A. Very Accurate
    B. Moderately Accurate
    C. Neither Accurate nor Inaccurate
    D. Moderately Inaccurate
    E. Very Inaccurate

11. I often do things I later regret.

    A. Very Accurate
    B. Moderately Accurate
    C. Neither Accurate nor Inaccurate
    D. Moderately Inaccurate
    E. Very Inaccurate

12. I feel sympathy for those who are worse off than I am.

    A. Very Accurate
    B. Moderately Accurate
    C. Neither Accurate nor Inaccurate
    D. Moderately Inaccurate
    E. Very Inaccurate

13. If a rule gets in the way of my doing my job well, I'll look for ways around it.

    A. Very Accurate
    B. Moderately Accurate
    C. Neither Accurate nor Inaccurate
    D. Moderately Inaccurate
    E. Very Inaccurate

14. I think a person's dress and appearance are important in the work environment.

    A. Very Accurate
    B. Moderately Accurate
    C. Neither Accurate nor Inaccurate
    D. Moderately Inaccurate
    E. Very Inaccurate

15. There have been times when my own personal use of drugs or alcohol has adversely affected my job performance.

    A. Very Accurate
    B. Moderately Accurate
    C. Neither Accurate nor Inaccurate
    D. Moderately Inaccurate
    E. Very Inaccurate

16. In past work or school experience, I have never been in a position to supervise the work of others.

    A. Very Accurate
    B. Moderately Accurate
    C. Neither Accurate nor Inaccurate
    D. Moderately Inaccurate
    E. Very Inaccurate

17. If I need to, I can talk other people into doing what I think is necessary.

    A. Very Accurate
    B. Moderately Accurate
    C. Neither Accurate nor Inaccurate
    D. Moderately Inaccurate
    E. Very Inaccurate

18. I usually prefer order to chaos.

    A. Very Accurate
    B. Moderately Accurate
    C. Neither Accurate nor Inaccurate
    D. Moderately Inaccurate
    E. Very Inaccurate

19. When I'm faced with an ethical dilemma, I listen to my conscience.

    A. Very Accurate
    B. Moderately Accurate
    C. Neither Accurate nor Inaccurate
    D. Moderately Inaccurate
    E. Very Inaccurate

20. When I communicate with other people, I can easily sense their emotional state.

    A. Very Accurate
    B. Moderately Accurate
    C. Neither Accurate nor Inaccurate
    D. Moderately Inaccurate
    E. Very Inaccurate

21. I set high standards for myself and others.

    A. Very Accurate
    B. Moderately Accurate
    C. Neither Accurate nor Inaccurate
    D. Moderately Inaccurate
    E. Very Inaccurate

22. In school or at work, I am never late.

    A. Very Accurate
    B. Moderately Accurate
    C. Neither Accurate nor Inaccurate
    D. Moderately Inaccurate
    E. Very Inaccurate

23. I sometimes make assumptions about people based on their racial or ethnic backgrounds.

    A. Very Accurate
    B. Moderately Accurate
    C. Neither Accurate nor Inaccurate
    D. Moderately Inaccurate
    E. Very Inaccurate

24. I tend to focus on the positive aspects of a complex situation, rather than the negatives.

    A. Very Accurate
    B. Moderately Accurate
    C. Neither Accurate nor Inaccurate
    D. Moderately Inaccurate
    E. Very Inaccurate

25. I can manage several tasks at the same time.

    A. Very Accurate
    B. Moderately Accurate
    C. Neither Accurate nor Inaccurate
    D. Moderately Inaccurate
    E. Very Inaccurate

4 (#2)

Experiences and Traits

For each of the 25 items, score your response according to the list below. Then add the scores of all 25 items to arrive at a single number.

1. A=0;B=1;C=2;D=3;E=4
2. A=0;B=1;C=2;D=3;E=4
3. A=0;B=1;C=2;D=3;E=4
4. A=0;B=1;C=2;D=3;E=4
5. A=4;B=3;C=2;D=1;E=0

6. A=0;B=1;C=2;D=3;E=4
7. A=4;B=3;C=2;D=1;E=0
8. A=0;B=1;C=2;D=3;E=4
9. A=0;B=1;C=2;D=3;E=4
10. A=0;B=1;C=2;D=3;E=4

11. A=0;B=1;C=2;D=3;E=4
12. A=4;B=3;C=2;D=1;E=0
13. A=0;B=1;C=2;D=3;E=4
14. A=4;B=3;C=2;D=1;E=0
15. A=0;B=1;C=2;D=3;E=4

16. A=0;B=1;C=2;D=3;E=4
17. A=4;B=3;C=2;D=1;E=0
18. A=4;B=3;C=2;D=1;E=0
19. A=4;B=3;C=2;D=1;E=0
20. A=4;B=3;C=2;D=1;E=0

21. A=4;B=3;C=2;D=1;E=0
22. A=4;B=3;C=2;D=1;E=0
23. A=0;B=1;C=2;D=3;E=4
24. A=4;B=3;C=2;D=1;E=0
25. A=4;B=3;C=2;D=1;E=0

The following scores serve as an approximate guide to your compatibility with a career in law enforcementbut should not be taken as the final word.

85-100 points	Most compatible
70-84 points	Compatible
50-69 points	Somewhat compatible
0-49 points	Incompatible

EXAMINATION SECTION

TEST 1

DIRECTIONS: Each question or incomplete statement is followed by several suggested answers or completions. Select the one that BEST answers the question or completes the statement. *PRINT THE LETTER OF THE CORRECT ANSWER IN THE SPACE AT THE RIGHT.*

1. While a senior in high school, I was absent
    A. never
    B. seldom
    C. frequently
    D. more than 10 days
    E. only when I felt bored

    1._____

2. While in high school, I failed classes
    A. never
    B. once
    C. twice
    D. more than twice
    E. at least four times

    2._____

3. During class discussions in my high school classes, I usually
    A. listened without participating
    B. participated as much as possible
    C. listened until I had something to add to the discussion
    D. disagreed with others simply for the sake of argument
    E. laughed at stupid ideas

    3._____

4. My high school grade point average (on a 4.0 scale) was
    A. 2.0 or lower
    B. 2.1 to 2.5
    C. 2.6 to 3.0
    D. 3.1 to 3.5
    E. 3.6 to 4.0

    4._____

5. As a high school student, I completed my assignments
    A. as close to the due date as I could manage
    B. whenever the teacher gave me an extension
    C. frequently
    D. on time
    E. when they were interesting

    5._____

6. While in high school, I participated in
    A. athletic and non-athletic extracurricular activities
    B. athletic extracurricular activities
    C. non-athletic extracurricular activities
    D. no extracurricular activities
    E. mandatory afterschool programs

    6._____

7. In high school, I made the honor roll
    A. several times
    B. once
    C. more than once
    D. twice
    E. I cannot remember

    7._____

8. Upon graduation from high school, I received _____ honors.
    A. academic and non-academic
    B. academic
    C. non-academic
    D. no
    E. I cannot remember

    8._____

9. While attending high school, I worked at a paid job or as a volunteer
    A. never
    B. every so often
    C. 5 to 10 hours a month
    D. more than 10 hours a month
    E. more than 15 hours a month

    9._____

10. During my senior year of high school, I skipped school
    A. whenever I could
    B. once a week
    C. several times a week
    D. not at all
    E. when I got bored

    10._____

11. I was suspended from high school
    A. not at all
    B. once or twice
    C. once or twice, for fighting
    D. several times
    E. more times than I can remember

    11._____

12. During high school, my fellow students and teachers considered me
    A. above average
    B. below average
    C. average
    D. underachieving
    E. underachieving and prone to fighting

    12._____

13. An effective leader is someone who
    A. inspires confidence in his/her followers
    B. inspires fear in his/her followers
    C. tells subordinates exactly what they should do
    D. creates an environment in which subordinates feel insecure about their job security and performance
    E. makes as few decisions as possible

    13._____

3 (#1)

14. While a student, I spent my summers and holiday breaks			14._____
    A. in summer or remedial classes
    B. traveling
    C. working
    D. relaxing
    E. spending time with my friends

15. As a high school student, I cut classes			15._____
    A. frequently
    B. when I didn't like them
    C. sometimes
    D. rarely
    E. when I needed the sleep

16. In high school, I received academic honors			16._____
    A. not at all
    B. once
    C. twice
    D. several times
    E. I cannot remember

17. As a student, I failed _____ classes.			17._____
    A. no
    B. two
    C. three
    D. four
    E. more than four

18. Friends describe me as			18._____
    A. introverted
    B. hot-tempered
    C. unpredictable
    D. quiet
    E. easygoing

19. During my high school classes, I preferred to			19._____
    A. remain silent during discussions
    B. do other homework during discussions
    C. participate frequently in discussions
    D. argue with others as much as possible
    E. laugh at the stupid opinions of others

20. As a high school student, I was placed on academic probation			20._____
    A. not at all
    B. once
    C. twice
    D. three times
    E. more than three times

21. At work, being a team player means to 21._____
    A. compromise your ideals and beliefs
    B. compensate for the incompetence of others
    C. count on others to compensate for your inexperience
    D. cooperate with others to get a project finished
    E. rely on others to get the job done

22. My friends from school remember me primarily as a(n) 22._____
    A. person who loved to party
    B. ambitious student
    C. athlete
    D. joker
    E. fighter

23. My school experience is memorable primarily because of 23._____
    A. the friends I made
    B. the sorority/fraternity I was able to join
    C. the social activities I participated in
    D. my academic achievements
    E. the money I spent

24. A friend who is applying for a job asks you to help him pass the 24._____
    mandatory drug test by substituting your urine sample for his. You should
    A. help him by supplying the sample
    B. supply the sample and insist he seek drug counseling
    C. supply the sample, but tell him that this is the only time you'll help in this way
    D. call the police
    E. refuse

25. As a student, I handed in my assignments when 25._____
    A. they were due
    B. I could get an extension
    C. they were interesting
    D. my friends reminded me to
    E. I was able to

KEY (CORRECT ANSWERS)

1. A	11. A	21. D
2. A	12. A	22. B
3. C	13. A	23. D
4. E	14. C	24. E
5. D	15. D	25. A
6. A	16. D	
7. A	17. A	
8. A	18. E	
9. E	19. C	
10. D	20. A	

TEST 2

DIRECTIONS: Each question or incomplete statement is followed by several suggested answers or completions. Select the one that BEST answers the question or completes the statement. *PRINT THE LETTER OF THE CORRECT ANSWER IN THE SPACE AT THE RIGHT.*

1. At work you are accused of a minor infraction which you did not commit. Your first reaction is to
    A. call a lawyer
    B. speak to your supervisor about the mistake
    C. call the police
    D. yell at the person who did commit the infraction
    E. accept the consequences regardless of your guilt or innocence

    1._____

2. As a student, I began to prepare for final exams
    A. the night before taking them
    B. when the professor handed out the review sheets
    C. several weeks before taking them
    D. when my friends began to prepare for their exams
    E. the morning of the exam

    2._____

3. At work, I am known as
    A. popular
    B. quiet
    C. intense
    D. easygoing
    E. dedicated

    3._____

4. The most important quality in a coworker is
    A. friendliness
    B. cleanliness
    C. good sense of humor
    D. dependability
    E. good listening skills

    4._____

5. In the past year, I have stayed home from work
    A. frequently
    B. only when I felt depressed
    C. rarely
    D. only when I felt overwhelmed
    E. only to run important errands

    5._____

6. For me, the best thing about school was the
    A. chance to strengthen my friendships and develop new ones
    B. chance to test my abilities and develop new ones
    C. number of extracurricular activities and clubs
    D. chance to socialize
    E. chance to try several different majors

    6._____

7. As an employee, my weakest skill is
    A. controlling my temper
    B. organizational ability
    C. ability to effectively understand directions
    D. ability to effectively manage others
    E. ability to communicate my thoughts in writing

8. As an employee, my greatest strength would be
    A. my sense of loyalty
    B. organizational ability
    C. punctuality
    D. dedication
    E. ability to intimidate others

9. If asked by my company to learn a new job-related skill, my reaction would be to
    A. ask for a raise
    B. ask for overtime pay
    C. question the necessity of the skill
    D. cooperate with some reluctance
    E. cooperate with enthusiasm

10. When I disagree with others, I tend to
    A. listen quietly despite my disagreement
    B. laugh openly at the person I disagree with
    C. ask the person to explain their views before I respond
    D. leave the conversation before my anger gets the best of me
    E. point out exactly why the person is wrong

11. When I find myself in a situation which is confusing or unclear, my reaction is to
    A. pretend I am not confused
    B. remain calm and, if necessary, ask someone else for clarification
    C. grow frustrated and angry
    D. walk away from the situation
    E. immediately insist that someone explain things to me

12. If you were placed in a supervisory position, which of the following abilities would you consider to be most important to your job performance?
    A. Stubbornness
    B. The ability to hear all sides of a story before making a decision
    C. Kindness
    D. The ability to make and stick to a decision
    E. Patience

13. What is your highest level of education?
    A. Less than a high school diploma
    B. High school diploma or equivalency
    C. Graduate of community college
    D. Graduate of a four-year accredited college
    E. Degree from graduate school

3 (#2)

14. When asked to supervise other workers, your approach should be to
    A. ask for management wages since you're doing management work
    B. give the workers direction and supervise every aspect of the process
    C. give the workers direction and then allow them to do the job
    D. hand the workers their job specifications
    E. do the work yourself, since you're uncomfortable supervising others

14._____

15. Which of the following best describes you?
    A. Need little or no supervision
    B. Resent too much supervision
    C. Require as much supervision as my peers
    D. Require slightly more supervision than my peers
    E. Require close supervision

15._____

16. You accept a job which requires an ability to perform several tasks at once. What is the best way to handle such a position?
    A. With strong organizational skills and close attention to detail
    B. By delegating the work to someone with strong organizational skills
    C. Staying focused on one task at a time, no matter what happens
    D. Working on one task at a time until each task is successfully completed
    E. Asking your supervisor to help you

16._____

17. Which of the following best describes your behavior when you disagree with someone? You
    A. state your own point of view as quickly and loudly as you can
    B. listen quietly and keep your opinions to yourself
    C. listen to the other person's perspective and then carefully point out all the flaws in their logic
    D. list all of the ignorant people who agree with the opposing point of view
    E. listen to the other person's perspective and then explain your own perspective

17._____

18. As a new employee, you make several mistakes during your first week of work. You react by
    A. learning from your mistakes and moving on
    B. resigning
    C. blaming it on your supervisor
    D. refusing to talk about it
    E. blaming yourself

18._____

19. My ability to communicate effectively with others is
    A. below average
    B. average
    C. above average
    D. far above average
    E. far below average

19._____

20. In which of the following areas are you most highly skilled? 20._____
    A. Written communication
    B. Oral communication
    C. Ability to think quickly in difficult situations
    D. Ability to work with a broad diversity of people and personalities
    E. Organizational skills

21. As a worker, you are assigned to work with a partner whom you dislike. 21._____
    You should
    A. immediately report the problem to your supervisor
    B. ask your partner not to speak to you during working hours
    C. tell your colleagues about your differences
    D. tell your partner why you dislike him/her
    E. work with your partner regardless of your personal feelings

22. During high school, what was your most common afterschool activity? 22._____
    A. Remaining after school to participate in various clubs and organizations (band, sports, etc.)
    B. Making up for missed classes
    C. Punishment or detention
    D. Going straight to an afterschool job
    E. Spending the afternoon at home or with friends

23. During high school, in which of the following subjects did you receive the 23._____
    highest grades?
    A. English, history, social studies
    B. Math, science
    C. Vocational classes
    D. My grades were consistent in all subjects
    E. Classes I liked

24. When faced with an overwhelming number of duties at work, your 24._____
    reaction is to
    A. do all of the work yourself, no matter what the cost
    B. delegate some responsibilities to capable colleagues
    C. immediately ask your supervisor for help
    D. put off as much work as possible until you can get to it
    E. take some time off to relax and clear your mind

25. Which of the following best describes your desk at your current or most 25._____
    recent job?
    A. Messy and disorganized
    B. Neat and organized
    C. Messy but organized
    D. Neat but disorganized
    E. Messy

KEY (CORRECT ANSWERS)

1. B	11. B	21. E
2. C	12. D	22. A
3. E	13. E	23. D
4. D	14. C	24. B
5. C	15. A	25. B
6. B	16. A	
7. E	17. E	
8. D	18. A	
9. E	19. C	
10. C	20. C	

TEST 3

DIRECTIONS: Each question or incomplete statement is followed by several suggested answers or completions. Select the one that BEST answers the question or completes the statement. *PRINT THE LETTER OF THE CORRECT ANSWER IN THE SPACE AT THE RIGHT.*

1. When asked to take on extra responsibility at work, in order to help out a coworker who is overwhelmed, your response is to
    A. ask for overtime pay
    B. complain to your supervisor that you are being taken advantage of
    C. help the coworker to the best of your ability
    D. ask the coworker to come back some other time
    E. give the coworker some advice on how to get his/her job done

1._____

2. At my last job, I was promoted
    A. not at all
    B. once
    C. twice
    D. three times
    E. more than three times

2._____

3. You are faced with an overwhelming deadline at work. Your reaction is to
    A. procrastinate until the last minute
    B. procrastinate until someone notices that you need some help
    C. notify your supervisor that you cannot complete the work on your own
    D. work in silence without asking any questions
    E. arrange your schedule so that you can get the work done before the deadline

3._____

4. When you feel yourself under deadline pressure at work, your response is
    A. make sure you keep to a schedule which allows you to complete the work on time
    B. wait until just before the deadline to complete the work
    C. ask someone else to do the work
    D. grow so obsessive about the work that your coworkers feel compelled to help you
    E. ask your supervisor immediately for help

4._____

5. Which of the following best describes your appearance at your current or most recent position?
    A. Well-groomed, neat and clean
    B. Unkempt, but dressed neatly
    C. Messy and dirty clothing
    D. Unshaven and untidy
    E. Clean-shaven, but sloppily dressed

5._____

6. Which of the following best describes the way you react to making a difficult decision?
   A. Consult with the people you're closest to before making the decision
   B. Make the decision entirely on your own
   C. Consult only with those people whom your decision will affect
   D. Consult with everyone you know, in an effort to make a decision that will please everyone
   E. Forget about the decision until you have to make it

6._____

7. If placed in a supervisory role, which of the following characteristics would you rely on most heavily when dealing with the employees you supervise?
   A. Kindness
   B. Cheeriness
   C. Honesty
   D. Hostility
   E. Aloofness

7._____

8. When confronted with gossip at work, your typical reaction is to
   A. participate
   B. listen without participating
   C. notify your supervisor
   D. excuse yourself from the discussion
   E. confront your coworkers about their problem

8._____

9. In the past two years, how many jobs have you held?
   A. None
   B. One
   C. Two
   D. Three
   E. More than three

9._____

10. In your current or most recent job, your favorite part of the job is the part which involves
    A. telling other people what they're doing wrong
    B. supervising others
    C. working without supervision to finish a project
    D. written communication
    E. oral communication

10._____

11. Your supervisor asks you about a colleague who is applying for a position which you also want. You react by
    A. commenting honestly on the colleague's work performance
    B. enhancing the person's negative traits
    C. informing your supervisor about your colleague's personal problems
    D. telling your supervisor that you would be better in the position
    E. refusing to comment

11._____

12. Which of these best describes your responsibilities in your last job?
    A. Entirely supervisory
    B. Much supervisory responsibility
    C. Equal amounts of supervisory and non-supervisory responsibility
    D. Some supervisory responsibilities
    E. No supervisory responsibilities

    12._____

13. How much written communication did your previous or most recent job require of you?
    A. A great deal
    B. Some
    C. I don't remember
    D. A small amount
    E. None

    13._____

14. In the past two years, how many times have you been fired from a job?
    A. None
    B. Once
    C. Twice
    D. Three times
    E. More than three times

    14._____

15. How many hours per week have you spent working for volunteer organizations in the past year?
    A. 10 to 20
    B. 5 to 10
    C. 3 to 5
    D. 1 to 3
    E. None

    15._____

16. Your efforts at volunteer work usually revolve around which of the following types of organizations?
    A. Religious
    B. Community-based organization working to improve the community
    C. Charity on behalf of the poor
    D. Charity on behalf of the infirm or handicapped
    E. Other

    16._____

17. Which of the following best describes your professional history? Promoted at _____ coworkers.
    A. a much faster rate than
    B. a slightly faster rate than
    C. the same rate as
    D. a slightly slower rate than
    E. a much slower rate than

    17._____

18. Which of the following qualities do you most appreciate in a coworker?
    A. Friendliness
    B. Dependability
    C. Good looks
    D. Silence
    E. Forgiveness

    18._____

19. When you disagree with a supervisor's instructions or opinion about how to complete a project, your reaction is to
    A. inform your supervisor that you refuse to complete the project according to his or her instructions
    B. inform your colleagues of your supervisor's incompetence
    C. accept your supervisor's instructions in silence
    D. voice your concerns and then complete the project according to your own instincts
    E. voice your concerns and then complete the project according to your supervisor's instructions

19._____

20. Which of the following best describes your reaction to close supervision and specific direction from your supervisors? You
    A. listen carefully to the direction, then figure out a way to do the job more effectively
    B. complete the job according to the given specifications
    C. show some initiative by doing the job your way
    D. ask someone else to do the job for you
    E. listen carefully to the directions, and then figure out a better way to do the job which will save more money

20._____

21. At work, you are faced with a difficult decision. You react by
    A. seeking advice from your colleagues
    B. following your own path regardless of the consequences
    C. asking your supervisor what you should do
    D. keeping the difficulties to yourself
    E. working for a solution which will please everyone

21._____

22. If asked to work with a person whom you dislike, your response would be
    A. to ask your supervisor to allow you to work with someone else
    B. to ask your coworker to transfer to another department or project
    C. talk to your coworker about the proper way to behave at work
    D. pretend the coworker is your best friend for the sake of your job
    E. set aside your personal differences in order to complete the job

22._____

23. As a supervisor, which of the following incentives would you use to motivate your employees?
    A. Fear of losing their jobs
    B. Fear of their supervisors
    C. Allowing employees to provide their input on a number of policies
    D. Encouraging employees to file secret reports regarding colleagues' transgressions
    E. All of the above

23._____

24. A fellow worker, with whom you enjoy a close friendship, has a substance abuse problem which has gone undetected. You suspect the problem may be affecting his job. You would
    A. ask the worker if the problem is affecting his job performance
    B. warn the worker that he must seek counseling or you will report him
    C. wait a few weeks to see whether the worker's problem really is affecting his job
    D. discuss it with your supervisor
    E. wait for the supervisor to discover the problem

25. In the past two months, you have missed work
    A. never
    B. once
    C. twice
    D. three times
    E. more than three times

KEY (CORRECT ANSWERS)

1. C	11. A	21. A
2. C	12. D	22. E
3. E	13. B	23. C
4. A	14. A	24. D
5. A	15. C	25. A
6. A	16. B	
7. C	17. A	
8. D	18. B	
9. B	19. E	
10. C	20. B	

PHILOSOPHY, PRINCIPLES, PRACTICES, AND TECHNICS OF SUPERVISION, ADMINISTRATION, MANAGEMENT, AND ORGANIZATION

TABLE OF CONTENTS

	Page
MEANING OF SUPERVISION	1
THE OLD AND THE NEW SUPERVISION	1
THE EIGHT (8) BASIC PRINCIPLES OF THE NEW SUPERVISION	1
I. Principle of Responsibility	1
II. Principle of Authority	2
III. Principle of Self-Growth	2
IV. Principle of Individual Worth	2
V. Principle of Creative Leadership	2
VI. Principle of Success and Failure	2
VII. Principle of Science	3
VIII. Principle of Cooperation	3
WHAT IS ADMINISTRATION?	3
I. Practices Commonly Classed as "Supervisory"	3
II. Practices Commonly Classed as "Administrative"	3
III. Practices Commonly Classed as Both "Supervisory" and "Administrative"	4
RESPONSIBILITIES OF THE SUPERVISOR	4
COMPETENCIES OF THE SUPERVISOR	4
THE PROFESSIONAL SUPERVISOR-EMPLOYEE RELATIONSHIP	4
MINI-TEXT IN SUPERVISION, ADMINISTRATION, MANAGEMENT, AND ORGANIZATION	5
I. Brief Highlights	5
A. Levels of Management	6
B. What the Supervisor Must Learn	6
C. A Definition of Supervision	6
D. Elements of the Team Concept	6
E. Principles of Organization	6
F. The Four Important Parts of Every Job	7
G. Principles of Delegation	7
H. Principles of Effective Communications	7
I. Principles of Work Improvement	7
J. Areas of Job Improvement	7
K. Seven Key Points in Making Improvements	8

	L.	Corrective Techniques for Job Improvement	8
	M.	A Planning Checklist	8
	N.	Five Characteristics of Good Directions	9
	O.	Types of Directions	9
	P.	Controls	9
	Q.	Orienting the New Employee	9
	R.	Checklist for Orienting New Employees	9
	S.	Principles of Learning	10
	T.	Causes of Poor Performance	10
	U.	Four Major Steps in On-the-Job Instructions	10
	V.	Employees Want Five Things	10
	W.	Some Don'ts in Regard to Praise	11
	X.	How to Gain Your Workers' Confidence	11
	Y.	Sources of Employee Problems	11
	Z.	The Supervisor's Key to Discipline	11
	AA.	Five Important Processes of Management	12
	BB.	When the Supervisor Fails to Plan	12
	CC.	Fourteen General Principles of Management	12
	DD.	Change	12
II.	Brief Topical Summaries		13
	A.	Who/What is the Supervisor?	13
	B.	The Sociology of Work	13
	C.	Principles and Practices of Supervision	14
	D.	Dynamic Leadership	14
	E.	Processes for Solving Problems	15
	F.	Training for Results	15
	G.	Health, Safety, and Accident Prevention	16
	H.	Equal Employment Opportunity	16
	I.	Improving Communications	16
	J.	Self-Development	17
	K.	Teaching and Training	17
		1. The Teaching Process	17
		a. Preparation	17
		b. Presentation	18
		c. Summary	18
		d. Application	18
		e. Evaluation	18
		2. Teaching Methods	18
		a. Lecture	18
		b. Discussion	18
		c. Demonstration	19
		d. Performance	19
		e. Which Method to Use	19

PHILOSOPHY, PRINCIPLES, PRACTICES, AND TECHNICS OF SUPERVISION, ADMINISTRATION, MANAGEMENT, AND ORGANIZATION

MEANING OF SUPERVISION

The extension of the democratic philosophy has been accompanied by an extension in the scope of supervision. Modern leaders and supervisors no longer think of supervision in the narrow sense of being confined chiefly to visiting employees, supplying materials, or rating the staff. They regard supervision as being intimately related to all the concerned agencies of society, they speak of the supervisor's function in terms of "growth," rather than the "improvement" of employees.

This modern concept of supervision may be defined as follows: Supervision is leadership and the development of leadership within groups which are cooperatively engaged in inspection, research, training, guidance, and evaluation.

THE OLD AND THE NEW SUPERVISION

TRADITIONAL
1. Inspection
2. Focused on the employee
3. Visitation
4. Random and haphazard
5. Imposed and authoritarian
6. One person usually

MODERN
1. Study and analysis
2. Focused on aims, materials, methods, supervisors, employees, environment
3. Demonstrations, intervisitation, workshops, directed reading, bulletins, etc.
4. Definitely organized and planned (scientific)
5. Cooperative and democratic
6. Many persons involved (creative)

THE EIGHT (8) BASIC PRINCIPLES OF THE NEW SUPERVISION

I. Principle of Responsibility
   Authority to act and responsibility for acting must be joined.
   A. If you give responsibility, give authority.
   B. Define employee duties clearly.
   C. Protect employees from criticism by others.
   D. Recognize the rights as well as obligations of employees.
   E. Achieve the aims of a democratic society insofar as it is possible within the area of your work.
   F. Establish a situation favorable to training and learning.
   G. Accept ultimate responsibility for everything done in your section, unit, office, division, department.
   H. Good administration and good supervision are inseparable.

II. Principle of Authority
The success of the supervisor is measured by the extent to which the power of authority is not used.
- A. Exercise simplicity and informality in supervision
- B. Use the simplest machinery of supervision
- C. If it is good for the organization as a whole, it is probably justified.
- D. Seldom be arbitrary or authoritative.
- E. Do not base your work on the power of position or of personality.
- F. Permit and encourage the free expression of opinions.

III. Principle of Self-Growth
The success of the supervisor is measured by the extent to which, and the speed with which, he is no longer needed.
- A. Base criticism on principles, not on specifics.
- B. Point out higher activities to employees.
- C. Train for self-thinking by employees to meet new situations.
- D. Stimulate initiative, self-reliance, and individual responsibility
- E. Concentrate on stimulating the growth of employees rather than on removing defects.

IV. Principle of Individual Worth
Respect for the individual is a paramount consideration in supervision.
- A. Be human and sympathetic in dealing with employees.
- B. Don't nag about things to be done.
- C. Recognize the individual differences among employees and seek opportunities to permit best expression of each personality.

V. Principle of Creative Leadership
The best supervision is that which is not apparent to the employee.
- A. Stimulate, don't drive employees to creative action.
- B. Emphasize doing good things.
- C. Encourage employees to do what they do best.
- D. Do not be too greatly concerned with details of subject or method.
- E. Do not be concerned exclusively with immediate problems and activities.
- F. Reveal higher activities and make them both desired and maximally possible.
- G. Determine procedures in the light of each situation but see that these are derived from a sound basic philosophy.
- H. Aid, inspire, and lead so as to liberate the creative spirit latent in all good employees.

VI. Principle of Success and Failure
There are no unsuccessful employees, only unsuccessful supervisors who have failed to give proper leadership.
- A. Adapt suggestions to the capacities, attitudes, and prejudices of employees.
- B. Be gradual, be progressive, be persistent.
- C. Help the employee find the general principle; have the employee apply his own problem to the general principle.
- D. Give adequate appreciation for good work and honest effort.
- E. Anticipate employee difficulties and help to prevent them.
- F. Encourage employees to do the desirable things they will do anyway.
- G. Judge your supervision by the results it secures.

VII. Principle of Science
Successful supervision is scientific, objective, and experimental. It is based on facts, not on prejudices.
   A. Be cumulative in results.
   B. Never divorce your suggestions from the goals of training.
   C. Don't be impatient of results.
   D. Keep all matters on a professional, not a personal, level.
   E. Do not be concerned exclusively with immediate problems and activities.
   F. Use objective means of determining achievement and rating where possible.

VIII. Principle of Cooperation
Supervision is a cooperative enterprise between supervisor and employee.
   A. Begin with conditions as they are.
   B. Ask opinions of all involved when formulating policies.
   C. Organization is as good as its weakest link.
   D. Let employees help to determine policies and department programs.
   E. Be approachable and accessible—physically and mentally.
   F. Develop pleasant social relationships.

WHAT IS ADMINISTRATION

Administration is concerned with providing the environment, the material facilities, and the operational procedures that will promote the maximum growth and development of supervisors and employees. (Organization is an aspect and a concomitant of administration.)

There is no sharp line of demarcation between supervision and administration; these functions are intimately interrelated and, often, overlapping. They are complementary activities.

I. Practices Commonly Classed as "Supervisory"
   A. Conducting employees' conferences
   B. Visiting sections, units, offices, divisions, departments
   C. Arranging for demonstrations
   D. Examining plans
   E. Suggesting professional reading
   F. Interpreting bulletins
   G. Recommending in-service training courses
   H. Encouraging experimentation
   I. Appraising employee morale
   J. Providing for intervisitation

II. Practices Commonly Classified as "Administrative"
   A. Management of the office
   B. Arrangement of schedules for extra duties
   C. Assignment of rooms or areas
   D. Distribution of supplies
   E. Keeping records and reports
   F. Care of audio-visual materials
   G. Keeping inventory records
   H. Checking record cards and books

      I.   Programming special activities
      J.   Checking on the attendance and punctuality of employees

  III.   Practices Commonly Classified as Both "Supervisory" and "Administrative"
      A.   Program construction
      B.   Testing or evaluating outcomes
      C.   Personnel accounting
      D.   Ordering instructional materials

RESPONSIBILITIES OF THE SUPERVISOR

A person employed in a supervisory capacity must constantly be able to improve his own efficiency and ability. He represent the employer to the employees and only continuous self-examination can make him a capable supervisor.

Leadership and training are the supervisor's responsibility. An efficient working unit is one in which the employees work with the supervisor. It is his job to bring out the best in his employees. He must always be relaxed, courteous, and calm in his association with his employees. Their feelings are important, and a harsh attitude does not develop the most efficient employees.

COMPETENCES OF THE SUPERVISOR

    I.   Complete knowledge of the duties and responsibilities of his position.
    II.   To be able to organize a job, plan ahead, and carry through.
    III. To have self-confidence and initiative.
    IV. To be able to handle the unexpected situation and make quick decisions.
    V.   To be able to properly train subordinates in the positions they are best suited for.
    VI. To be able to keep good human relations among his subordinates.
    VII. To be able to keep good human relations between his subordinates and himself and to earn their respect and trust.

THE PROFESSIONAL SUPERVISOR-EMPLOYEE RELATIONSHIP

There are two kinds of efficiency: one kind is only apparent and is produced in organizations through the exercise of mere discipline; this is but a simulation of the second, or true, efficiency which springs from spontaneous cooperation. If you are a manager, no matter how great or small your responsibility, it is your job, in the final analysis, to create and develop this involuntary cooperation among the people whom you supervise. For, no matter how powerful a combination of money, machines, and materials a company may have, this is a dead and sterile thing without a team of willing, thinking, and articulate people to guide it.

The following 21 points are presented as indicative of the exemplary basic relationship that should exist between supervisor and employee:

1. Each person wants to be liked and respected by his fellow employee and wants to be treated with consideration and respect by his superior.
2. The most competent employee will make an error. However, in a unit where good relations exist between the supervisor and his employees, tenseness and fear do not exist. Thus, errors are not hidden or covered up, and the efficiency of a unit is not impaired.

3. Subordinates resent rules, regulations, or orders that are unreasonable or unexplained.
4. Subordinates are quick to resent unfairness, harshness, injustices, and favoritism.
5. An employee will accept responsibility if he knows that he will be complimented for a job well done, and not too harshly chastised for failure; that his supervisor will check the cause of the failure, and, if it was the supervisor's fault, he will assume the blame therefore. If it was the employee's fault, his supervisor will explain the correct method or means of handling the responsibility.
6. An employee wants to receive credit for a suggestion he has made, that is used. If a suggestion cannot be used, the employee is entitled to an explanation. The supervisor should not say "no" and close the subject.
7. Fear and worry slow up a worker's ability. Poor working environment can impair his physical and mental health. A good supervisor avoids forceful methods, threats, and arguments to get a job done.
8. A forceful supervisor is able to train his employees individually and as a team, and is able to motivate them in the proper channels.
9. A mature supervisor is able to properly evaluate his subordinates and to keep them happy and satisfied.
10. A sensitive supervisor will never patronize his subordinates.
11. A worthy supervisor will respect his employees' confidences.
12. Definite and clear-cut responsibilities should be assigned to each executive.
13. Responsibility should always be coupled with corresponding authority.
14. No change should be made in the scope or responsibilities of a position without a definite understanding to that effect on the part of all persons concerned.
15. No executive or employee, occupying a single position in the organization, should be subject to definite orders from more than one source.
16. Orders should never be given to subordinates over the head of a responsible executive. Rather than do this, the officer in question should be supplanted.
17. Criticisms of subordinates should, whoever possible, be made privately, and in no case should a subordinate be criticized in the presence of executives or employees of equal or lower rank.
18. No dispute or difference between executives or employees as to authority or responsibilities should be considered too trivial for prompt and careful adjudication.
19. Promotions, wage changes, and disciplinary action should always be approved by the executive immediately superior to the one directly responsible.
20. No executive or employee should ever be required, or expected, to be at the same time an assistant to, and critic of, another.
21. Any executive whose work is subject to regular inspection should, wherever practicable, be given the assistance and facilities necessary to enable him to maintain an independent check of the quality of his work.

MINI-TEXT IN SUPERVISION, ADMINISTRATION, MANAGEMENT, AND ORGANIZATION

I. Brief Highlights

Listed concisely and sequentially are major headings and important data in the field for quick recall and review.

A. Levels of Management
Any organization of some size has several levels of management. In terms of a ladder, the levels are:

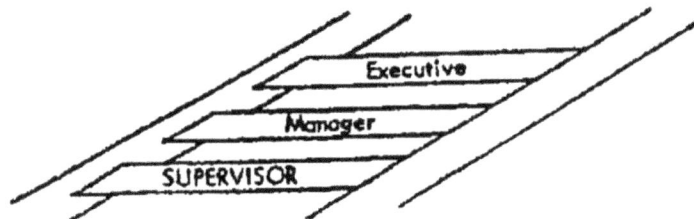

The first level is very important because it is the beginning point of management leadership.

B. What the Supervisor Must Learn
A supervisor must learn to:
1. Deal with people and their differences
2. Get the job done through people
3. Recognize the problems when they exist
4. Overcome obstacles to good performance
5. Evaluate the performance of people
6. Check his own performance in terms of accomplishment

C. A Definition of Supervisor
The term supervisor means any individual having authority, in the interests of the employer, to hire, transfer, suspend, lay-off, recall, promote, discharge, assign, reward, or discipline other employees or responsibility to direct them, or to adjust their grievances, or effectively to recommend such action, if, in connection with the foregoing, exercise of such authority is not of a merely routine or clerical nature but requires the use of independent judgment.

D. Elements of the Team Concept
What is involved in teamwork? The component parts are:
1. Members
2. A leader
3. Goals
4. Plans
5. Cooperation
6. Spirit

E. Principles of Organization
1. A team member must know what his job is.
2. Be sure that the nature and scope of a job are understood.
3. Authority and responsibility should be carefully spelled out.
4. A supervisor should be permitted to make the maximum number of decisions affecting his employees.
5. Employees should report to only one supervisor.
6. A supervisor should direct only as many employees as he can handle effectively.
7. An organization plan should be flexible.

8. Inspection and performance of work should be separate.
9. Organizational problems should receive immediate attention.
10. Assign work in line with ability and experience.

F. The Four Important Parts of Every Job
1. Inherent in every job is the *accountability* for results.
2. A second set of factors in every job is *responsibilities*.
3. Along with duties and responsibilities one must have the *authority* to act within certain limits without obtaining permission to proceed.
4. No job exists in a vacuum. The supervisor is surrounded by key *relationships*.

G. Principles of Delegation
Where work is delegated for the first time, the supervisor should think in terms of these questions:
1. Who is best qualified to do this?
2. Can an employee improve his abilities by doing this?
3. How long should an employee spend on this?
4. Are there any special problems for which he will need guidance?
5. How broad a delegation can I make?

H. Principles of Effective Communications
1. Determine the media.
2. To whom directed?
3. Identification and source authority.
4. Is communication understood?

I. Principles of Work Improvement
1. Most people usually do only the work which is assigned to them.
2. Workers are likely to fit assigned work into the time available to perform it.
3. A good workload usually stimulates output.
4. People usually do their best work when they know that results will be reviewed or inspected.
5. Employees usually feel that someone else is responsible for conditions of work, workplace layout, job methods, type of tools/equipment, and other such factors.
6. Employees are usually defensive about their job security.
7. Employees have natural resistance to change.
8. Employees can support or destroy a supervisor.
9. A supervisor usually earns the respect of his people through his personal example of diligence and efficiency.

J. Areas of Job Improvement
The areas of job improvement are quite numerous, but the most common ones which a supervisor can identify and utilize are:
1. Departmental layout
2. Flow of work
3. Workplace layout
4. Utilization of manpower
5. Work methods
6. Materials handling

7. Utilization
8. Motion economy

K. Seven Key Points in Making Improvements
1. Select the job to be improved
2. Study how it is being done now
3. Question the present method
4. Determine actions to be taken
5. Chart proposed method
6. Get approval and apply
7. Solicit worker participation

L. Corrective Techniques of Job Improvement
Specific Problems
1. Size of workload
2. Inability to meet schedules
3. Strain and fatigue
4. Improper use of men and skills
5. Waste, poor quality, unsafe conditions
6. Bottleneck conditions that hinder output
7. Poor utilization of equipment and machine
8. Efficiency and productivity of labor

General Improvement
1. Departmental layout
2. Flow of work
3. Work plan layout
4. Utilization of manpower
5. Work methods
6. Materials handling
7. Utilization of equipment
8. Motion economy

Corrective Techniques
1. Study with scale model
2. Flow chart study
3. Motion analysis
4. Comparison of units produced to standard allowance
5. Methods analysis
6. Flow chart and equipment study
7. Down time vs. running time
8. Motion analysis

M. A Planning Checklist
1. Objectives
2. Controls
3. Delegations
4. Communications
5. Resources
6. Manpower

7. Equipment
8. Supplies and materials
9. Utilization of time
10. Safety
11. Money
12. Work
13. Timing of improvements

N. Five Characteristics of Good Directions
In order to get results, directions must be:
1. Possible of accomplishment
2. Agreeable with worker interests
3. Related to mission
4. Planned and complete
5. Unmistakably clear

O. Types of Directions
1. Demands or direct orders
2. Requests
3. Suggestion or implication
4. volunteering

P. Controls
A typical listing of the overall areas in which the supervisor should establish controls might be:
1. Manpower
2. Materials
3. Quality of work
4. Quantity of work
5. Time
6. Space
7. Money
8. Methods

Q. Orienting the New Employee
1. Prepare for him
2. Welcome the new employee
3. Orientation for the job
4. Follow-up

R. Checklist for Orienting New Employees   Yes   No
1. Do you appreciate the feelings of new employees
   when they first report for work?   ___   ___
2. Are you aware of the fact that the new employee must
   make a big adjustment to his job?   ___   ___
3. Have you given him good reasons for liking the job and
   the organization?   ___   ___
4. Have you prepared for his first day on the job?   ___   ___
5. Did you welcome him cordially and make him feel needed?   ___   ___

	Yes	No

6. Did you establish rapport with him so that he feels free to talk and discuss matters with you? ___ ___
7. Did you explain his job to him and his relationship to you? ___ ___
8. Does he know that his work will be evaluated periodically on a basis that is fair and objective? ___ ___
9. Did you introduce him to his fellow workers in such a way that they are likely to accept him? ___ ___
10. Does he know what employee benefits he will receive? ___ ___
11. Does he understand the importance of being on the job and what to do if he must leave his duty station? ___ ___
12. Has he been impressed with the importance of accident prevention and safe practice? ___ ___
13. Does he generally know his way around the department? ___ ___
14. Is he under the guidance of a sponsor who will teach the right way of doing things? ___ ___
15. Do you plan to follow-up so that he will continue to adjust successfully to his job? ___ ___

S. Principles of Learning
1. Motivation
2. Demonstration or explanation
3. Practice

T. Causes of Poor Performance
1. Improper training for job
2. Wrong tools
3. Inadequate directions
4. Lack of supervisory follow-up
5. Poor communications
6. Lack of standards of performance
7. Wrong work habits
8. Low morale
9. Other

U. Four Major Steps in On-The-Job Instruction
1. Prepare the worker
2. Present the operation
3. Tryout performance
4. Follow-up

V. Employees Want Five Things
1. Security
2. Opportunity
3. Recognition
4. Inclusion
5. Expression

W. Some Don'ts in Regard to Praise
1. Don't praise a person for something he hasn't done.
2. Don't praise a person unless you can be sincere.
3. Don't be sparing in praise just because your superior withholds it from you.
4. Don't let too much time elapse between good performance and recognition of it

X. How to Gain Your Workers' Confidence
Methods of developing confidence include such things as:
1. Knowing the interests, habits, hobbies of employees
2. Admitting your own inadequacies
3. Sharing and telling of confidence in others
4. Supporting people when they are in trouble
5. Delegating matters that can be well handled
6. Being frank and straightforward about problems and working conditions
7. Encouraging others to bring their problems to you
8. Taking action on problems which impede worker progress

Y. Sources of Employee Problems
On-the-job causes might be such things as:
1. A feeling that favoritism is exercised in assignments
2. Assignment of overtime
3. An undue amount of supervision
4. Changing methods or systems
5. Stealing of ideas or trade secrets
6. Lack of interest in job
7. Threat of reduction in force
8. Ignorance or lack of communications
9. Poor equipment
10. Lack of knowing how supervisor feels toward employee
11. Shift assignments

Off-the-job problems might have to do with:
1. Health
2. Finances
3. Housing
4. Family

Z. The Supervisor's Key to Discipline
There are several key points about discipline which the supervisor should keep in mind:
1. Job discipline is one of the disciplines of life and is directed by the supervisor.
2. It is more important to correct an employee fault than to fix blame for it.
3. Employee performance is affected by problems both on the job and off.
4. Sudden or abrupt changes in behavior can be indications of important employee problems.
5. Problems should be dealt with as soon as possible after they are identified.
6. The attitude of the supervisor may have more to do with solving problems than the techniques of problem solving.
7. Correction of employee behavior should be resorted to only after the supervisor is sure that training or counseling will not be helpful.

8. Be sure to document your disciplinary actions.
9. Make sure that you are disciplining on the basis of facts rather than personal feelings.
10. Take each disciplinary step in order, being careful not to make snap judgments, or decisions based on impatience.

AA. Five Important Processes of Management
1. Planning
2. Organizing
3. Scheduling
4. Controlling
5. Motivating

BB. When the Supervisor Fails to Plan
1. Supervisor creates impression of not knowing his job
2. May lead to excessive overtime
3. Job runs itself—supervisor lacks control
4. Deadlines and appointments missed
5. Parts of the work go undone
6. Work interrupted by emergencies
7. Sets a bad example
8. Uneven workload creates peaks and valleys
9. Too much time on minor details at expense of more important tasks

CC. Fourteen General Principles of Management
1. Division of work
2. Authority and responsibility
3. Discipline
4. Unity of command
5. Unity of direction
6. Subordination of individual interest to general interest
7. Remuneration of personnel
8. Centralization
9. Scalar chain
10. Order
11. Equity
12. Stability of tenure of personnel
13. Initiative
14. Esprit de corps

DD. Change

Bringing about change is perhaps attempted more often, and yet less well understood, than anything else the supervisor does. How do people generally react to change? (People tend to resist change that is imposed upon them by other individuals or circumstances.

Change is characteristic of every situation. It is a part of every real endeavor where the efforts of people are concerned.

1. Why do people resist change?
   People may resist change because of:
   a. Fear of the unknown
   b. Implied criticism
   c. Unpleasant experiences in the past
   d. Fear of loss of status
   e. Threat to the ego
   f. Fear of loss of economic stability

2. How can we best overcome the resistance to change?
   In initiating change, take these steps:
   a. Get ready to sell
   b. Identify sources of help
   c. Anticipate objections
   d. Sell benefits
   e. Listen in depth
   f. Follow up

II. Brief Topical Summaries

   A. Who/What is the Supervisor?
      1. The supervisor is often called the "highest level employee and the lowest level manager."
      2. A supervisor is a member of both management and the work group. He acts as a bridge between the two.
      3. Most problems in supervision are in the area of human relations, or people problems.
      4. Employees expect: Respect, opportunity to learn and to advance, and a sense of belonging, and so forth.
      5. Supervisors are responsible for directing people and organizing work. Planning is of paramount importance.
      6. A position description is a set of duties and responsibilities inherent to a given position.
      7. It is important to keep the position description up-to-date and to provide each employee with his own copy.

   B. The Sociology of Work
      1. People are alike in many ways; however, each individual is unique.
      2. The supervisor is challenged in getting to know employee differences. Acquiring skills in evaluating individuals is an asset.
      3. Maintaining meaningful working relationships in the organization is of great importance.
      4. The supervisor has an obligation to help individuals to develop to their fullest potential.
      5. Job rotation on a planned basis helps to build versatility and to maintain interest and enthusiasm in work groups.
      6. Cross training (job rotation) provides backup skills.

7. The supervisor can help reduce tension by maintaining a sense of humor, providing guidance to employees, and by making reasonable and timely decisions. Employees respond favorably to working under reasonably predictable circumstances.
8. Change is characteristic of all managerial behavior. The supervisor must adjust to changes in procedures, new methods, technological changes, and to a number of new and sometimes challenging situations.
9. To overcome the natural tendency for people to resist change, the supervisor should become more skillful in initiating change.

C. Principles and Practices of Supervision
1. Employees should be required to answer to only one superior.
2. A supervisor can effectively direct only a limited number of employees, depending upon the complexity, variety, and proximity of the jobs involved.
3. The organizational chart presents the organization in graphic form. It reflects lines of authority and responsibility as well as interrelationships of units within the organization.
4. Distribution of work can be improved through an analysis using the "Work Distribution Chart."
5. The "Work Distribution Chart" reflects the division of work within a unit in understandable form.
6. When related tasks are given to an employee, he has a better chance of increasing his skills through training.
7. The individual who is given the responsibility for tasks must also be given the appropriate authority to insure adequate results.
8. The supervisor should delegate repetitive, routine work. Preparation of recurring reports, maintaining leave and attendance records are some examples.
9. Good discipline is essential to good task performance. Discipline is reflected in the actions of employees on the job in the absence of supervision.
10. Disciplinary action may have to be taken when the positive aspects of discipline have failed. Reprimand, warning, and suspension are examples of disciplinary action.
11. If a situation calls for a reprimand, be sure it is deserved and remember it is to be done in private.

D. Dynamic Leadership
1. A style is a personal method or manner of exerting influence.
2. Authoritarian leaders often see themselves as the source of power and authority.
3. The democratic leader often perceives the group as the source of authority and power.
4. Supervisors tend to do better when using the pattern of leadership that is most natural for them.
5. Social scientists suggest that the effective supervisor use the leadership style that best fits the problem or circumstances involved.
6. All four styles—telling, selling, consulting, joining—have their place. Using one does not preclude using the other at another time.

7. The theory X point of view assumes that the average person dislikes work, will avoid it whenever possible, and must be coerced to achieve organizational objectives.
8. The theory Y point of view assumes that the average person considers work to be a natural as play, and, when the individual is committed, he requires little supervision or direction to accomplish desired objectives.
9. The leader's basic assumptions concerning human behavior and human nature affect his actions, decisions, and other managerial practices.
10. Dissatisfaction among employees is often present, but difficult to isolate. The supervisor should seek to weaken dissatisfaction by keeping promises, being sincere and considerate, keeping employees informed, and so forth.
11. Constructive suggestions should be encouraged during the natural progress of the work.

E. Processes for Solving Problems
1. People find their daily tasks more meaningful and satisfying when they can improve them.
2. The causes of problems, or the key factors, are often hidden in the background. Ability to solve problems often involves the ability to isolate them from their backgrounds. There is some substance to the cliché that some persons "can't see the forest for the trees."
3. New procedures are often developed from old ones. Problems should be broken down into manageable parts. New ideas can be adapted from old one.
4. People think differently in problem-solving situations. Using a logical, patterned approach is often useful. One approach found to be useful includes these steps:
   a. Define the problem
   b. Establish objectives
   c. Get the facts
   d. Weigh and decide
   e. Take action
   f. Evaluate action

F. Training for Results
1. Participants respond best when they feel training is important to them.
2. The supervisor has responsibility for the training and development of those who report to him.
3. When training is delegated to others, great care must be exercised to insure the trainer has knowledge, aptitude, and interest for his work as a trainer.
4. Training (learning) of some type goes on continually. The most successful supervisor makes certain the learning contributes in a productive manner to operational goals.
5. New employees are particularly susceptible to training. Older employees facing new job situations require specific training, as well as having need for development and growth opportunities.
6. Training needs require continuous monitoring.
7. The training officer of an agency is a professional with a responsibility to assist supervisors in solving training problems.

8. Many of the self-development steps important to the supervisor's own growth are equally important to the development of peers and subordinates. Knowledge of these is important when the supervisor consults with others on development and growth opportunities.

G. Health, Safety, and Accident Prevention
1. Management-minded supervisors take appropriate measures to assist employees in maintaining health and in assuring safe practices in the work environment.
2. Effective safety training and practices help to avoid injury and accidents.
3. Safety should be a management goal. All infractions of safety which are observed should be corrected without exception.
4. Employees' safety attitude, training and instruction, provision of safe tools and equipment, supervision, and leadership are considered highly important factors which contribute to safety and which can be influenced directly by supervisors.
5. When accidents do occur, they should be investigated promptly for very important reasons, including the fact that information which is gained can be used to prevent accidents in the future.

H. Equal Employment Opportunity
1. The supervisor should endeavor to treat all employees fairly, without regard to religion, race, sex, or national origin.
2. Groups tend to reflect the attitude of the leader. Prejudice can be detected even in very subtle form. Supervisors must strive to create a feeling of mutual respect and confidence in every employee.
3. Complete utilization of all human resources is a national goal. Equitable consideration should be accorded women in the work force, minority-group members, the physically and mentally handicapped, and the older employee. The important question is: "Who can do the job?"
4. Training opportunities, recognition for performance, overtime assignments, promotional opportunities, and all other personnel actions are to be handled on an equitable basis.

I. Improving Communications
1. Communications is achieving understanding between the sender and the receiver of a message. It also means sharing information—the creation of understanding.
2. Communication is basic to all human activity. Words are means of conveying meanings; however, real meanings are in people.
3. There are very practical differences in the effectiveness of one-way, impersonal, and two-way communications. Words spoken face-to-face are better understood. Telephone conversations are effective, but lack the rapport of person-to-person exchanges. The whole person communicates.
4. Cooperation and communication in an organization go hand in hand. When there is a mutual respect between people, spelling out rules and procedures for communicating is unnecessary.
5. There are several barriers to effective communications. These include failure to listen with respect and understanding, lack of skill in feedback, and misinterpreting the meanings of words used by the speaker. It is also common

practice to listen to what we want to hear, and tune out things we do not want to hear.
6. Communication is management's chief problem. The supervisor should accept the challenge to communicate more effectively and to improve interagency and intra-agency communications.
7. The supervisor may often plan for and conduct meetings. The planning phase is critical and may determine the success or the failure of a meeting.
8. Speaking before groups usually requires extra effort. Stage fright may never disappear completely, but it can be controlled.

J. Self-Development
1. Every employee is responsible for his own self-development.
2. Toastmaster and toastmistress clubs offer opportunities to improve skills in oral communications.
3. Planning for one's own self-development is of vital importance. Supervisors know their own strengths and limitations better than anyone else.
4. Many opportunities are open to aid the supervisor in his developmental efforts, including job assignments; training opportunities, both governmental and non-governmental—to include universities and professional conferences and seminars.
5. Programmed instruction offers a means of studying at one's own rate.
6. Where difficulties may arise from a supervisor's being away from his work for training, he may participate in televised home study or correspondence courses to meet his self-development needs.

K. Teaching and Training
1. The Teaching Process
Teaching is encouraging and guiding the learning activities of students toward established goals. In most cases this process consists of five steps: preparation, presentation, summarization, evaluation, and application.

   a. Preparation
   Preparation is two-fold in nature; that of the supervisor and the employee. Preparation by the supervisor is absolutely essential to success. He must know what, when, where, how, and whom he will teach. Some of the factors that should be considered are:
   1) The objectives
   2) The materials needed
   3) The methods to be used
   4) Employee participation
   5) Employee interest
   6) Training aids
   7) Evaluation
   8) Summarization

   Employee preparation consists in preparing the employee to receive the material. Probably the most important single factor in the preparation of the employee is arousing and maintaining his interest. He must know the objectives of the training, why he is there, how the material can be used, and its importance to him.

b. Presentation
In presentation, have a carefully designed plan and follow it. The plan should be accurate and complete, yet flexible enough to meet situations as they arise. The method of presentation will be determined by the particular situation and objectives.

c. Summary
A summary should be made at the end of every training unit and program. In addition, there may be internal summaries depending on the nature of the material being taught. The important thing is that the trainee must always be able to understand how each part of the new material relates to the whole.

d. Application
The supervisor must arrange work so the employee will be given a chance to apply new knowledge or skills while the material is still clear in his mind and interest is high. The trainee does not really know whether he has learned the material until he has been given a chance to apply it. If the material is not applied, it loses most of its value.

e. Evaluation
The purpose of all training is to promote learning. To determine whether the training has been a success or failure, the supervisor must evaluate this learning.
In the broadest sense, evaluation includes all the devices, methods, skills, and techniques used by the supervisor to keep himself and the employees informed as to their progress toward the objectives they are pursuing. The extent to which the employee has mastered the knowledge, skills, and abilities, or changed his attitudes, as determined by the program objectives, is the extent to which instruction has succeeded or failed.
Evaluation should not be confined to the end of the lesson, day, or program but should be used continuously. We shall note later the way this relates to the rest of the teaching process.

2. Teaching Methods
A teaching method is a pattern of identifiable student and instructor activity used in presenting training material.
All supervisors are faced with the problem of deciding which method should be used at a given time.

a. Lecture
The lecture is direct oral presentation of material by the supervisor. The present trend is to place less emphasis on the trainer's activity and more on that of the trainee.

b. Discussion
Teaching by discussion or conference involves using questions and other techniques to arouse interest and focus attention upon certain areas, and by doing so creating a learning situation. This can be one of the most

valuable methods because it gives the employees an opportunity to express their ideas and pool their knowledge.

    c. Demonstration

The demonstration is used to teach how something works or how to do something. It can be used to show a principle or what the results of a series of actions will be. A well-staged demonstration is particularly effective because it shows proper methods of performance in a realistic manner.

    d. Performance

Performance is one of the most fundamental of all learning techniques or teaching methods. The trainee may be able to tell how a specific operation should be performed but he cannot be sure he knows how to perform the operation until he has done so.
As with all methods, there are certain advantages and disadvantages to each method.

    e. Which Method to Use

Moreover, there are other methods and techniques of teaching. It is difficult to use any method without other methods entering into it. In any learning situation, a combination of methods is usually more effective than any one method alone.

Finally, evaluation must be integrated into the other aspects of the teaching-learning process.

It must be used in the motivation of the trainees; it must be used to assist in developing understanding during the training; and it must be related to employee application of the results of training.

This is distinctly the role of the supervisor.

www.ingramcontent.com/pod-product-compliance
Lightning Source LLC
Chambersburg PA
CBHW081758300426
44116CB00014B/2157